National
—and—
Ethnic Identity
—in the—
European Context

DAVID DUNKERLEY
LESLEY HODGSON
STANISŁAW KONOPACKI
TONY SPYBEY
ANDREW THOMPSON

ŁÓDŹ UNIVERSITY PRESS · ŁÓDŹ 2001

REVIEWERS: *Joseph D. Lewandowski, Andrzej Weseliński*

PUBLISHING HOUSE EDITOR: *Elżbieta Marciszewska-Kowalczyk*

TECHNICAL EDITOR: *Maria Wojciechowska*

COVER DESIGN: *Barbara Grzejszczak*

PUBLISHED: The University of Łódź Publishing House, 2001
34 Jaracza Street, Łódź (PL)

PRINTED AND BOUND: Agencja Reklamowo-Wydawnicza „ARA"
35 Sienkiewicza Street, Łódź (PL)

This publications has been made possible through the financial, organizational and academic sponsorship of the European Union project TEMPUS JEP 13492-98/00: "European Studies' Modules in the Curriculum of the Institute of International Studies, University of Łódź". The project's author, contractor and coordinator was Professor *Krystyna Kujawińska-Courtney* representing the University of Łódź, Poland.

ISBN 83-7171-448-3

Contents

Acknowledgements

This volume has arisen from a TEMPUS PHARE (DG XXII) project (#AC-JEP-13492-98) that enabled co-operation between present and prospective European Union member countries in the generation of under-graduate courses geared to a rapidly expanding EU. The three countries involved in the enterprise were Poland, Sweden and the United Kingdom and were represented by the Universities of Łódź, Växjö and Glamorgan respectively. The representative of the Contractor was Krystyna Kujawińska-Courtney.

Professor Witold Ostrowski acted as our energetic critical reviewer and his considerable efforts are greatly appreciated, especially his valiant attempts to get two Englishmen, one Irishman, a Pole and a Welsh woman to learn how not to regularly split an infinitive!

We are also grateful to Urszula Krzemińska and Penny Byrne for their very considerable administrative assistance.

The forbearance of Teresa de Villiers, Hugh Dunkerley, Natalie, Abigail, Daniel and Harriet Hodgson, Elżbieta and Mateusz Konopacki and Cerys Davies has been beyond expectation. Their tolerance towards, and understanding of, our need regularly to meet in our respective countries over a two-year period has enabled the project to be completed on time.

David Dunkerley, Lesley Hodgson, Stanisław Konopacki,
Tony Spybey & Andrew Thompson

Introduction: European Identities in Context

The basic aim of this book is to provide an accessible text for undergraduate students that examines a wide range of issues of national and ethnic identity in the context of a rapidly expanding European Union (EU). The basic objective is thus to provide a fresh approach to problems raised by current developments in the EU.

There is currently considerable speculation about the likely future of the nation-state. In the EU, and for those states who are in the process of applying to join the EU such as Poland, this is an issue that is, arguably, of greater significance than for states elsewhere in the world. As most commentators, and even national politicians, recognise, membership of the EU comes at some cost with respect to the degree of control that national governments may exert over affairs within the territory over which they have *de jure* control. At such a time, then, it is necessary that we give hard consideration to the past and future trajectory of the nation-state in Europe.

Accordingly, Chapter Two begins by assessing the genesis of the modern nation-state in the late-eighteenth century and asks what are the principal features of this form of polity. The chapter proceeds to reflect on how the fortunes of the European nation-state have changed over the course of the twentieth century, from its political peak in the aftermath of the 1st World War to its putative nadir in the opening decade of the 21st century. The final section of the chapter considers the impact of European integration on the nation-states of the EU.

The modern conception of the nation-state is of European origin and the model has been accepted as more-or-less universal. The foundation of the United Nations in 1945 with its General Assembly of representatives of virtually all the nation-states in the world may be taken as a form of confirmation of this. All nations that have established their constitutional independence have sought to join. In 1945 there were 51 members but with the break-up of the European colonial empires and other struggles for independence the number is now approaching 200.

One of the factors that set European civilisation apart from the other great civilisations during the last millennium was its development not as a single imperial hierarchy but as a collection of competing nation-states. The competition between states consistently provided the driving force for the extension of European politico-economic institutions around the world. In a sense, therefore, the integration of Europe into the European Union represents the reversal of something like 600 years of European expansion. However it was this very expansion that created the global system in which during the last century Europe has found it increasingly difficult to maintain its supremacy. Hence the creation of the European Economic Community and now the European Union.

European colonial settlement gave rise to many post-colonial states and above all to the United States of America. The two world wars of the twentieth century began as European 'civil wars' and were immensely destructive to Europe leaving the USA in 1945 as incontrovertibly the world's most powerful state. Since then Japan has progressed to the position of the second largest economy and therefore the idea of something approaching a 'United States of Europe' has, despite much resistance, gained ground.

Following such historical description and explanation, in Chapters Three and Four the notion of the nation-state is explored in some detail particularly within a European context. The modern conception of the nation-state is a European institution or more accurately a set of European institutions. There are many variations to the model because it was not constructed intentionally *per se*, rather it developed from a complex series of historical events. The absolutist monarchs of Europe are credited with establishing effective centralised state administration during the 16th and 17th centuries. But the state and the monarch were hardly separate and it was in later centuries that the struggles for citizenship and democracy achieved success. What emerged was the model familiar to us today of democratic government served by a permanent bureaucracy but counter-balanced by an independent judiciary and police.

The British Parliament regards itself as the 'mother' of parliaments having achieved reasonably effective independence from royal edict by the end of the 17th century but the French Revolution represents a more sweeping end to the *ancien régime*. Contemporary governments vary in form and content but the combination of elected assembly and executive is universal in all modern forms of the state.

State bureaucracy owes much in concept to the centralising aims of the absolutist states and, in particular, to the reforms of Colbert under Louis XIV in France. The basic equation is that an administration efficient enough to contain an excise process delivering undiluted revenues to the central exchequer enables a state to augment its power in all kinds of ways. What was loyal to the monarch in the absolutist example should now be loyal to the democratic state.

It cannot be claimed that law is a European invention. However, inasmuch as European institutions followed European colonisation the basis for post-colonial legal systems is mostly European especially if this is broadened to encompass the European influence in the USA. Even within Europe, however, the form of the law and of the judicial system differs quite widely. The basis for English law is common law with the insertion of case law and especially property law that owes something to Roman law. In France there is the *code Napoleon*. The distinctive principle of modern European law is that the judiciary is supposed to be independent.

The organisation of the European Union does not, to-date, conform to this configuration and this is precisely because of the power of the individual states of which it is comprised. There is, however, the European Parliament and the bureaucratic European Commission which tend to be the reverse in order of importance. There is also the European Court of Justice as a court of appeal for member states and InterPol as a form of police co-operation that, in fact, predates the European Union.

In Chapter Five the political developments unfolding across Europe in recent years are explored. They testify to the continuing salience of nationalism and national identity as major political forces. From the war in Kosovo to the on-going disputes about the implications of European integration, it is evident that reconciling nationalism with social change will remain a key policy issue for the immediate future. For the process of European integration, the reproduction of national identities is an issue of paramount importance. For national politicians who advocate participation in this process, sentiments of national identity must be addressed carefully. As the situations in all EU states illustrate, although to varying degrees, failure to do so can open a space for far-right nationalisms. In seeking to understand the role of nationalism in the politics of contemporary Europe, it must first be recognised that the subject of enquiry is not nationalism in the singular sense but national*isms*, as a plurality of differing forms. Although common traits between different kinds of nationalisms can be identified, it is nevertheless impossible to explain all using one model.

Chapter Five begins by examining some of the recent theoretical analyses of nationalism and national identity. Of especial importance here are the importance of considering how nationalisms and national identities are sustained across generations and societies. From this starting-point the relevance of these questions for the EU, and, in particular, the process of European integration is explored. The chapter concludes by considering the development of policy measures for accommodating nationalisms and European integration.

Interestingly, the term *Europe* did not come into common use until after 1500 (the term *Christendom* being used before that). The breaking of the Venetian monopoly of trade with the outside world during the 16th century came about as the result of European maritime expansion and colonialism. This was pioneered by the Portuguese and Spanish and carried on in even greater measure by the Dutch, the British, the French and others. By this time a European identity had been firmly established and it was one that over-arched the individual European states despite their linguistic and cultural differences.

The contemporary propagation of European identity by the EU might therefore be seen as a reincarnation of something that has existed for 500 years but that has to a great extent been at odds with the growing power of nation-states. This forms the central debate in Chapter Six.

The initial *raison d'être* for the European Union was to put an end, once and for all, to the recurring conflict between the French and Germans that had, above all, sparked off two world wars. The expansion of the EU has been a process of attracting more and more of the European nation-states to the idea. The aim of economic union, however, inevitably leads to the erosion of elements of nationalism, as, for instance, when the introduction of the Euro as everyday currency will require the abolition not only of national currencies but of the nationalistic emblems that they bear.

Chapter Seven addresses the issue of the enlargement of the EU. It places the process of enlargement in an historical context, briefly outlining the processes undergone through previous enlargements, the rapid political/social changes in Central and East European countries (CEECs) after 1989 and the strategy used by the Commission to assess whether a *prima facie* case existed for exploring further which countries might gain entry and which, in the first wave, might not.

Discussion within the chapter takes the form of answers to a series of questions including whether the entry of the first five CEECs (including Poland) followed by a further five will create new divisions and new conflicts in Europe (and beyond). Of course, it is not at all clear whether all five CEECs will join at the same time so it needs to asked what is a reasonable timetable.

As part of the enlargement process, the EU needs to present itself as more open, democratic, transparent, efficient and representative as it gets larger and larger. Similarly reforms of the major spending programmes (agriculture, regional policies) will need to take place in order to accommodate the new members.

There are clear problems of enlargement. There has never been such an ambitious programme of enlargement. Never has there been entry of countries with such low relative incomes and the consequent problem of how to address the commitment to income redistribution. Enlargement is taking place in the wider context of increased economic globalisation. At the same time, Euroscepticism within existing EU countries cannot be ignored. And, there is the issue of how the enlarged EU will be seen by those countries at its new borders, especially Russia. In turn, this also raises the question of European foreign policy and international relations.

The chapter concludes with an examination of the EU's *political* role, its *economic* role and the impact of enlargement on the net budget contributors to the EU such as Germany, the UK and the Netherlands and aspects of European *social policy*.

Over the course of the post-war period, and particularly since the 1970s, a number of those states now incorporated within the EU have sponsored varying degrees of regionalisation and this forms the basis of the discussion in Chapter Eight. The federal system of government in the former Federal Republic of Germany had been established in 1949 as part of the post-war settlement. The governments in Italy and Spain introduced programmes of regional devolution in 1970 and 1978, respectively, while France also initiated similar reforms beginning in 1982. Most recently, in the United Kingdom, formerly one of the most centralised of unitary states in the EU, a devolved Assembly has been established in Northern Ireland, while Scotland and Wales have acquired regional forms of government since 1999.

In other member states, regional and local government have differing forms of relations with central government: Austria, for example, has a form of federalism not unlike that of Germany; Portugal has granted autonomy to The Azores and Madeira island groups, but the rest of the country remains strongly centralised; Denmark, Finland and Sweden have strong local government, but have not undergone regionalisation; in Greece, the Republic of Ireland and Luxembourg government remains firmly centralised with little indication of moves towards the introduction of a regional level of administration. Across the member states, then, there are varying degrees of involvement of the sub-national tier of government, although in some states the role of directly elected regional assemblies is considerably stronger than in others. In all member states, however, there have been growing calls for the devolution of political power to sub-national agencies in order to promote regional and local development.

The EU itself has been a major influence in the development of regionalism, especially through the disbursement of the Structural Funds. Other pressures have come from regional organisations and sub-state politicians. Chapter Eight traces the development of these processes in Europe in the post-war period, before moving on to assess the particular role played by EU policy. In this context, the discussion examines some of the considerable differences between regions across the EU (and within the associate member states). It also assesses the rise of the 'new regionalism'. The chapter concludes by examining the potential impact of current EU policy, most notably the application of the contentious issue of 'subsidiarity' and the development of the Committee of the Regions.

Set in historical context, Chapter Nine examines the changing face of race, racism, immigration and ethnic identity in contemporary European societies (including those in the proposed first wave of enlargement) and in the EU as a whole. The issue of whether 'European racism' can be identified is raised together with its potential impact of political and social policies in the EU.

If it is indeed possible to identify the emergence of a 'European identity' then this suggests problems for 'migrants', 'foreigners' and 'blacks'. As such the types of policy and political interventions to deal with the position of minority communities are examined as is the impact on Europe and European societies of mass migration from the CEECs and from the Mahgreb.

Different European societies have addressed the issue of 'race' and 'race relations' in different ways (Britain has been a particular example of this difference) yet there is no doubt that migration and settlement patterns themselves have shaped both national and EU political contexts.

There has been a significant impact in Europe of the growing numbers of refugees and asylum seekers (from natural disasters, genocide, political instability, etc.) and this is explored in the chapter. Similarly, the resurgence of racist and extreme nationalist movements in some European countries (e.g. France, Belgium, Germany, Austria) is discussed particularly in terms of how this has affected the debate about the 'new' Europe.

Chapter Ten continues in similar vein by arguing that human rights have traditionally been bound up with national sovereignty and that moves to internationalise rights have largely been hampered by a lack of commitment and implementation at nation-state level. The wide disparity between proclaimed ideals, expressed intentions and the actual situation can therefore be emphasised.

The role of the nation-state in the implementation of human rights treaties is analysed, tracing the development of rights alongside the rise of the nation-state. Issues surrounding globalising processes are also examined with respect to the internationalising of rights issues. Post-war rights processes are examined, including the Nuremberg International Tribunal and the setting up of the League of Nations and the United Nations and the development of more recent rights documents and supra-national organs. All are addressed in the light of the dichotomy between national sovereignty and international human rights.

Issues such as race, ethnicity and human rights have, in part, led to a growing interest in the idea of citizenship over the last ten years. It is agreed that the source of the revival of the concept lies in three political developments. First, there is the liberation of Central and East Europe and German reunification. Second, there is the issue of European integration marked by the Maastricht Treaty, the Single Market in 1993, the Amsterdam Treaty, the Treaty of Nice and the challenge of further enlargement. Third, there is the increasing number of immigrants coming to Europe from different parts of the world which raises the question of universal values and the principles of constitutional democracies.

In the first of three chapters exploring various facets of citizenship, Chapter Eleven examines the idea of citizenship perceived within the context of the European tradition of political thought. The starting point is Aristotle's concept as presented in his *Politics* which treats 'man' as a political animal whose identity is determined by participation in the *polis*. Then the development of the citizenship idea is discussed in relation to the traditions of the Roman Empire, the Middle Ages, the Renaissance and modernity. The following part is devoted to Marshall's concept of citizenship, this being the crucial reference point for all contemporary discussions of the problem. Finally, four modern philosophical doctrines – liberalism, republicanism, communitarianism and neo-republicanism – are presented with the focus on understanding the idea of citizenship.

The chapter therefore aims to provide grounds for answering the important questions of whether the tradition of the idea of citizenship is of any relevance to the contemporary world and which strands of the entire tradition of citizenship preserve their significance in meeting the challenges of globalisation, post-modernisation and European integration.

In the context of Western Europe growing interest in the idea of citizenship results from the increase of the perceived 'power gap' between the governed and government. This raises the question of 'rights' and the possibilities for subjects truly to become 'citizens'. Another issue concerns the contemporary failure of the welfare state and its ability to provide citizens with the social conditions of life that they have come to enjoy during over half a century. A third issue refers to the enlargement of the European Union and the challenge that this presents to the privileges of Western societies as enjoyed so far and now preserved within the concept of European citizenship.

Chapter Twelve examines the objectives behind the idea of European Union citizenship, the main purpose of which has been to enhance the rights and freedoms of member state nationals; to reduce the so-called democratic deficit; to create European identity enabling individual nationals to identify with the European Union; and to delineate those who belong to the EU. The specific provisions of European citizenship as envisaged in the Maastricht Treaty, the Amsterdam Treaty and the Nice Treaty are discussed enabling the following parts to concentrate on the weaknesses and limitations of the citizenship concept.

Globalisation has become rather a fashionable term to refer to developments in the contemporary world that include the world-wide operation of financial markets, trans-national corporations, trade patterns, flows of information, international organisations and international law. Each of these challenges the authority of the nation-state. Moreover, the essential feature of the global condition is a compression of time and space due to the development of new means of transport and communication. It is sometimes said that we witness not 'the end of history' but 'the end of geography'.

These developments result in the polarisation of social space which seems to be divided between elites travelling and investing more (and faster) than ever before and others tied to the local space that they inhabit. The privileged are emancipated from the constraints of local conditions while those excluded are cut off from the benefits of technological achievements.

The separation of the well-off from the poor sectors of society leads often towards increasing suspicion of others, resentment of strangers and intolerance. The process of globalisation is accompanied by the parallel phenomenon of territorialisation. In other words, these are two sides of the same coin sometimes referred to as *glocalisation.*

In this context Chapter Thirteen addresses two aspects of citizenship in the age of globalisation. One is devoted to the rights and obligations of the individual realised on the global scale in that ideas such as world/global and cosmopolitan citizenship; multiple citizenship; ecological citizenship; universal citizenship; and post-national/trans-national model of citizenship are analysed. The other addresses the question of citizenship from the perspective of the local and excluded. Here, issues such as the politics of identity and difference; citizenship and feminism; and post-modern citizenship are key.

A European based 'modern world-system' has its origins in the sixteenth century. The implication of this term is that there have been other 'world-systems' but that the 'modern world-system' supplanted them. The emergence of this system coincides with European maritime expansionism and the extension of European colonialism all around the world. Thus the 'modern world-system' is not based upon a single imperial hierarchy as was the case with other 'world-systems' but is the creation of the European *state* system. In fact, as the European states commenced their transition from feudal agriculture to capitalist industry, a process that took something like four centuries, the 'modern world-system' grew – based as it is upon the capitalist world-economy. It is to this and its association with cultural aspects of European identity that Chapter Fourteen turns

A different and newer approach to the broad concept of 'modern world system' is that of globalisation particularly as it emphasises the cultural aspects of European influence in the world. Arguably, globalisation has existed for 2000 years or, to put it another way, for the same period as Christianity. It might also be argued that European (or Western) culture is the world's first truly global culture, but that true globalisation has occurred only with the electronic communications revolution of the past two or three decades. Other civilisations may have liked to think that they dominated the world but the culture that emerged from Europe is the first to have actually achieved this and it did so by cultural means rather than by the time honoured pathway of military conquest. The cultural imperative appears to be stronger than either the perceived ambitions of individuals such as Genghis Khan.

The spatial dimension of globalisation is explicit in the term itself but the effects are unevenly distributed and the old inequalities remain or else are replaced by new ones. A 'global triad' in which the full benefits of globalisation are concentrated in three geographic areas has been identified: North America, Europe and East Asia especially Japan. By Europe is meant the European Union, the existence of which may in large part be explained in terms of the growth of the other two parts of this 'triad'. This may be taken to suggest that there is more in the concept of a capitalist world-economy than may be dismissed on the grounds of culture. However, it is the attractiveness of European culture that has brought about globalisation whilst its emulation and further development in other parts of the world that provides the driving force for European integration and identity quite apart from national and ethnic identity.

Andrew Thompson

The Nation-State in Europe

Introduction

Throughout the closing decade of the last century a debate intensified on the future of the nation-state, enveloping policy-makers, academics, and activists. However one seeks to conceptualise this debate, the basic question concerns the future of the nation-state. Most politicians will defend the idea of the nation-state – not surprising given that they are dependent on the votes of a national electorate – but, increasingly, they argue that globalisation is changing the role of national government. Some observers remain defensive of the nation-state, while others, more particularly, remain convinced of the capacity of national governments to exercise a greater degree of control over the fate of their citizens than government politicians currently claim is possible. For others, however, these commentators are the flat-earthers of the twenty-first century, failing to envisage political life beyond the nation-state. Kenichi Ohmae, a leading strategy adviser to large corporations and influential writer, argues that the nation-state is 'increasingly a nostalgic fiction' (1996: 13), and he advocates the development of smaller, 'region-states' to replace what he views as the cumbersome and largely ineffective nation-state as the organising unit of the global economy. Others offer a less radical vision of the future, although they speak of the need for global institutions of governance and civil society. George Soros (1998), the market speculator and philanthropist, proposes that we need a global legislature to create international law that could bind states together in a global society.

In the European Union discussion of these kinds of issues are, arguably, more intense – and more heated – than in other parts of the world, for the EU represents the most significant movement towards international integration. Soros, for example, describes the EU as a 'gigantic experiment in social engineering' (1998: 227), one which, in his opinion, has not gone far enough. Other states across the world have ceded varying degrees of authority to supranational organisations – to the United Nations and the World Trade

Organisation, for example – but nowhere like the voluntary surrender of authority on the part of the member states of the European Union. European Monetary Union, launched on the 1st January 1999, established the Euro as the common currency for the 11 states that took part in this launch, and their national currencies will cease to circulate early in 2002. Imagine the governments of the United States, Japan, and China, for example, surrendering the dollar, yen, or renimibi, then one begins to gain a sense of the level of integration among the majority of the member states of the European Union. Other European states will almost certainly sign-up to EMU during the first decade of the twenty-first century. Even for those EU member states that did not take part in the launch of EMU, integration of national economies is nevertheless at a very advanced stage. Integration is not, however, confined to the economic sphere, although it is most advanced in these matters. The 1992 Treaty of the European Union, for example, formally accorded citizens of the EU political rights in addition to the rights they possess by virtue of their citizenship of their national states.

With such developments occurring, particularly since the mid 1980s, it is not surprising that the debate on the future of the nation-state has assumed a special significance in Europe. This unit will explore some of the issues relating to the impact of European integration on the nation-state. It begins, however, by examining the rise and consolidation of the nation-state in Europe.

The rise of the nation-state in Europe

At the outset it is necessary to mention that there is an important difference between the concepts of state and nation-state. A number of the issues we drew to attention in the introduction refer to debates about the changing functions of the state, such as the question of the extent the ability of the state to exercise authority over economic affairs is diminishing. To employ the concept of nation-state is to raise questions about the impact of any putative changes for the relationship between state and national citizens, or to query the effect of change on the ability of the state to represent the interests of the nation. 'Nation-state', understood correctly, must involve some notion of a relationship between the state and the nation, of the ability of the state to embody the will of 'the people'. The concept of nation involves an idea of the national people – a populace itself subject to change over time, as we show below – sharing common interests and values. Government, a key state institution, claims to represent these national interests and values, thus invoking a claim to popular legitimacy. If the concept of state refers to the ability to exercise a range of powers, the concept of nation-state refers to the ability to exercise these powers in the interests of the nation.

David Held (1995) argues that the modern nation-state is characterised by four principal characteristics: territoriality; control of the means of violence; impersonal structure of power; and legitimacy. From the seventeenth century onward, European states have developed these characteristics, although, as we shall show, the development of separate European nation-states has not been one of linear progression. As Held points out, in the latter half of the seventeenth century the idea of sovereignty gradually came to be no longer restricted to the monarch, but was extended to refer to the territory over which the monarch ruled. Absolutist states were nevertheless characterised by the dominance of the monarch in affairs of state, whether Henry VIII in sixteenth century England or Frederick the Great in eighteenth century Prussia. In England a more radical change came in the mid-seventeenth century, when Charles I was executed and parliamentary sovereignty replaced the sovereign monarch. From this stage on, the monarch performed an increasingly residual role in the politics of the state. The restoration of the monarchy in 1688 did not diminish the significance of parliament, which continued to exercise growing executive and legislative authority. Of broader significance, however, was the 1789 French Revolution, which fostered the principle of the sovereign people – the nation – as the source of power and the state as the representative of the general will of the sovereign people.

In each of these instances, however, the state came to exercise a growing influence over affairs within the national territory. From the seventeenth century, the state became increasingly involved in the development of a national economy through promoting exports while seeking to restrict imports. The state also increasingly developed an administrative function, such as tax gathering and, in some European states (such as Prussia), an extensive state bureaucracy. Through this function the state came to have a greater involvement in the lives of those living in the national territory. The growing administrative role, especially the development of bureaucratic systems and the increasing use of public law, is also closely linked to Held's notion of an impersonal structure of power. Incidences of direct and indirect discrimination against certain groups living in national territories across Europe, clearly illustrate that establishing a genuinely impersonal structure of power continues to be a problem in the early twentieth century (although less so than in the eighteenth and nineteenth centuries).

Undoubtedly the most important way in which the state came to link public and private affairs was through the development of a permanent military infrastructure and personnel. In marked contrast to the powerful Portuguese and Spanish absolutist states of the sixteenth century, which relied on mercenary armies to support their expansion, the Great Powers of the eighteenth and nineteenth century – Britain, France, Prussia, and Russia – had developed well-equipped standing armies and navies. Building these forces required vast expenditure on the military, and by the beginning of the nineteenth century was spending the majority of its finances on either waging war or preparing for it, as writers such as Michael Mann (1986) and Paul Kennedy (1988) show. A key element of this militarisation, was the mobilisation of large numbers of civilians. Kennedy (1988) notes that the numbers of military personnel of the major European powers were expanding further, although Britain experienced a temporary reduction after the end of the Napoleonic wars. In 1816 France had 132000 military personnel and the Habsburg Empire had 22000 men-at-arms; by 1890 these figures had increased considerably to 542000 and 346000 men, respectively. Therefore, throughout the course of the nineteenth century we see, all across Europe, significant expansions in the number of men who are called on to defend, and advance, the national interests.

Linda Colley (1992) notes the expansion, in Britain, of both the army and the navy in a remarkably short period of time. By 1789, the British army numbered 40,000 regular soldiers, and the navy 16,000 men; by 1814, the army had grown to over a quarter of a million soldiers, while the navy consisted of 140,000 regular seamen. Additionally, she adds that there were nearly half a million men organised into civil defence units by 1804. The mobilisation of such large numbers of men, a pattern mirrored by developments in other European states, was brought about by a range of factors, among them patriotism, state propaganda, the threat of invasion, as well as economic factors such as unemployment. The price the state had to pay for this commitment was political reform. As Colley argues, in bringing together men as patriots the 'authorities ran an obvious risk of encouraging demands for political change in the future', but, she adds, they 'ran this risk knowingly, because they recognised they had no choice' (1992: 336).

Thus, a side effect of mass mobilisation was the growing politicisation of those, and others, who had been called up to fight. State elites actively fostered nationalism, and employed the rhetoric of national identity, to aid mobilisation, while for the masses this incorporation into the nation stimulated demands for further rights as members of the nation (influenced also, in the early nineteenth century, by the growth political radicalism in Europe). Held (1995) cautions against viewing the relationship between war and the development of the democratic nation-state in simple causal terms, but adds that the higher the costs of war to the citizen the more the state was willing to negotiate the terms of membership of the political community.

The use of nationalism to win popular support for, and involvement in, war brings us to the fourth characteristic identified in Held's model of the nation-state:

legitimacy. As he suggests, the 'loyalty of citizens became something that had to be *won* by modern states' (1995: 49). Some states introduced measures of social welfare in order to stem potential support for social radicalism. The German state under Bismarck, for example, began to introduce relatively large-scale welfare provisions in the 1890s, covering sickness, infirmity, and old age. More extensively, states began to develop more interventionist policies with respect to education. Between 1879–1891, the French government introduced a raft of legislation concerned with education, while the Italian government similarly embarked on an extensive school-building programme (Stone, 1999). European states also extended universal male suffrage throughout the latter part of the nineteenth and early twentieth centuries, as in the cases of Denmark (1849), Germany (1871), France (1875), Switzerland (1879), the United Kingdom (1884), and Norway (1898). Such extensions of the franchise did not mean that governments necessarily behaved in a radically different manner than before. Combined with the growth of an increasingly literate public, however, and the changing contours of the official nation – those who now had a formal stake in the political community – the need to shape public opinion became more important.

The need to generate a sense of national community on the part of the state – to justify war or to confront alternative sources of political ideology, such as socialism – is also evident in other practices. In *The Invention of Tradition* (1983), Eric Hobsbawm provides a number of interesting examples of the state, and allied elites, seeking to deliberately inculcate a sense of national tradition. In France the 1789 Revolution was commemorated on Bastille Day, celebrated for the first time in 1880. On this occasion, Hobsbawm argues, state and citizen were connected through a mass of public ceremonies. In Germany, during the closing decades of that century, architects, sculptors, and craftsmen busied themselves with constructing public monuments that marked key events in the unification of Germany, or which were concerned with establishing a linear, *German* national past back beyond unification. In a similar manner, in European states of this period the organisation of a linear national past through historical research was indispensable to the process of nation-building. Moretti (1999), examining historiography in Italy shortly after unification in 1870, discusses how a growing number of professional historians dedicated their efforts to demonstrating the ancient origins of unified Italy. Indeed, he quotes one such figure as arguing that such research was not 'merely of scientific need, but also a patriotic duty' (Moretti 1999: 114).

By the early twentieth century, then, the idea of the nation-state was assuming form. The legitimacy of the state (or lack of it) was now more readily associated with a mode of mass, democratic legitimacy that had its roots in the nation, than with any notion of God given right on the part of a monarch. The extension of the activities of the state, both in terms of establishing a national territory and in making connections with the lives of the masses through a variety of mechanisms, established the nation-state as an increasingly powerful source of loyalty. As the twentieth century opened, European states planned further social intervention, in education, increases in the provision of social welfare, and bureaucratic management. Allied to the formal activities of the state, the nation was also given life by nationalist historiography and by public monuments celebrating events in the carefully spun national past. The state clearly had still much work to do in order to build a strong national consensus, which allied divergent class interests, as well as the respective experiences of the industrial and agricultural populations. In Germany, for example, 510,000 people went on strike in 1905, while in 1913 250,000 workers struck, while in Italy there were 1,255 strikes involving 327,000 workers in 1911 (Stone 1999). The Great War, of course, killed large sections of the labouring classes, while the prospect of revolutionary socialism (outside of Russia) was largely stymied by the nationalist emotions generated by the war. After the War, however, the challenges to the nation-state returned, as in the case of the 1926 General Strike in Britain, and the state would have to engage in further nation-building in order to strengthen collective identity in European societies.

Building the nation-state

The Great War, and the effect of the propaganda that accompanied it, nevertheless illustrated how effective state-sponsored nationalism and xenophobia were in mobilising popular opinion. The English poet Siegfried Sassoon, who had served in the trenches during the War, does not disguise his vitriol at the manner in which he saw the British public so blindly taken in by war propaganda that they could treat the war, in performances in music halls, as a subject of humour. The behaviour and attitudes against which Owen had railed were replicated in other European states during the first years of the Great War. Ferro (1999: 301) argues that during the war 'pacifist groups were not able to make themselves heard at all', and records that the writer René Benjamin alone sold 150,000 copies of his pro-war publications. In Germany the celebratory tenor of the performances in the music halls was lowered as, by 1915, awareness of the scale of German losses was becoming clearer to the German public (Jelavich 1999). In those regions that would emerge as independent states after 1918, such as Poland and the Kingdom of Serbs, Croats, and Slovenes (to become Yugoslavia in 1926), propaganda was utilised by the aspiring elites to engender national consciousness (Segel 1999; Wachtel 1999).

Hopes that, after the war, stability would grow in the newly independent states were dashed as a combination of economic problems, political in-fighting, and continued ethnic conflict led to domestic strife and international concern. In many of the east European states, the established elites refused to give ground to the pressures of democratic politics. Yugoslavia, a hybrid creation of the Great Powers while the dust was still settling across Europe in the aftermath of World War 1, involved a precarious fusion of multinationalism from its beginnings. During the inter-war years, when Serb elites dominated the political apparatus with little involvement from those of the other nationalities, the hostilities between Serbs and Croats, in particular, endured in spite of the veil of national unity. Indeed, as one commentator observed prior as the 1991 civil war was unfolding, the 'Yugoslav idea was discredited in the eyes of non-Serbs even before the Second World War' (Lendvai 1991: 254). Other states went the same way: Bulgaria, Hungary, Poland, and Romania. The problems were not restricted to the states that had emerged out of the shadows of the old empires. As Eric Hobsbawm (1994) points out in *Age of Extremes*, the only European societies with 'adequately democratic political institutions that functioned without a break during the entire inter-war period were Britain, Finland (only just), the Irish Free State, Sweden, and Switzerland' (1995: 111).

As Hobsbawm and other writers have suggested, among the major forces behind the rise of fascism and the right in the inter-war years were the fears of social revolution and the general collapse of economic conditions in the 1930s. With regard to the former, the greatest concerns were among the middle classes, a situation that was compounded with the deterioration in economic circumstances in the 1930s and, with them, the social order on which this class existed. With the divisions running through European societies of this period, it was difficult to speak of a broad social and political consensus. The old elites had little interest in securing the support of the masses, as they feared the consequences of any extension in the power base of those who represented their greatest threat. The radical right was the direct challenger to the left workers' movement, and, as such, was more likely to draw its support from the middle classes who also feared the consequences of a militant left. The social situation, then, becomes fractious, and where the state refuses to acknowledge the demands of the industrial masses or the concerns of the middle classes, then the appeal of alternative positions, such as fascism, became greater. Of all the lessons the post-war state would learn, it was the need to build a nation-state, forging a stronger and wider social consensus, which would be the most valuable for the reconstruction of Europe.

The nation-state and European integration. 1950–1985

There is no doubt that the experiences of the war contributed much to the drive towards formal political integration in western Europe. The desire to negate the potential for the national rivalry that led to war in Europe twice in the first half of the century was a common concern, not restricted to the early architects of integration. It would nevertheless be stretching the limits of this idealism – that nation-states would agree to surrender some of their autonomy in exchange for the greater west European good – to suggest that this was the principal motor of integration. That the plan to create a Franco-German common market for the coal and steel industries, proposed by the French Foreign Minister Robert Schuman in 1950, was extended to include Belgium, the Netherlands, Luxembourg, and Italy, must more correctly be viewed as calculated decisions taken by national governments to *advance* domestic interests.

What, then, were these interests in the immediate post-war period? Three major interests can be identified. First, the need to broaden the base of popular legitimacy within the nation-state. As the historian Alan Milward (1992) argues in his acclaimed study, *The European Rescue of the Nation-State*, the rise of fascism and the collapse of nation-states across continental Europe in the 1930s highlighted the weakness of liberal parliamentary democracy. As a consequence, he maintains, a primary concern for national governments in the immediate post-war period was to construct a much more inclusive social consensus within European nation-states. Thus, in these societies governments developed policy agendas designed to foster the support of the working masses, both in industry and agriculture. It is in this period, therefore, that we witness the beginning of a long period of extensive state investment in welfare systems. As we noted above, states were providing some measure of public welfare support prior to this period, but post-war state investment was far in advance of these earlier initiatives. Milward (1992) calculates that in western Europe welfare expenditure (including on education, housing, public health, and social security) rose from approximately 25 per cent of Gross National Product in 1950 to around 45 per cent in the mid-1970s. Milward also points out that the conditions of those reliant on agriculture as a particular concern of the post-war consensus builders, as it was among rural populations in Austria, Germany, and Italy that authoritarian political parties had found a rich vein of support in the 1930s.

A second major interest for post-war governments in western Europe was economic, both in the need to rebuild economies and to prevent the high levels of inflation and unemployment that contributed to the popular turn to fascism and to the general weakness of most European nation-states in the 1930s. The objective of raising employment levels was secured through a number of policies, among them: state intervention to modernise industrial and agricultural production; increased government consumption of national commodities and services, thus aiding demand; and state ownership of successful and/or vital industries (such as Renault in France, Volkswagen in Germany, and the coal industry in the UK), combined with mercantilist policies designed to protect growing sectors (such as the car industry in Italy) from foreign competition.

Relatedly, governments developed taxation policies that would ensure that, with a measure of redistribution, a greater mass of the population could engage in the consumption that was necessary to sustain increased production in, for example, the manufacturing industries. Thus, national economic policies, designed to help build the new post-war consensus in west European societies, contributed significantly to the post-war economic boom and, in turn, helped to maintain the legitimacy of the nation-state.

The third main interest was the containment of Germany. For France, in particular, the need to rein the Federal Republic of Germany into a framework that would reduce, or eliminate, the possibility of a resurgent Germany militarism, was a major objective. Thus, just months after Schuman had put forward his proposal for the French and German coal and steel industries, the French government presented another plan for a common European alliance: the European Defence Community. A treaty establishing this institution was signed by the six states that had agreed to Schuman's plan in 1952, but was never ratified by the French National Assembly. Schuman's proposals did, however, meet with success, and the European Coal and Steel Community was established in Paris in 1952.

Why, then, had the six national governments signed the Treaty of Paris that brought the ECSC to life? The desire for peace? Certainly, although this was not the driving force. Arguably the main reason why these governments chose to surrender a portion of their powers in order to create the ECSC was national pragmatism. Integration suited the economic, political, and social objectives of the six founder member states. As Milward (1992) contests, integration enabled domestic policies to be pursued that would otherwise have been more difficult to execute. For example, when the Belgian coal industry, hitherto one of the main employers in the country, initiated a restructuring plan that involved making large numbers of workers redundant in 1958, the ECSC provided generous subsidies for retraining and to aid the restructuring and modernisation of the industry. Similarly, when the 1957 Treaty of Rome created the European Economic Community, Milward argues that the rationale for national governments committing to this new community was the desire to continue to preserve both the post-war social and political consensus through further economic growth and, ultimately, to further the reassertion of the west European nation-state. As he suggests, it was rising prosperity that maintained the legitimacy of the nation-state and the 'importance of foreign trade to that prosperity was great and was magnified in the political and economic thought of the time' (1992: 223).

European integration throughout the 1960s continued to be shaped by national pragmatism. On two occasions, 1963 and 1967, the United Kingdom sought entry to the EEC, in large part because of the declining importance of the

Commonwealth as a market for UK exports. Why France vetoed both of the UK's applications for membership is not entirely clear, although both the challenge that the UK would bring to France's role as one of the two senior partners of the EEC (the other being the FRG) and the opposition to the number of caveats that the UK's application involved were arguably among the principal determining factors. The development of the Common Agricultural Policy, beginning in the late 1950s, also suited the interests of national policies. The creation of this supranational institution had significant implications for all member states of the EEC, but, with the possible exception of the FRG, the advantages of obligating member states to seek imports from each other before turning to agricultural producers outside outweighed the disadvantages. Thus, while common prices for certain commodities may have proved costly for some producers, they nevertheless gained preferential access to markets for other produce. Again, the desire to further the interests of the nation-state and to preserve domestic political consensus were primary objectives in the negotiations on the CAP.

In contrast to the advances of the 1950s and 1960s, the 1970s were characterised by the increasingly inter-governmental nature of integration advance relative to the Commission-driven supranational agenda. There were certainly advances in integration, notably with the accession of three new member states in 1973: Denmark, the Republic of Ireland, and the United Kingdom. Moreover, membership negotiations began with Greece, Portugal, and Spain in the latter part of the decade. Institutionally, the 1970s also witnessed a number of new developments. In 1970 the existing member states agreed, under the umbrella of European Political Co-operation, to work towards a common position on foreign policy matters. In 1974 the meetings between the heads of member states was formally established as part of the framework of the EEC, as the European Council. 1979 saw the first direct elections to the European Parliament, and the creation of a new European politician: the Member of the European Parliament. Finally, in 1979 the European Monetary System was launched with the objective of, among other matters, bringing the currencies of the member states into closer alignment.

Each of these advances demonstrated a willingness to consider the possibility of working towards a common position, but much of the energy of both national governments and the Commission was dedicated to the negotiations on enlargement. Moreover, the accession of the United Kingdom, after Harold Wilson replaced Edward Heath as British Prime Minister, added further complications to the idea of furthering integration outside the realm of economic affairs. Problems within each of the nine member states, caused by inflation, the rising cost of social welfare, the decline of major industrial sectors, and two oil crises, led to fractious in-fighting, as governments sought to preserve the national social consensus that had been built during the post-war period. Finally, the rising costs for national governments – in demands for higher wages, support for declining industries, and social welfare – contributed significantly to the growing challenge to the power of the trade unions, an institution that had been central to creating the post-war consensus within European nation-states.

Events in the early 1980s did little to improve relations between the member states (joined by Greece in 1981). A further oil crisis in 1979–1980, combined with a recession in the face of competition from Japan and other economies in south east Asia, led to defensive economic and monetary policies designed to try to protect national markets from the worst effects. Margaret Thatcher, British Prime Minister from 1979, engaged in the first of a series of negotiations about the UK's financial contribution to the budget of the European Community. At the same time, discussions over common agricultural and fishery policies and prices became the subject of protracted discussions between member states.

This period was, in spite of outward appearances, the beginning of a period of major change, comparable to the first movements towards integration in the early post-war period, and one that would lead to a further change in the domestic consensus within member states. As with the events of the early post-war period, this new momentum led to changes in the form of European integration. Gradually, this momentum came to be directed towards the advance of the single market, which had begun with the 1951 Treaty of Paris and was widened with the 1957 Treaty of Rome. For member states, then, economic policy gradually moved away from supporting key national industries towards a European Community within which the remaining borders to trade would be removed.

Until a monetary crisis in 1983, the French socialist government fought to maintain the economic strategy that had been so successful for much of the post-war period, including fiscal policies designed to ensure demand on the part of poorer sections of society along with support for the agricultural sector. After this, however, the French government began to move more towards the policies pursued by other member states. The actions of the French government illustrated that the need to preserve the idea of the nation-state remained a paramount concern. The commitment to progress the internal market, and the change in economic and monetary policy on the part of member states, indicated the beginning of a period of change, it was also apparent that the chosen policies of the French government may have differed to those of other member states, its aim – the preservation of the French nation-state – was in keeping with that of other states.

The nation-state and European integration 1985–2000

The discussions on the 1985 Single European Act, which formally set in motion the move towards the completion of the Single European Market, revealed that negotiations continued to centre on maintaining key areas of domestic support. Middlemas (1995) points out that, for example, both the Republic of Ireland and Greece received assurances of extra EC funding to enable their respective economies to adapt to the new pressures created by the single market, while Belgium and the Netherlands won measures of further political cooperation that would aid their own national interests. France secured a commitment to work towards European Monetary Union, which it had been championing as a method of ensuring that German monetary policy did not dominate European monetary affairs. Baun (1996: 25) suggests that since 'within European institutions Paris would presumably have some voice, it would thereby regain a degree of control over monetary policy', which it had lost after its monetary crisis in the early 1980s. There can be little argument, however, that the SEA strengthened the transnational integrationist hand relative to the machinations of inter-governmental cooperation. The SEA extended the procedure of qualified majority voting within the Council of Ministers, thus making it more difficult to halt the progress of integration, and buttressed the scrutinising role of the European Parliament. Moreover, the SEA also included provisions declaring the intentions to work towards producing a common European foreign policy, under the guise of European political co-operation.

More significantly, the SEA marked the beginning of renewed commitment to the integration process, especially the drive to complete, by 1992, the single European market. Just as in the early post-war period integration had been driven by the imperatives of the founding members to establish a common framework within which they could advance their domestic interests, so the SEA seemed to represent a similar coming together of interests to work towards a new period of growth. It is nevertheless necessary to add that, as with earlier stages in the development of European integration, the emphasis during the 1980s was primarily on extending the process of economic integration, notably through the completion of the single market, in an effort to boost prosperity and to maintain the support of national voters. The hostility of the Thatcher administration in the UK to perceived threats to British national identity were evidence that incursions into the relationship between state and citizen, beyond economic integration, raised hackles. Moreover, while the SEA gave some limited increase in powers to the European Parliament, it was evident that national governments had little intention of allowing the Parliament to develop as an alternative to national parliaments. Finally, while the SEA gave recognition to EPC, there was no *obligation* to develop a Community foreign policy (Holland 1994). Finally, while the 1980s witnessed the emergence of common symbols of the European Community, in the form of common passports and the creation of a European Community flag, moves to establish a broader popular consciousness on the part of citizens of the Community as a political entity would have to wait until the early 1990s to take legal form.

Events in the late-1980s and early-1990s did, however, lead to a significant step forward in the integration process. Firstly, in the back end of the 1980s the French government put forward a paper concerning the progress of European Monetary Union (of which there had been no explicit coverage in the SEA), and in 1988 it was agreed, under the German Presidency, to establish a committee to look into EMU. After discussions, it was agreed at the European Council in Rome in 1990 that an Inter-Governmental Conference on EMU would take place in December 1990. Secondly, after the events in Eastern and Central Europe, and especially after the unification of Germany in 1990, momentum gathered for a strengthening of political union. Driven primarily by French concerns about a larger Germany, which were acknowledged the German Chancellor, Helmut Kohl, the objective of further political integration was agreed as the subject of a second IGC, also to be held in Rome in December 1990. The issues of EMU and EPC were nevertheless more substantively advanced at IGCs in France in the first half of 1991, and concluded in two IGCs later that year in the Netherlands, from which the Member States moved towards the next stage of integration: the 1992 Treaty on European Union (more usually referred to as the Maastricht Treaty, after the city in which the Treaty was signed).

What are we to make of these events with regard to the relationship between the nation-state and European integration? In general, we can say that the same principle that Milward identifies in the early stage of integration, is present in the events in the years preceding the Maastricht Treaty. That is, integration will progress while the Member States are of the collective view that it benefits their domestic interests to do so. Thus, the desire to progress EPC was the product not only of French concerns about German unification, but also of changes in the external security framework due to events in central and eastern Europe, and the former-Soviet Union, as well as the Gulf War and the civil war in the Federal Republic of Yugoslavia. The subsequent situation in Yugoslavia nevertheless illustrated that the European Community was not capable of acting in concert to establish a peace settlement in spite of the statement issued by Jacques Poos, Chair of the EC Foreign Ministers, in 1991, that the civil war in Yugoslavia could be solved by the collective efforts of the Member States. The wranglings, and negotiations over the implosion of Yugoslavia, succeeded in highlighting the differing national interests. In August 1991 the EC established the Badinter Commission to arbitrate between the various domestic parties in Yugoslavia (see Rady 1996). Meanwhile, the Austrian, German, and Italian governments moved to a common position – in clear opposition to the EC requirements for a common agreement among all Member States – that would, they held, lead to the recognition of Croatian and Slovenian independence by the end of 1991. After negotiations between EC ministers in December 1991, at which it was agreed that the republics could apply for international recognition, Germany broke rank and made public its recognition on 23rd December 1991. The EC itself followed this, recognising Croatia and Slovenia in January 1992. Recognition therefore progressed in spite of warnings from a number of international participants that such measures could well exacerbate problems, rather than create solutions (Roberts 1995; Woodward 1995). Moreover, despite Macedonia meeting the criteria on rights to be accorded to minorities and specified democratic standards laid down by the Badinter Commission, it was refused recognition by the EC as part of a deal to secure the support of the Greek government for the Maastricht Treaty, while the UK supported the German move to recognise the independence of Croatia and Slovenia as part of an agreement that would enable it opt out of the 'Social Chapter' in the Maastricht Treaty.

The Maastricht Treaty did nevertheless give formal recognition to the need to work towards a Common Foreign and Security Policy, as well as to advance similar co-operation in the field of Justice and Home Affairs. That the Member States should commit to an obligation to co-ordinate, and consult, on matters of defence and foreign policy should be viewed as a significant step forward in the integration process, given that these are areas which nation-states have conventionally jealously guarded. These developments must be viewed against the backdrop of the end of the Cold War, of the changes in wider Europe, as well as the desire of some Member States to step out of the shadow of the US. The Member States differed, however, in their opinions towards cooperation in these fields, with France and the UK, for example, keen to ensure that national interests were not compromised. That the Maastricht Treaty did not transfer powers to the EU over deployment of military forces was indicative of the opposition on the part of a number of Member States to any such move.

Like the CFSP, EMU also involves co-ordination between the Member States, but with the latter, as outlined in the Maastricht Treaty, there is a real transfer of sovereign powers to a supranational institution. As has been noted earlier, discussions on EMU had progressed in the late 1980s, but the Maastricht Treaty advanced it by settling on the timetables for the next two stages of EMU (the first being the completion of the single market), as well as on the convergence criteria. The Treaty also established the framework for the European Central Bank, the independent supranational institution that would be responsible for monetary policy among those Member States participating in EMU. The agreement on the progress of EMU, therefore, was a significant integrationist measure, since, unlike the CFSP, it did envisage the loss of monetary tools on the part of the nation-state, and the creation of a governing entity that would operate independently of either the Member States or the main institutions of the EU. Perhaps more significantly, the negotiations on EMU were underpinned, however one might view the disputes between Member States, by a remarkable degree of political commitment. As will be noted below, the failure of the single currency will reflect badly on the EU more widely; the success of the euro will be a judgement on the standing of the EU. Moreover, governments will need to make a strong public commitment to the euro in order to maintain the support of national voters in the face of certain domestic political opposition. For these reasons, it would be erroneous to view EMU as merely the logical extension of the single market project, although, clearly, EMU is central to the working of the single market.

The Maastricht Treaty also makes formal recognition of EU citizenship. As is noted in the chapter on the social dimensions of European integration, the period since the mid-1970s has seen growing interest for some parties, although especially in the European Commission, for a strengthening of the popular legitimacy of integration and for a closer links to be made between the Community and the citizen. The Maastricht Treaty creates a status of EU citizen, although the provisions are limited in scope. While some states, such as Spain (which, in 1990, had initiated the discussions on Community citizenship), have been supportive of a strengthening of citizenship, Member States are protective of the relationship with national citizens. The status of citizen of the EU derives from firstly being a national of a Member State; the EU cannot by itself confer citizenship rights on a third country national. Within the TEU (under the pillar of justice and home affairs) there are provisions for promoting joint positions on, for example, conditions of residence for third country nationals and immigration policy, but such positions must be preceded by a unanimous decision by the Council of Ministers. Member states nevertheless remain, by and large, guarded against common action in these areas, and continue to hold that policy and legislation on nationality and immigration should derive from the national level. Thus, in contrast even to the CFSP, the advances in the area of EU citizenship have been limited. The Committee of the Regions, established by the Maastricht Treaty to add a tier of government that would bring representatives operating at the level closest to the citizen, provided a formal sub-national dimension to decision-making in the EU, but it holds few powers by which to check the power of the Member States.

In the period since the Maastricht Treaty, the dominant events in European integration have been the launch of the first wave of EMU on 1st January 1999 and the negotiations on the enlargement of the EU. Other matters, such as the CFSP or Justice and Home Affairs, have taken back seats in relation to the

former matters. The 1997 Treaty of Amsterdam, and more especially the
following period, saw some movement towards advancing the CFSP, largely
because the UK (which has long resisted incorporating the West European
Union into the EU) has indicated that it is willing to work towards a compromise
that would be more acceptable to its EU partners. The Treaty of Amsterdam did
nevertheless incorporate provisions that would enable the EU to act together to
perform collective humanitarian or peace-keeping tasks. The extent to which this
capacity of the EU progresses further, or is enhanced, will, as always, depend on
whether it is viewed to be in the wider interests of the Member States. The
agreement signed in Amsterdam illustrated just how difficult it will be to
commit EU states to a CFSP; the 'constructive abstention' procedure, for
example, enables a Member State not to take part in a common policy while not
blocking the move.

If the lack of movement on the CFSP, as well as the slow progress of any
policy relating to the citizenship or the social dimensions of the EU, demonstrate
that the nation-state in the EU remains a real force, the progress of EMU
represents the other side of the debate. The weakness of the Euro on the global
currency markets since its launch on 1st January 1999 does not detract from the
significance of the venture undertaken by the eleven Member States taking part
in the first wave. The implications of a centralised monetary policy will be
important for many aspects of EU policy-making, and it will be difficult for
those Member States not participating in EMU to be at the heart of decision-
making in the EU. The governments of Denmark and the UK had negotiated opt-
outs from the second stage of EMU during the discussions preceding Maastricht,
while Sweden also chose to pursue the cautious approach adopted by the other
two (Greece had openly failed to meet the convergence criteria for EMU). The
Danish electorate delivered a crushing blow to the Danish government, when it
voted in September 2000 against joining EMU, an event that had ramifications
for the British government that faces the arguably more difficult challenge of
persuading the British electorate to join EMU. Even so, that it will be strange if
either the Danish, Swedish or UK governments embark on policies that would
jeopardise their option of joining EMU at a future stage, highlights how, even
for the 'outsiders', the euro-states will be the pace setters for the other Member
States in some of the key policy areas.

Summary: the twilight of the nation-state?

- Where do these events leave the nation-state at the start of the twenty-first
  century? It is necessary to refrain from polemics: the nation-state is neither
  fading nor is it a case of 'business-as-usual'. In the EU, in particular, the

nation-state is adapting to changes in the external environment by entering into binding agreements with others. For EU member states, as well as for those who will enter over the next decade, this means that some of the conventional dimensions of the nation-state have altered, such as in the area of economic policy.

- The notion of 'sovereignty' should be qualified, therefore. Technically, sovereignty is never completely given away, because even if a treaty is signed that gives primacy to the laws of another legislature (such as the EU), the relevant legislation can be repealed at a future date by the domestic legislature. Such a zero-sum conception of sovereignty does not, however, do justice to the way in which European integration alters the environment in which the European nation-state operates. Some aspects of EU law have 'direct effect', and, as such, do not require any action by the national legislature in order to make provisions binding within the national territory. Clearly, then, the concept of 'territoriality' cannot mean that the national state is the sovereign power within the national territory.

- Moreover, harmonisation of policy-making, especially in the realm of economic affairs, greatly limits the ability of national executives to unilaterally direct policy. EMU, for example, establishes a body – the European Central Bank – that is independent of the Member States; it is, therefore, a genuinely transnational institution.

- We should not be quick to declare the end of the era of the nation-state in Europe. European nation-states still retain significant control over foreign and defence policy, and, most especially, they remain the most powerful actor for individual citizens. All the evidence in Europe suggests that, for a good time to come, European governments will remain protective against any challenges to the relationship between state and citizen, or to efforts to enable bodies other than the nation-state powers to award citizenship rights.

Further Reading

Gowland, D., B. O'Neill & R. Dunphy (eds) (2000), *The European Mosaic. Contemporary Politics, Economics, and Culture*. Harlow: Longman.

Lynch, P., N. Neuwahl & W. Rees (eds) (2000), *Reforming the European Union – from Maastricht to Amsterdam*. Harlow: Longman.

Milward, A. S. (2000), *The European Rescue of the Nation-State*. London: Routledge.

Stone, L. (1999), *Europe Transformed, 1878–1919*. Oxford: Blackwell.

References

Baun, M. (1995), *An Imperfect Union*. Boulder: Westview Press.

Colley, L. (1992), *Britons. Forging the Nation 1707–1837*. London: Vintage.

Ferro, M. (1999), "Cultural life in France, 1914–1918". In: **Roshwald**, A. and R. **Stites** (eds), *European Culture in the Great War*. Cambridge: Cambridge University Press.

Held, D. (1995), *Democracy and the Global Order*. Cambridge: Polity.

Hobsbawm (1995), *Age of Extremes*. London: Abacus.

Hobsbawm, E. and T. **Ranger** (eds) (1983), *The Invention of Tradition*. Cambridge: Cambridge University Press.

Jelavich, P. (1999), "German culture in the Great War". In: **Roshwald**, A. and R. **Stites** (eds), *European Culture in the Great War*. Cambridge: Cambridge University Press.

Kennedy, P. (1988), *The Rise and Fall of the Great Powers*.

Lendvai, P. (1991), "Yugoslavia without Yugoslavs: the roots of the crisis". *International Affairs*. 67, 2: 251–261.

Mann, M. (1986), *The Sources of Social Power*. Vol. 1. Cambridge: Cambridge University Press.

Middlemas, K. (1995), *Orchestrating Europe*. London: Fontana.

Milward, A. S. (2000), *The European Rescue of the Nation-State*. London: Routledge.

Moretti, M. (1999), "The search for a 'national' history: Italian historiographical trends following unification". In: **Berger**, S., M. **Donovan** and K. **Passmore** (eds), *Writing National Histories*. London: Routledge.

Ohmae, K. (1996), *The End of the Nation-State*. London: HarperCollins.

Rady, M. (1996) "Self-determinaton and the dissolution of Yugoslavia". *Ethnic and Racial Studies*. 19: 379–389.

Roberts, A. (1995), "Communal conflict as a challenge to international organization: the case of the former Yugoslavia". *Review of International Studies*. 21: 389–410.

Segel, H. B. (1999), "Culture in Poland during World War I". In: **Roshwald**, A. and R. **Stites** (eds), *European Culture in the Great War*. Cambridge: Cambridge University Press.

Soros, G. (1998), *The Crisis of Global Capitalism*. London: Little, Brown and Co.

Stone, L. (1999), *Europe Transformed, 1878–1919*. Oxford: Blackwell.

Wachtel, A. (1999), "Culture in the South Slavic lands, 1914–1918". In: **Roshwald**, A. and R. **Stites** (eds), *European Culture in the Great War*. Cambridge: Cambridge University Press.

Woodward, S. L. (1995), *Balkan Tragedy: Chaos and Dissolution After the Cold War*. Washington: The Brookings Institution.

Tony Spybey

The Nation-State and European Integration

It has been asserted in several chapters of this book that the nation-state is essentially a European political form or, more specifically, a political form created and developed by Europeans. Historically, since medieval times the continent of Europe developed in the form of a number of increasingly powerful states and no empire emerged to rule the whole of Europe after Roman times. There were of course attempts to do this by Charlemagne and later Napoleon and Hitler but they never achieved their goal. The so-called Holy Roman Empire of the Habsburgs which attempted to carry on the aspirations of Charlemagne was always piecemeal, ruling parts of Europe but not the whole. The more cynical observers have remarked that it was not holy, Roman or an empire! Its last existence ended with the First World War and the way that Europe has been organised since is quite clearly as a collection of independent sovereign nation-states, interrupted only by Nazi occupation during the Second World War. This means that no other form, such as a single continental state or federation, has existed and this in itself may account for some of the misgivings exhibited by some Europeans in the face of progressive European integration. That is, the European Union appears to some to threaten the continued existence of the nation-states in favour of some form of federation or even a single 'super-state'.

There is also the further observation that the European model of the nation-state has become universalised – adopted throughout the world. An alternative word for universalisation is globalisation and in a round about way this is one of the reasons for European integration. In order for Europeans to protect themselves and maintain their standards of living in a progressively globalising and competitive world, the European Union promises to be the largest and therefore potentially the most powerful politico-economic entity in the world. There is therefore a paradox. The political form which the Europeans devised and in which they are accustomed to living is the nation-state and yet the continued existence of this appears to be threatened by the very measures being taken to protect Europe from global competition.

The Nation-State and the Federation

Reference to the universalisation of the nation-state model has to be qualified. That we live in a world of nation-states cannot be doubted, but some nation-states are in themselves organised as federations. In Europe there are the familiar examples of Germany and Austria, which are members of the European Union, and Switzerland which is not. However, the most significant example of a large federal state is of course the United States of America. After the Declaration of Independence in 1776, the USA might conceivably have developed as a number of independent states and these could very well have come into conflict with each other during the two centuries since. Indeed the American Civil War (1861–65) was fought to maintain the Union against the secession of some southern states as the Confederacy and we may be sure that the determination to do this was derived in some part from an awareness of the history of European conflict in a continent consisting of independent states. The Union prevailed and contemporary observation might contrast the success of the USA as a federated super-state with the neighbouring example of Latin America where the former Spanish and Portuguese colonial territories remained as independent states with many subsequent conflicts and little co-operation.

The Threat to the Nation-State

The European Union is often taken to be a threat to the integrity of the nation-state. Indeed it is, but that is not necessarily the same thing as a threat to the rights and freedoms of the people who make up the nation-state. When all is said and done the nation-state is nothing more than a contrived arrangement for the government of the people who inhabit a bounded parcel of land. Indeed it was the development of the nation-state that brought with it fixed territorial boundaries – or borders as they are commonly referred to. Previous political arrangements, notably military empires, had frontiers that fluctuated with the success or failure of virtually constant military campaigns. It is not unknown for the borders of nation-states to change but that is not the norm. Borders between states set apart specific populations but these may or may not have in common straightforward ethnic identity or cultural heritage. This is because the nation-state is essentially an administrative device and in few cases does it coincide with a single undisputed nation. Once fixed the border contains the people who live within it and they are encouraged, and in some cases enforced, to recognise a particular nationality – that of the nation-state itself. On the other hand, the many political struggles over nationality, as in Belgium or Northern Ireland, or over peripheral nationality, as in the Basque region of Spain, serve to draw our attention to the contrived nature of the nation-state and the particular form of nationality that it propagates.

The Case for a Federal Europe

In contrast with the singular nature of the unitary nation-state, the federal form can produce tiers of government and administration which may bring decision-making over many matters closer to the people. In the case of the USA, as well as the federal government there are the state governments with different approaches to many issues. The more sensational instances of these differences are those states that have retained or revived the death penalty for murder, or the few with restrictions over the consumption or even the prohibition of alcohol. These are examples which come immediately to mind but there are many other distinctions which have appeal to the people who live in particular states within the federation. In the European Union there is the case of the German *lande* and their differing approaches to agriculture, for instance, which have emerged in relation to the Common Agricultural Policy or, more recently, to the prohibition of British beef in the face of BSE ('mad cow disease').

There is another factor in relation to peripherality in the nation-state. There are those instances in which the European Union, as an overarching political entity, has offered finance to the peripheral regions of Europe when their state governments have tended towards neglect. The EU symbol is exhibited on many civil engineering and building developments that it has financed in part if not in total. In effect, therefore, the European Union has already demonstrated that it can offer benefits at a number of levels across Europe regardless of nation-states or their governments.

In fact, if national sovereignty is considered as largely an emotive issue, the real benefits which the European Union may be able to confer could be considered as much more important. In the case of Britain and the proposed introduction of the Euro, for instance, the significance which is attached to retaining the Queen's head on banknotes may prove to be very shallow indeed when considered in the context of what precise advantages the independent pound can provide in the future for the people who use it and depend upon it. In fact the currently strong pound, at the time of writing, has serious disadvantages because the price of exports is too high and jobs are being lost as result of British industry's inability to compete, even in Europe let alone in the rest of the world. Yet if the living standards of people are taken to be paramount rather than a form of national pride then support for the pound may be swept away in favour of the Euro. The Queen's head may be a potent national symbol but it does little for Britain's GNP.

An Integrated Europe in the Wider World

In many issues there can be little doubt that the size and strength of a fully integrated Europe, in whatever form that takes, would protect the interests of the people of Europe and their standard of living in a progressively globalising world. The European Union (or perhaps even a future United States of Europe) is one part of what Kenichi Ohmae (1985) has described as the 'global triad', the other two parts being the North America and Japan. In terms of trade, North America is now NAFTA – the North American Free Trade Area that includes Canada and Mexico. A future East Asian trade alliance might contain or, according to some observers, even be lead by China – already there are many cross-national commercial and industrial partnerships within China's 'special development areas' and beyond.

In this scheme of things the existing European Union, plus those several countries from the former Eastern European bloc and the Balkans which are regarded as the next wave of entrants, would become by far the largest economic entity for the foreseeable future – although China would still of course make any East Asian alliance the largest conglomeration of people. In fact China would, if translated into consumer society on the scale of the West, be the largest market in the world with all that this implies for economic expansion and the balance of economic power. It is this kind of scenario that lends much weight to the argument for an integrated European Union.

There is a further paradox in that Europeans need the European Union to protect themselves against the progressive globalisation of the world when it was in fact Europeans who set the globalisation process in motion in the first place. Many writers have contributed to the argument that from the sixteenth century onwards Europeans precipitated the exchange of goods and services – and culture too – on an increasingly global scale. Recently André Gunder Frank has gone so far as to claim that this outpouring of European global activity involved the 'high-jacking' of an existing Chinese 'world economy' – China, the 'middle kingdom', had hitherto dominated all of its surrounding areas. This take-over was financed chiefly by the acquisition of prodigious amounts of silver from the Spanish American colonies. Initially, the Spanish used this silver to buy the requirements of empire which they lacked and in this way the wealth passed into the pan-European economy. For their part, the Chinese regarded their culture as naturally superior to any other and the consequence of this was that they desired nothing from Europe. Therefore, it was only the large amounts of silver that enabled Europeans to buy their way into China and establish trading enclaves at Macao, Hong Kong, Canton and Shanghai. In later centuries Opium was introduced into the trade as a less honourable substitute for the silver.

Gunder Frank's further argument is that with the contemporary success of East Asian industry and in particular those applications in vehicle building and electronics which have improved on the European original, the core of the world economy is gradually gravitating back towards East Asia and, he claims, ultimately China. This is of course a long-term view and is taken regardless of economic recession in East Asia, which in any case appears to have been of a temporary nature. It could be interpreted therefore as another dimension to the case for a powerful and integrated European Union in the global economy.

The Structure of an Integrated Europe

European institutions of government, of one kind or another, have existed ever since the Treaty of Rome produced the European Economic Community of the original six nation-states back in 1957. What is more, in principle, they have changed little since, despite the addition of nine more states. David Arter (1993) distinguishes between what he terms 'the supranational institutions', those made up of people employed by the European Union, and 'the intergovernmental institutions', those made up of people from the governments and administrations of member states. This distinction in itself shows up the inherent tension within the European Union which encompasses integration and association at the same time.

Foremost of the supranational institutions is the **European Commission**, a permanent body charged with a largely bureaucratic role but also with responsibility for upholding the principles of the European Union. It consists of a president who is selected through a process of bargaining in the European Council, which is not a supranational but an intergovernmental institution, as described below. The president of the Commission then has to work with the commissioners who are appointed by the governments of member states. Every member state has at least one commissioner and the larger states of France, Italy, Germany, Spain and the UK each has two (although at the time of writing this advantage is under review especially in the face of enlargement). An important factor here is that it is the prerogative of member states to maintain or replace their commissioners at any time, without necessarily any reference to the president. This is another facet of the tension between supranational and intergovernmental influences. However, the president does have the responsibility for assigning roles to the commissioners.

An indicator of the practical role played by Commissioners is provided by those occasions when the governments of member states have come to regard 'their' commissioners, the commissioners appointed by them, as 'going native'. That is, they have appeared to operate exclusively in the interests of the European Union without heed for those of the member-state government. There have been several instances of this and it demonstrates another aspect of the broad tension between the EU and its member states.

The history and status of the European Commission has been mixed and this has most often depended upon the personality and capabilities of its president. The political leaders of member states have sometimes worked strongly against the Commission, particularly in the case of progressive European integration. The first president of the Commission was Jean Monnet, one of the founders of European union, and his term was as might be expected extremely influential. Later during the 1960s, however, President Charles de Gaulle of France worked strongly against the power of the president. Following that, during the 1970s and 1980s there was a series of strong presidents, but then in 1988 Margaret Thatcher made her Bruges speech in which she retaliated against the integrative tendencies of Jacques Delors, the president at the time.

More damaging still, during the 1990s and particularly the latter part of that decade, the Commission became mired in corruption scandals to the extent that in the end almost the entire commission was made to resign en masse. There is now an anti-corruption commissioner! This harmed the cause of European integration immeasurably and yet the Commission is still charged with implementing the principles of the Treaty of Rome and successive treaties and declarations, principally the Single European Act of 1985 and the Treaty on European Union of 1992.

A second supranational institution is the **European Parliament**. In the first place this was merely an assembly with representatives of political parties in member states. Direct elections did not come until as late as 1979 and even now there are different methods of election in different countries. As with the Commission the larger countries have more representation and with the re-unification of Germany it has more than any other in recognition of its large population. The precise numbers have become almost a permanent item on the political agenda in the European Union as well as in member states.

With the coming of direct elections the European Parliament was able to establish itself much more powerfully as a component of European Union government. Since then it can truly claim to have influenced decision-making and policy formation when before there was really little evidence of this. It has produced two major party groupings: the Socialist Group which has been consistently the largest and the centre-right European People's Party (Christian Democrat/Conservative), the next largest. These were derived from the political alignments of member states but it can be claimed that a European party system is developing with trans-national policies and programmes – not only astride the traditional left-right divide but also in the form of the 'Rainbow Alliance' which consists of 'green' and other alternative positions.

The third supranational institution is the **European Court of Justice**. This is a court operating along familiar lines whose judges are appointed from its member states, one from each state for a term of six years, and there is also a smaller number of advocates general. It is a constitutional court in that its role is to uphold the principles of those treaties which have served to form the European Union and also the laws which have been enacted by the constituent parts of the European Union, as described above and below. Its business is largely transgressions of these principles and laws and its work may take a number of forms including actions by the Commission against member states or by one member state against another. Individual citizens or groups of citizens can apply to the court, especially under the terms of the European Convention on Human Rights, although this is gradually being absorbed into the legal systems of member states.

From here we should move to the intergovernmental institutions, the **European Council** and the **Council of Ministers**. It should be made clear straight away that these are councils of ministers of member state governments who meet together from time to time. For all of the most important issues there is a council of member-state prime ministers or their equivalents; this is the European Council. It meets twice a year to discuss broad issues and form strategic policy. In the case of lesser important or more specific issues, other ministers meet under the aegis of a Council of Ministers. For instance, agricultural issues will be dealt with by a meeting of agriculture ministers, foreign issues by foreign ministers, etc. The most important of these have assumed a permanent existence and there is the Agricultural Council, the Economic and Financial Council and the Foreign Affairs Council, each of which meets monthly.

The ground is prepared for these councils by civil servants and diplomats from member states who meet twice weekly to plan the meetings and prepare agenda and papers.

These councils form the medium by which member state governments maintain their overall power in the European Union. To date the balance of power has remained firmly in the favour of member states with the supranational institutions having only a partial contribution to European Union decision-making. The European Council and to a lesser extent the Council of

Ministers can have absolute power within the Union. The raison d'être for this is that, notwithstanding the existence of the European Parliament, the democratic institutions of Europe reside essentially in the electorates of member states and in the existence of member-state governments who therefore maintain their precedence over decision-making within the European Union.

References

Arter, D. (1993), *The Politics of European Integration in the Twentieth Century*. Aldershot: Dartmouth.

Gunder, F. A. (1998), *Re-Orient: Global Economy in the Asian Age*. Berkeley, Cal.: University of California Press.

Henig, S. (1997), *The Uniting of Europe*. London: Routledge.

Holland, M. (1993), *European Community Integration*. London: Pinter.

Ohmae, K. (1995), *Triad Power: The Coming Shape of Global Competition*. New York: Free Press.

Wistrich, E. (1989), *After 1992: The United States of Europe*. London: Routledge.

Tony Spybey

The Nation-State and European Institutions

First of all we must be careful to understand what we mean here. The nation-state with all its constituent features is itself a European institution or more accurately a set of institutions. That is, the nation-state emerged from the political development of Europe and, as part of Europe's influence on the rest of the world, became adopted globally. The contemporary world is a world of nation-states as confirmed by the existence of the United Nations Organisation with its membership comprising of virtually all the nation-states of the world currently numbering 188. Now we perceive that Europe's nation-states, each with its own government and administration, are well advanced in the process of coming to terms with the European Union which is an overarching constitutional entity developing its own state-like forms of organisation.

Therefore, we must look at the development of those long-standing European institutions, government, administration, law, etc., which gave us the Europe of the nation-states and then go on to see how this is affected by the newer pan-European institutions. These were created firstly by the Treaty of Rome in 1957 in the form of the European Economic Community which developed into the European Community during the late 1980s. But more significantly, since the early 1990s, there is the development of the European Union with the Maastricht Treaty of 1991, the Single Market of 1993 and the moves to introduce a single currency, the Euro, around 1998.

The prior existence of the European nation-states does of course provide the matrix against which all subsequent European developments have taken place. The EEC, EC and EU have successively arisen from Europe's reconstruction after the Second World War and its subsequent response to a globalised world the form of which, it must not be forgotten, was also created by people of European origin. It was Europeans who began the globalisation process and it was those Europeans who crossed the Atlantic for a separate existence as Americans who have notably contributed to it during the twentieth century. Subsequently, the Europeans who are most in favour of European integration see a future United States of Europe as a politico-economic entity that is capable of matching in all respects the superpower status of the United States of America.

Antecedents

The arrangements that societies have made for their government and administration are commonly referred to as the state. This implies permanent or at least lasting institutions of government that originally played a significant part in distinguishing a society with a settled urbanised core from a nomadic or semi-nomadic tribal society. The existence of the state is taken to be one of the hallmarks of civilisation.

The earliest states were city-states, that is arrangements for government – and also belief-system and trade – located within the walls of city. Such walls served not only to protect the polity but also as a barrier at which to tax the passage of goods in trade. In the case of Europe, we like to look back to the city-states of Ancient Greece as the origins of our political institutions: the polity, democracy, etc. Moving forward in time many centuries, the city-states of the Italian Renaissance are often linked with these, largely because of their patronage of the reproduction of many aspects of the classical arts. In writing about the Renaissance, however, Peter Burke counsels against making too simplistic a connection either between Ancient Greece and Renaissance Italy or between these city-states and our modern European ideas of polity, liberty and democracy.

…examples (from ancient Greece or northern Italy c.1100–1500, not to say 'Athens and Florence') present a misleadingly clear picture of the city-state as a small but autonomous political unit, the home of liberty and democracy . . .(Burke 1986: 137).

Nevertheless, the example of these city-states clearly serves to illustrate the development of the state, that is the institutions for the governance and administration of society that have been and continue to be significant for Europeans. There is no example of a perfect society in terms of its governance and administration but the significance of such things as polity, liberty and democracy, in principle at least, is clear in the governance and administration of European society especially since the nineteenth century. Furthermore, these have become the principles not only for the nation-state societies of Europe but also for other societies where European influence has been felt. That is virtually the whole world.

To move directly from classical city-states to the contemporary world would be to miss out other examples of European state building. For instance, the so-called absolutist states of the Reformation are examples of the concentration of power by the state, although in this case in the name of the king. The lesson is not lost, however, that the facility to centralise government and administration makes possible the concentration of revenue collection. This makes possible the financing of permanent military power that assures the continued existence of the state. It is a circular process of the empowerment of the state. Those states that were successful survived. In fact, not only did they survive, they swallowed up the weaker states that were unsuccessful. Charles Tilly estimates that the 500 or so states of Europe in 1500 were reduced to only 25 by 1900 (Tilly 1975: 12).

The principles of centralisation in state administration, with its attendant advantages in the concentration of fiscal revenues, is evident in the modern nation-state which in addition has much greater administrative capabilities. The absolutists monarchs used the concentration of revenue to equip their armies and navies with the latest military technology, principally in the form of artillery which enabled adversaries' defences to be literally blown away. The modern nation-state has an accepted monopoly of much greater armed force with the industrialisation of weapons production and the application of advanced technology. Moreover, the armed forces of the state are accepted as legitimate whilst the existence of any other is regarded as criminal or terrorist.

Expressed very simply, the modern nation-state is characterised by a democratically elected government, served by a permanent and impartial administration, upheld by an independent judiciary, backed up by a police force for internal order and armed forces for external defence. In real life examples there are breaches in the nature of this simple structure of which we are only too well aware, but the remarkable thing is the resilience and ubiquity of the model as an idealised form.

However, it should not be assumed that there is a simple straightforward evolution of the European state form from the city-state, through the absolutist state, to the modern nation-state. The nature of the development of European institutions is that they emerged from centuries of history involving much struggle which ensured that developments did not always go in the same direction. The result however is the state institutions that we see and recognise today. Now, the independent nation-states of Europe are attempting to accommodate these institutions of government with the emerging administrative structure of the European Union. Quite clearly, attitudes towards the progressive development of the European Union vary enormously across Europe and so in this continuing development there will be no simple evolution either.

European Institutions

This is quite obviously a broad category and can be taken to mean all kinds of things. However, from the foregoing it can be seen that the definition employed here is those institutions which Europeans have devised for their government and administration and which are currently in an as yet partial and incomplete process of absorption into the European Union. The outcome and the balance of authority between the Union itself and the nation-states of which it consists is unclear and is likely to remain unclear in the foreseeable future. This can only be further complicated by the admission to the Union of those eastern European states which were formerly dominated by the Soviet Union. Despite their economic disadvantages they are now amongst the most fervent advocates not only of membership but of progressive integration too.

The development of European institutions based upon the nation-state is inseparable from the experience of the people who live within the European nation-states and now the European Union. The existence of the modern nation-state brought with it the principles of citizenship and citizenship rights. The rights of the individual as citizen, including principally equality before the law, suffrage and welfare, are vested in the nation-state. Moreover, even to exist in the modern world one needs to be the citizen of a nation-state. Manifestly, the existence of stateless persons is uncomfortable and often hazardous.

For example, it may be seen that as part of the restructuring of the modern Middle East with the collapse of the Ottoman Empire after the First World War, the Kurds were unlucky enough to miss out on the state building process that produced Turkey, Syria, Iraq, the Lebanon, Jordan, etc. Consequently their existence now is at the mercy of the Turkish and Iraqi nation-states in particular, which as recent experience shows has tended to result in their persecution.

Within the established nation-state, however, the recognised citizen can expect to contribute to democratic government at least through the right to vote in elections, but also through the freedom to form political parties and pressure groups and put forward candidates for election to government. Such a government will be served by a permanent and impartial bureaucracy to which entry is achieved by qualification derived from an education system which the state also underwrites. The principle of education for all has been one of the cornerstones and defining features of the modern nation-state, albeit that resources may be limited and elite forms continue to exist.

Equality before the law is upheld in principle by the existence of an independent judiciary to which even the elected government may be taken to task if it steps outside the statutes that it creates. Equally independent should be the police force that in this scheme of things is charged with the maintenance of order within the society of the nation-state. As mentioned earlier the police together with the armed forces, which exist for external defence, are the only bodies with the right to carry arms and exercise legitimate force and they do this on behalf of the nation-state as directed by government through decision-making and legislation. These are the European institutions which form the components of the nation-state and they have become globalised because the contemporary world is organised as nation-states which conform more or less to this model in a nation-state system. Confirmation of this is provided by the existence of the United Nations Organisation. Here it is necessary to emphasise once again that despite the ineffectualities and corruptions of this system, which undoubtedly exist, the most remarkable thing is the pervasiveness of the model.

The point of all this is to illustrate that what are referred to here as European institutions have developed from the centuries of development of Europe as a collection of separate independent, sovereign states. Historically the European states have been politically independent. This is what has distinguished Europe from other civilisations organised as singular hierarchical empires. Yet they have developed constitutional structures in common.

Of particular significance is the separation of polity and economy in Europe. This has left economy free to develop the capitalist form that has been so effective in wealth creation, allowing Europe to be so powerful in the world. As described above, the development of the European state although never a simple evolutionary process, allowed for the centralisation of administration and therefore of fiscal income which in turn enabled the state to finance increased military power. The freeing up of economy to create private wealth provided the potential for increased fiscal income and the state's military power could then amongst other things protect its national trading enterprise. Nevertheless economy became increasingly interdependent between states which brought about both the process of globalisation and the creation of large economic blocs like the European Union.

Modernity

The combination of state power and burgeoning trade arose with the absolutist states and these were very significant in the development of European institutions. But in the absolutist state the power was invested in the person of the monarch. With the transition to modernity the power of the king was removed to be replaced by that of democratic government and with this European institutions became transformed into more or less what we see today.

Arguably the first really significant and influential example of this was the English civil war and the later Glorious Revolution of the seventeenth century. The civil war was between the king, Charles I, and parliament. The victory of parliament involved the trial and execution of the king. However, after the death of the parliamentary leader, Oliver Cromwell, the crown was restored with the reinstatement of the king's son, Charles II. This turned out to be a temporary restoration because, with the replacement of the Stuart dynasty by the house of Orange in the Glorious Revolution towards the end of the seventeenth century, the power of parliament over the king was firmly established once and for all. Even then it was more than a century before a long process of reform began to bring rights of citizenship in law, elections and social welfare.

A much more dramatic and even more influential example was the American Revolution, or Declaration of Independence, when those Europeans who had settled in North America decided they had had enough of the rule of kings. These were principally British and they were rebelling against the rule of the Hanoverian dynasty in the person of King George III and his colonial rule. The outcome was not just the establishment of the United States of America but of the rights of man and the citizen as embodied in the American Constitution, following the writings of Thomas Paine. This was the first time that the principles of government of a nation-state had been set out in an all-encompassing legal document. As such it represents the codification of state institutions, albeit geographically on another continent, in legal-rational form consistent with the spirit of the Enlightenment. Whatever the shortcomings of the American Constitution, and we know that they are many, full credit has to be given to the attempt to establish government on rational principles putting behind and removing for good government vested in kings, hereditary succession and aristocracy.

The American Revolution began with the Declaration of Independence in 1776 and a little while later a similar and just as significant establishment of the rights of man and the citizen took place with the French Revolution beginning in 1789. In this case not only was the king executed but the aristocracy as well and many others connected with it in the Reign of Terror. The transformation of state institutions was comprehensive, at first even to the extent of introducing a new calendar commencing at the revolution. Even the emergence of Napoleon and his self-declaration as emperor brought widespread reform, as for instance in a new legal system, the *Code Napoleon*, and a new education system based upon the state rather than the church.

These three major examples of radical change in European institutions were historically very different and yet all three contributed significantly to the establishment in principle of the familiar organs of the state: elected government, permanent and impartial administration, independent judiciary, backed up by a monopoly of the means of violence embodied in police and armed forces.

Weber's Rational-Legal Bureaucracy

It was notably Max Weber who recognised and defined the rational-legal form of authority as it applied to the organisation of the state. He distinguished this from rationality based upon tradition or charismatic leadership. These latter two were of course the hallmarks of the state in traditional societies before the onset of modernity. With the Enlightenment had come the desire for explanation based upon science and, in the state, a form of government which avoided either the stasis of tradition or the foibles of rule by kings and their successors. The revolutions described above, therefore, represent the constitutional equivalents of breakthroughs in scientific explanation of the physical world, as stimulated by Isaac Newton, and the natural world, by Charles Darwin. No longer were people prepared just to accept the government they were given. Instead they wanted to play a part in its creation through the ballot box. Along with equality before the law, these are the two fundamental principles of citizenship, the recognition of the individual as a legal entity with rights. Only after that comes the pressure for a range of welfare benefits which, writ broadly, encompass health, education and care especially in old age.

Mass education in particular has been held up as one of the hallmarks of a civilised society, although in fact it is a reciprocal arrangement. The state requires educated citizens in order that they understand what is at stake in elections and government and that they are able to contribute to the economy of a modern society. Citizens require education in order to be able to participate fully in the institutions of a modern society and fulfil their duties to the state, to work and to the armed forces when necessary. This is the social contract as recognised by Jean-Jaques Rousseau. The citizen must contribute to society as well as enjoy its benefits and education potentates this. The arrangement is eminently rational in the sense referred to here and in all respects a product of the Enlightenment. From the perspective of the twenty-first century the flaws in the contemporary outcome are all too apparent but we should not lose sight of the significance of this in European institutions. Only then can we begin to grapple with the possibilities for the European Union as it struggles to find a formula for integration and at the same time enlarge itself by admitting the growing number of mainly eastern European states which are queuing up to join.

Legal Institutions

The essence of the rational state is codification. This has been carried to a high degree with complex legal systems, giving employment to a burgeoning legal profession, and beyond that regulations covering many aspects of modern life, for instance agriculture, food hygiene, etc. To a great extent this is the way that public sector state administration intercedes in private sector economy. Additionally, today, it is the arena in which the legal systems of the nation-states interact with and potentially come into conflict with the directives of the European Union. Gradually, the European Union is preparing for a single society with European citizenship, whilst the member states resist changing things which they hold dear. At the time of writing the EU was attempting to regulate the selling of food in open air markets and in the process coming into conflict with the desire of the French not to lose the range of foodstuffs for which their cuisine is justifiably famous. They tend to be produced locally and not under the control of factory regulation, refrigeration, etc. This is only one example but the struggle continues in all kinds of milieu.

Europe developed as a collection of independent, sovereign nation-states each with its own legal system. These vary considerably and range from the incrementally developed British system at one extreme to the codified French system at the other. British law is based to a great extent upon precedent established through case law, derived originally from common law, but with several other influences such as the Roman principles that are so evident in the British law of property and commercial law. French law by contrast is based upon the nineteenth century *Code Napoleon* which transformed the whole system at a stroke in the aftermath of the French Revolution.

The Forces of Coercion

In the European states law is upheld by the police who serve to enforce internal order whilst the nation-state itself is protected from external aggression by its armed forces. This model has been bequeathed upon the world but nowhere is the distinction more evident than in Europe or those parts of the world where Europeans have settled: the USA and Canada, Australia and New Zealand. It is only in extreme circumstances in Europe when the armed forces are seen in an active role on the streets. Clearly this is not so elsewhere in some other parts of the world.

Yet even within Europe there are differences. In Italy, for example, the *carabinieri* are a form of militia organised quite separately from the local police and in Spain there are three kinds of police: the heavily armed *guardia civil*, the *policia nacional* and the local police. In Britain and the Scandinavian countries by contrast there is only one kind of police force although it has a number of branches.

These differences represent a further dimension to the problem of European integration. In fact the organisation called InterPol, which was formed to facilitate co-operation between Europe's police forces given the internationalisation of crime, actually pre-dates the European Union or its earlier forms the EEC and the EC. Against this, there have been instances when European countries have not even co-operated to extradite criminals who have fled from the country in which they committed their crimes. There was the notorious case of the so-called 'Costa del Crime' in Spain where many British criminals took refuge, although it has to be said that this was mainly before Spain's entry to the European Union.

The organisation of the military tends to have become globalised in recent times largely because of the industrialisation of weapons production which has brought about a globalisation of military weapons and the training for their use. From the American Armalite and the Russian Kalashnikov infantry rifles, through Semtex explosive, to jet fighters and Sam missiles, the supply is hugely standardised and this systematises the procedures for their use. Before this, however, the basic forms of military organisation which have emerged in modern military manuals and procedures were derived from the development of European states particularly during the absolutist period. Celebrated examples are infantry drill that was introduced by the Dutch Prince Maurice of Orange, the platoon system and salvo shots of King Gustavus Adolphus of Sweden, and the rigid chain of command of Count Wallenstein of Bohemia. During the process of state building European states introduced officer academies and gunnery schools to improve their armed forces and these have been emulated since wherever nation-states have employed armed forces.

As with InterPol in the case of police, the military alliance NATO (the North Atlantic Treaty Organisation) pre-dates the European Union and of course extends beyond it since the USA is by far its most powerful member. Nor has it been a completely Western European alliance since it was boycotted for many years by the French who preferred to maintain their own *Force de Frappe*. Above all NATO is a product of the Cold War when it faced the opposing Warsaw Pact alliance of the former Soviet Union and its Eastern European satellites. Since the collapse of the Soviet Union after 1989 some of its former Eastern European allies have applied for and been admitted to NATO. Previous to that the former Warsaw Pact countries joined the NATO countries in a North Atlantic Co-operation Council in 1991 immediately following the end of the Cold War.

There is, therefore, to date no military arm to the European Union but the issue has appeared on agenda in recent times. The Western European Union, a putative European pillar of NATO, has long existed but has been little used as a formal alliance of the Western European states. Now, with a queue of east

European states waiting to join the EU, its relevance would appear to have passed. Yet as the European Union increasingly assumes the identity of a state it seems almost inevitable that there should be armed forces attached to it.

The Global Significance of European Institutions

As Europeans colonised so many parts of the world from the sixteenth to the nineteenth centuries they took with them their social, political and economic institutions. That is, the means to govern the colonies were the same in principle as those used to govern the home societies in Europe, although colonial populations were generally treated much worse than home populations! Moreover, such institutions were established and reproduced amongst local populations through the medium of education, so that they lasted beyond colonialism.

The emerging political leaders who strove for constitutional independence in the colonies were themselves educated to the European pattern. Many of them had continued their studies in Europe or North America. They used the familiar forms of political parties and trade unions to further their claims for independence. And when independence came the 'emergent nations' as they were called were nations from the European mould.

They attempted to install democratically elected governments, although many examples subsequently collapsed to be replaced by military coups and dictatorships. The old colonial administration, with the Europeans removed, took over the civil service, although many examples became mired in corruption. The legal systems were modelled on those of their former colonial masters, although all too often they broke down in the face of dictatorship and corruption. Police and armed forces were based upon Western models but they suffered in the face of the same problems. Expenditure on arms in the former colonies has tended to be greater than on anything else.

The post-colonial state, therefore, has inherited the language, law, education and many other institutions of colonialism. This is the legacy of both the rise and decline of the West. The world now works largely on the basis of Western institutions. The United Nations Organisation is a form of confirmation of the global acceptance of the European model of the nation-state. The World Bank, the International Monetary Fund and the World Trade Organisation are extensions of European banking and trade, albeit dominated by the USA. The International Court of Justice is to all intents and purposes a court to the European model. It seems that all aspects of international organisation have come to terms with European ways of doing things. That is not surprising, they were after all organised overwhelmingly by people of European origin.

The Emergence of the European Union

Two Frenchmen, Jean Monnet and Robert Schuman, are recognised as setting in motion the concrete proposal for European union. The driving force came with the end of the Second World War and the belief that the only reliable guarantee of future peace lay in combining the interests of France and Germany. The original European Coal and Steel Community dated from 1951 and included Belgium, the Netherlands and Luxembourg as well as France and Germany (then West Germany of course). These same countries formed a customs union, the European Economic Community, with the Treaty of Rome in 1957.

The saga of Britain's role is well known. The Conservative governments of the 1950s were against joining in favour of Imperial Preference, the trading system of the British Empire. Although empire was fast transcending into commonwealth. The Labour governments of the 1960s were refused admission by the French and in particular by President Charles de Gaulle who, it is said, was merely getting revenge for shabby treatment during the war. Although he claimed that it was because Britain would be a disruptive member. It fell, therefore, to Conservative Prime Minister Edward Heath, a strong pro-European, to negotiate Britain's admission in January 1973, when Denmark and Ireland joined too.

The poorer countries of southern Europe took longer to prepare and first had to shed extreme right wing governments. Greece was admitted in January 1981 and Spain and Portugal in January 1986. Much later, in January 1995, Austria, Finland and Sweden joined leaving only Norway and Switzerland in Western Europe as non-members. At the beginning of the twenty-first century there is a long queue of countries in Eastern Europe, the Balkans and the Mediterranean eagerly awaiting entry.

The implications of this impending substantial increase in membership are enormous and yet the institutions of the European Union are to date the same in principle as they were when the EEC was formed in 1957. The main decision making body is the European Council (of Ministers) which is made up, as the name suggests, of ministers from member governments. For all major issues this means prime ministers or equivalents and decisions have to be unanimous. Lesser issues are decided by appropriate ministers. As for instance when decisions on agriculture are discussed by agriculture ministers, health by health ministers, etc.

The European Commission acts as a kind of permanent civil service for the European Union. Each country has at least one Commissioner and the larger countries have two, with a term of office of four years. The presidency of the Commission is decided by the member states. Commissioners are of course served by extensive administrative staff mostly based in Brussels. There has been extensive criticism of the power of the Commissioners. This came to a head over corruption scandals during the late 1990s so that most of the Commissioners were forced to resign and be replaced. Now there is a Commissioner whose job is solely to root out malpractice.

Despite its title, the least powerful body is the European Parliament. At the time of writing, 626 members are elected from constituent countries to well paid positions with generous expenses for accommodation and travel. Yet their decision-making capability is small when compared with the Council and the Commission, despite several declarations of intent to remedy this. Given the national party allegiances from which members emerge, a composite spectrum of alliances has been formed in the European Parliament but with two large groups, the socialists and the Christian-democrats (Conservatives). The Parliament has in the past met in Brussels, Luxembourg and Strasbourg but now has a new home in Strasbourg that may or may not be permanent.

In some ways the weakness of the European Parliament and the strength of the Council/Commission only reflects the imbalances of the cabinet-assembly relationship in the governments of member states. One thing that can be observed is that whilst the European Parliament and the parliaments of member states, like the European Commission and the civil services of member states, are quite separate, it is the ministers of member state governments who make up the European Council. This may be illustrated thus:

Member states		**EU institutions**
ministers	$\longrightarrow$	Council of Ministers
civil service	$\longleftrightarrow$	European Commission
parliament	$\longleftrightarrow$	European Parliament

The strategic decision-making of the European Union is currently carried out by ministers of governments of member states and this is taken to reflect the democracies of member states. These are then put into practice by the Commissioners who must put the detailed proposals before the European Parliament for approval. These are the basic principles although, of course, in practice they are more complicated and it is the less visible or even invisible workings that tend to cause suspicions about the so-called 'rule from Brussels'.

With the Maastricht Treaty of 1991, the Single Market of 1993 and foundation of the single currency at the turn of the century, there can be no doubt that the intention of the most pro-European politicians is closer political as well as economic union. The outcome of existing developments will take the European Union of the nation-states towards a European federation. With the use of words this can be seen as a federated Europe or even a federal Europe which to all intents and purposes would be a single political entity. There is no doubt, however, that the goal of some is an outright United States of Europe, a politico-economic state that would be larger and potentially more powerful than the United States of America.

References

Burke, P. (1986), "City states". In: **Hall**, J. A. (ed.), *States in History*. Oxford: Blackwell.

Tilly, C. (1975), "Reflections on the history of European state-making". In: **Tilly**, C. (ed.), *The Formation of National States in Western Europe*. Princeton N.J.: Princeton University Press.

Andrew Thompson

Nationalism in Europe

Introduction

In the opening sentences of his book *Nationalism* (1960), Elie Kedourie remarks that nationalism 'is a doctrine invented in Europe at the beginning of the nineteenth century', adding caustically that it is one that 'we might well have been without'. Subsequent studies, notably Benedict Anderson's (1983) *Imagined Communities*, have challenged the argument that Europe is the birthplace of nationalism. Events in Europe were nevertheless crucial in the early development of nationalism; it was Europe, notably its central and eastern regions, which would be the laboratory for implementing the Wilsonian concept of national self-determination.

In the late-twentieth century, Europe has, again, figured prominently in the history of nationalism. Events in central and eastern Europe have provided us with powerful reminders of the continuing potency of this ideology. Moreover, the development of European integration has sponsored a new twist, whereby nationalisms have learned to coexist with, and even thrive in relation to, the supranational European Union. Against the backdrop of these happenings, any discussion of the end of nationalism must be viewed as little more than wishful thinking

This chapter is concerned with exploring two facets of the development of nationalism in Europe. The first section examines three key stages in the rise and spread of nationalism in Europe. The second part of the discussion considers the relationship between nationalism and European integration.

The development of the 'national question' in Europe 1870–1914

It is difficult to establish a date that can be taken as marking the beginning of a qualitatively unique era in the history of nationalism in Europe. The back end of the nineteenth century was, however, a period marked by events of enormous importance, with the unification of Italy in 1870 and the unification of Germany a year later. These particular events were themselves preceded by lengthy campaigns that had begun in the opening decades of the century. The nationalisms that had, in the main, inspired the eventual unification of Germany and Italy, respectively, were not characterised by cultural, or ethnic visions of the nation. Such visions were certainly in circulation, among a small section of the elites in these territories, but they do not appear to have had a significant bearing on the form of nationalism that underpinned events in Germany and Italy. Historians, such as John Breuilly (1993) and Eric Hobsbawm (1990), have convincingly argued that the leaders of the campaigns for unification were underpinned by more nakedly political concerns, and that it was only after these new states were established that ethnic notions of the nation gained a wider currency.

In the period leading up to the end of World War 1, a number of other nationalist movements in continental Europe achieved independence, such as Romania (1878), Norway (1905), Bulgaria (1908), and Albania (1912). By the late-nineteenth century there were few states or regions in Europe that were not experiencing nationalist independence movements. The Balkans, for example, by the mid-1870s were the focus of political attention on the part of all the major European powers, when nationalist revolts erupted in opposition to the Ottoman rulers. Moreover, in the 1880s a nationalist movement emerged in Bulgaria, supported by Austria, to breakaway from its place in the Russian empire. On the fringes of Europe, the United Kingdom was facing internal nationalist challenges on a number of fronts, although most seriously from Ireland.

It is important to note that during this period nationalism is not confined to unification or separatist nationalisms, but is also crucial to understanding the politics of established European states. Eugen Weber's (1979) study, *Peasants into Frenchmen*, explains how, during the forty years preceding the outbreak of World War 1, the modernisation of the French state succeeded in establishing a widespread national consciousness among the population. The 1871 Forster's Education Act in the UK, which instructed that the medium of primary education must be English, met with opposition from speakers of the Irish, Scottish and Welsh languages but was nevertheless a central policy in an effort to strengthen Britishness. For those central and east European states that gained independence during this period, similar strategies were employed in order to forge popular attachments to the new states and their rulers.

What is evident in the closing decades of the nineteenth century is that the matter of ethnic or cultural identity became increasingly important for nationalist politics in its various forms. This is what Hobsbawm (1990) terms the 'transformation of nationalism'. This period also witnessed a growth in the number of movements across Europe seeking independence, a phenomenon that highlights the growing appeal of the nationalism and the idea of the nation. The 1878 Congress of Berlin, at which the major European powers sought to resolve territorial disputes in the Balkans, demonstrated the continuing power of empire, yet the result of this diplomatic agreement was the creation of more independent states (Montenegro, Romania, and Serbia). Although the great imperial powers continued to carve up the continent of Europe in accordance with their interests, the age of empire in Europe was rapidly coming to an end. The age of nationalism was beginning.

The age of nationalism 1918–1945

The end of the Great War signalled the growing international significance of nationalism. With the collapse of empires across Europe, in the period after 1917/1918, the principles of the nation-state and of national self-determination moved to the fore of the political agenda in Europe. As one leading commentator, James Mayall (1991), remarks, after 1918 'the dominant political form was the nation-state rather than the multi-national empire. The days of coexistence between popular sovereignty and dynasticism were numbered' (1991: 45). The League of Nations, created by the 1919 Treaty of Versailles, asserted the principle of national self-determination in the face of the multi-national empires that had hitherto existed on the European continent. With the exception of the territory of the USSR, in which the issue of national identity would continue to remain problematic, the principle of linking state (the political unit) with nation (the cultural entity) became the guiding principle for the Great Powers carving out the new European order in the aftermath of the War.

The post-World War 1 settlement established a number of new European states. In 1919, Austria, Czechoslovakia, Hungary, the Kingdom of the Serbs, Croats, and Slovenes (to become the Federal Republic of Yugoslavia in 1926), and Poland emerged as independent states. As we know today, the multinational human constitution of even some of these new hybrid entities has proved too much. Moreover, even states where the fault-lines were considerably weaker than in Yugoslavia and Czechoslovakia, contained sizeable ethnic minority populations that represented anomalies for the arbiters of the post-war peace settlement. It was within the states that had brought together two, or more, nationalities, however, that relations were at their most strained. In Yugoslavia, for example, during the inter-war years, when Serb elites dominated the political apparatus with little involvement from those of the other nationalities, the hostilities between Serbs and Croats, in particular, endured in spite of the veil of national unity. Indeed, as one commentator observed as the 1991 civil war was unfolding, the 'Yugoslav idea was discredited in the eyes of non-Serbs even before the Second World War' (Lendvai 1991: 254).

The influence of the Wilsonian settlement did not stop at the redrawing of the political map in central and eastern Europe. In western Europe, the concept of self-determination was embraced by newly-emergent nationalist political parties committed to seceding from their host states. In Wales, for example, Plaid Cymru, the Welsh nationalist party, was formed in 1925. Other influences on Plaid Cymru, however, illustrated how increasingly significant was nationalism in this period. For the founders of Plaid Cymru, events in nearby Ireland were clearly a strong influence. Further, the ruralism of Plaid Cymru is also characteristic of a form of nationalism which played particularly heavily on physical connections to the homeland, and which was also emphasised by Action Francaise.

A further repercussion of the 1919 Versailles peace settlement – one that would have more substantial implications for politics in Europe – was the reaction among Germans. Weimar Germany had been virtually united – from the Left to the Right – in opposition to the Treaty of Versailles. This national consciousness, when combined with the disastrous socio-economic circumstances of the early-1930s, produced great unease among the population. With the intervention of leaders who would fuel, and convert, these sentiments into full-bodied nationalisms, events took a darker turn. As Eric Hobsbawm (1995) argues, 'political liberalism was in full retreat throughout the Age of Catastrophe, a retreat which accelerated sharply after Adolf Hitler became Germany's chancellor in 1933' (1995: 112).

Right-wing fascist and nationalist political movements flourished in a number of continental European states during the 1930s, including Germany, Italy, Spain, Portugal, Hungary, and Romania. Britain was not immune to the influence of fascism, although the spell here was shortly broken. It should also be noted that nationalism was not the sole property of the extreme right. Political leaders who would be prominent in the war against fascism, such as Churchill and de Gaulle, could hardly be accused of failing to promote nationalistic emotions.

The revival of nationalism in western Europe 1945–2000

In the aftermath of World War Two, and against the backdrop of a period of considerable economic growth in western Europe, it is perhaps understandable that many observers felt that the days of European states splintering as a consequence of nationalism were over. Commentators, such as Karl Deutsch

(1966), advocated that the benefits of modernisation and rising prosperity would ensure that support for secessionist nationalist movements would be negligible. In the case for most west European states support for such movements was, indeed, limited for the first two decades of the post war period. By the mid-1960s, however, secessionist nationalist movements were achieving some notable victories.

In the United Kingdom, for example, Plaid Cymru, the nationalist party in Wales, secured its first seat in the British parliament as a result of a remarkable by-election victory in 1966. By 1974, the Scottish National Party had secured 30 per cent of the vote in Scotland, Plaid Cymru had won three parliamentary seats, while in Northern Ireland the British Army was involved in a counter-insurgency campaign against the irredentist Provisional IRA. Other west European states also experienced began to experience increases in support for nationalist political parties during the 1970s, notably in the Basque Country and Catalonia in Spain. Until the death of Franco in 1975 membership of the nationalist parties in these regions was illegal. At the first election in the new Basque 'autonomous community' in 1980, however, the Basque National Party (PNV) secured 37.6 per cent of the vote and Herri Batasuna, the separatist party, won 16.3 per cent (Kellas 1991). During this period nationalist political parties emerged elsewhere across Europe, such as the Breton Democratic Union (UDB) in Brittany, though with markedly less success than their counterparts in the UK and parts of Spain. Other regions also saw the advent of violent separatists activities seen in the United Kingdom (although mostly in Northern Ireland), such as the Basque Country and the island of Corsica.

It is difficult to establish universal explanations for the resurgence of nationalism in western Europe in the 1960s and 1970s. Socio-economic explanations are not particularly helpful. Nationalist successes in Wales and Scotland may partly be attributed to relative economic differences between 'core' and 'peripheral' regions, but the Basque Country and Catalonia are among the most prosperous autonomous communities in Spain.

A more fruitful explanation may be lie in an understanding of the political relations between central government and its regions, and any changes to the structure of political relations within a state. In the case of the Basque country, for example, aspects of Basque cultural identity were banned from public life under Franco's regime. The constitutional change of 1978 (see the chapter on regionalism for further discussion of this development) created institutional spaces for the public activities of nationalist parties. In the United Kingdom, although voters in Scotland and Wales had declined the opportunity for a measure of self-government at a special referendum in 1979, in 1997 devolved administrations were established in Northern Ireland, Scotland, and Wales following referendums. The success of the most recent referendums, in contrast to those in 1979 may be largely be attributed to the growing opposition to a central government which held a decreasing number of parliamentary seats in Scotland and Wales and a consequent desire to establish local centres of decision-making.

In Belgium, political changes have more significantly undermined the national government, and reinforced regionalist and nationalist divisions. Since the mid-1960s nationalist differences between Flemish and Walloons has resulted in the main political parties fracturing into their regional blocs. In Flanders in 1998, the two nationalist parties – the Vlaams Blok (11) and the smaller Volksunie (5), together held 16 seats in the federal parliament. Since 1988, when the federal system was established in Belgium, subsequent reforms have transferred increasing powers to the 'communities' and 'regions' from the federal level. Decentralising political changes have been taking place in other west European states since the early 1980s, and these have, again, enabled nationalist parties to have a more public role.

These changes represent challenges to national governments, at a time when, as a consequence of European integration and global changes, they are facing challenges from above. As we will highlight later, the former in particular has contributed to nationalist policies and rhetoric among national governments in the European Union. Thus, nationalisms against the state are not the only form of nationalisms that have emerged in the post-war period in western Europe.

The resurgence of nationalism in central and eastern Europe 1945–2000

Nationalism may have gradually moved back on to the political agenda in western Europe during the post-war period, but it is central and eastern Europe that has been the location for the most significant resurgence of nationalism in this period. The nationalisms of central and eastern Europe, along with those that have emerged in the former-Soviet Union, were significant in precipitating the demise of the communist regimes in the region. Other factors certainly contributed to this larger change, but nationalism acted as the vehicle that channelled popular opposition to communism. Though, in a number of instances, nationalist feelings would shortly led to conflict within the newly-liberated states, for Misha Glenny (1993), a noted commentator on these changes, 'nineteen eighty-nine was the finest hour of East European nationalism, when the desire for liberation was expressed through a reassertion of national identity' (1993: 204).

The build-up to the changes of 1989, the year that saw the symbolic collapse of the Berlin Wall, involved a growth in national consciousness among populations in states across central and eastern Europe. In the case of the former-Yugoslavia the beginning of the end came in 1990 when the Slovenian and Croatian delegations refused to participate any longer in the federal League of Communists of Yugoslavia. This had, however, been preceded by a growth in nationalist politics. A swell in support for Serbian nationalism had been engineered by Slobodan Miloševic, and had led to him assuming leadership of the Serbian League of Communists in 1987. Miloševic had mobilised popular support by directing attention towards tensions in the Serbian province of Kosovo, playing on what he portrayed as a terrorist threat on the part of ethnic Albanians towards the Montenegrin and, especially, the Serbian minorities resident in Kosovo. The domino effect of developments in Serbia was that politicians in Croatia and Slovenia became increasingly unsettled, and, in the immediate instance, relations between the respective League of Communists in Serbia and Slovenia deteriorated to breaking point in 1990. By the time, in 1990, when agreement had been reached among the eight constituent LC across the former-Yugoslavia to move towards the first multi-party elections, it was clear that, among the leading opposition parties in Slovenia and Croatia, the question of secession from the federation was of primary importance.

The situation in the former – Yugoslavia prior to the late – 1980s was also marked by nationalist tensions between the republics. The relative autonomy of the republics, for example can be traced back to political reforms in the early-1970s, when President Tito, in an effort to take some of the thunder from separatists in the constituent republics, devolved some powers down to the LC within the republics. After Tito's death in 1980 these powers were further strengthened, with the result that, by the late-1980s, the constituent LC were operating with varying degrees of autonomy.

In other states, too, across the region nationalism and the promotion of national consciousness was held by the political elites to be compatible with the governance of a communist state. In Romania, Ceaucescu actively promoted a popular sense of Romanian identity in order to strengthen his control, and moved Romanians from different regions of the country to Transylvania in order to increase the number of Romanians relative to ethnic Hungarians. Equally, the return of Transylvania to Romania from Hungary at the 1948 Treaty of Trianon met with opposition from Hungarian nationals. In Czechoslovakia, which would splinter in 1991, differences between distinctly Czech and Slovak agenda remained a constant throughout the post-war era. In the former-Soviet Union, nationalism was regarded as a bourgeois preoccupation (as it was in other Soviet bloc states), but this did not prevent the Soviet state from categorising its population by ethnic group, or 'nationality'. As Rogers Brubaker (1996) argues, the Soviet state effectively institutionalised nationhood and ethno-national identity, and thus ensured that tension would develop between national groups.

For example, the Soviet purges of opposition in Ukraine, and some of the other wealthier Soviet republics, in the early-1970s were a response to nationalist intellectuals. National hostility to Soviet domination also played a part in the revolts in, for example, Hungary in 1956, Czechoslovakia in 1968, and in Poland in 1980–81.

Nationalism was, then, in various forms, a feature of communist central and eastern Europe in the post-war period. The communist regimes in the states of this region succeeded, temporarily, in containing tensions between national groups, but this was only achieved temporarily and, often, by the use of repressive mechanisms. What, then, led to the heightened significance of nationalism in the region? Firstly, as we have already noted, national rivalries within and between states were not erased during the communist era. On the contrary, whether because regimes exploited ethno-national ideas, or because of what Brubaker terms the 'institutionalisation' of nationhood, national differences grew during the communist era. Relatedly, a second factor was the changing economic situation. In the case of the former – Yugoslavia, the general downturn in the economy, beginning in the late-1970s, led to growing calls (most notably from the International Monetary Fund) for political reforms, specifically the return to a greater degree of federal control over the economy and for greater restrictions on wages and credit facilities. In Slovenia, in particular, the most prosperous of the republics, the implementation of these reforms was met with stiff opposition. Rising levels of unemployment, as a consequence of the collapse of sectors of industry within the republics, and increased hardship, translated into growing hostility both towards the federal structure and towards the other republics. Woodward (1996) notes that, within Croatia and Slovenia, these economic changes were the catalysts for the growing appeal of 'right-wing symbols and ideas' (1996: 162). In the former – Soviet Union, national tensions were exacerbated by the Soviet system of redistribution, which saw wealth transferred out of the more successful republics (Hutchinson, 1994). Finally, there is the failure of the ideology of communism to defeat the challenge of nationalism. As Schöpflin (1995) explains, the 'communist experiment in the creation of identities was undermined because it lacked the capacity to construct the affective bonds that sustain states' (1995: 90).

Nationalism and European integration 1945–2000

The European Union, in contrast, has taken seriously the need to build a cultural dimension to European integration. Since the early-1970s, an increasingly important policy concern within the EU has been the objective of establishing a common cultural ground between the populations of the member states (since 1992, citizens of the European Union). The extent to which these policies in this area have, together, had the desired effect, but research undertaken by the European Commission holds that just under half of all EU citizens feel a dual sense of loyalty to their country and the EU (CEC 1996).

The EU must nevertheless continue to contend with its constituent nations for the loyalty of citizens. The same research cited above illustrates that 40 per cent of all EU citizens feel loyalty to their country only, a figure that rises to over 50 per cent with respect to citizens in Austria, Germany, Finland, Denmark, the United Kingdom, and Sweden. Undoubtedly, since the 1970s the positive presence of the EU in the daily lives of citizens, whether in terms of receipt of funding or through visual symbols, has increased markedly. The media of representation, so crucial in enhancing national identity in the early twentieth century, remain focused on the national arena. Education, a vital institution in developing national consciousness from the late-nineteenth century onwards, is similarly nationally organised. Disputes between national governments and the EU, as well as between national opposition parties and governments over EU affairs, has often created emotionally charged and nationalistic confrontations. Refracted through the media, especially the tabloid press, these developments can lead to opposition to European integration.

As we explain below, however, it would be erroneous to argue that the relationship between nationalism and the supranational EU agenda is of a zero-sum nature. In the discussion that follows we isolate two areas of activity: nationalism at the level of the state, and sub-state nationalism and national identity.

Nationalism and supra-nationalism

The launch of European Monetary Union on 1st January 1999 was a remarkable achievement, one that illustrated how far the process of European integration has progressed since the establishment of the European Coal and Steel Community in 1952. When national currencies disappear from circulation in 2002, people across the world – not just in the EU – will witness a significant transformation in the nation-state. At a symbolic level, images and icons that that have been inextricably linked to national identities will cease to have the public place they have occupied for, in some cases, hundreds of years.

Commentators have good reason, then, to speculate on the future of the European nation-state. As we comment in the unit on the nation-state in Europe, the gradual diminution of national autonomy has been a feature of European integration since the early post-war years, and has advanced considerably from the 1980s onwards. As these changes have unfolded, national governments have often had to reinvent the 'national interest' in order to convince voters of the benefits of continued participation in the formal integration process. Tony Blair, the British Prime Minister, has argued that the 'real patriotic case... for those who want Britain to maintain its traditional global role, is for leadership in Europe' (Blair 1996: 210). Thus, Blair seeks to convert the issue that had put the final nail in the coffin of the previous, Conservative government – that of the schismatic relationship between the national interest and European integration – into a position that allies patriotism with pro-Europeanism.

Other national governments have, however, been less ambivalent than those in the UK about linking state nationalism to European integration. One such case is the Republic of Ireland. In the three referenda held in 1992 on the Treaty of the European Union, 69.1 per cent of voters in the Republic of Ireland expressed their support for the Treaty, in contrast to 49.3 per cent in Denmark and 51 per cent in France. In the Republic of Ireland the issue of European integration is central to competing visions of the direction in which Ireland should progress. It is necessary to point out that this debate is about more than economics. As Joseph Ruane (1994) suggests, it is very much about what the nation will represent in the future, in which different nationalist traditions influence how the EU is perceived.

The cases of those central and eastern European states that are making preparations for joining the EU provide different examples of how the interests of the nation have been aligned with the process of European integration. At a session of the National Assembly of the Republic of Slovenia held on 17 December 1999, members adopted a Declaration of Foreign Policy that stressed that 'Slovenian foreign policy is based on maintaining the Slovenian national identity and, at the same time, an openness to the world', and a 'priority task' in developing the latter would be to seek membership of the EU. Other governments in the region have similarly stressed the compatibility between national identity and membership of the EU. In Poland, the 1997 National Strategy for Integration spoke of how 'Poles perceive the idea of including their country in the integration of Europe as part and parcel of political and economic transformation.' Similarly, at the opening of Estonia's accession negotiations with the EU in March 1998, the Minister for Foreign Affairs, Toomas Hendrik Ilves, remarked that for Estonians membership of the EU is a 'natural part of our development'. In each instance, the claim to know what the nation desires, and to speak on behalf of it, are important devices in furthering the legitimacy of government policy.

The response of national governments in central and eastern Europe highlight how, in spite of some domestic opposition, nationalism can be reconciled with the supranational programme of European integration. As we have suggested, such responses are, largely, mirrored by the positions increasingly adopted by national governments of existing member states. These positions can nevertheless be altered when policies are perceived to run counter to the national interest they have been elected to further, and, in these instances, governments are quite willing to play the national card in opposition to the EU. For example, in 1965 the French government, headed by Charles de Gaulle, refused to take part in Community business, in defiance of what it perceived to be the irreconcilable gulf between Community agricultural policy and French national interests. Later, the British government, led by Margaret Thatcher, was involved in a number of confrontations with the Community, in spite of its leading role in the launch of the Single European Market in the mid-1980s. In 1992, Thatcher's Conservative successor as Prime Minister, John Major, employed the language of nationalism to assuage concerns within his own party (and the electorate) about the Treaty of the European Union, attacking those who, he remarked, 'have in mind to haul down the Union Jack and fly high the star-spangled banner of a United States of Europe' (cited in Billig 1995). Tony Blair, despite his generally pro-European temper, has also not been averse to use similar language. In the build-up to the 1997 general election, and on the day prior to St. George's Day (the patron saint of England) he used the mythological dragon-slaying deeds of St. George as a metaphor for Labour's policy on the EU, stating that his party wants a 'Britain strong in Europe, leading in Europe, building a Europe on Britain's terms... St. George did not slay a dragon so that England could follow the rest. He did it so that we could be strong, and ready to lead' (*The Sun*, 22nd April 1997).

These examples may, in tone, run contrary to the more positive statements by other political leaders (and, sometimes, to the same political leader), yet together they illustrate the same phenomenon: the continued salience of appeals to the nation as a key source of political legitimacy. There may, for example, be a considerable discrepancy in practice between the rhetoric of Slovenian foreign policy strengthening 'Slovenian statehood' and the aspirations of its National Assembly for 'full membership' of the EU, but this does not diminish the importance of the latter for bolstering national pride in Slovenia. Similarly, among the current member states of the EU national governments will continue to utilise nationalism to justify and win support for their own involvement in the EU. As the process of integration exacts further prices from EU member states the issue of who represents the national interest will intensify within domestic political arenas. In this environment it will be difficult for governments not to employ the same nationalist rhetoric, albeit to redefine the national interest, used by opposition parties.

European integration and sub-state nationalisms

State nationalism is not the only example of how the national interest is being redefined in light of developments in the process of European integration. At the sub-state level, too, political parties have increasingly come to view the EU as a forum within which to further the interests of the nations they represent. Ieuan Wyn Jones (1996), a member of the British parliament representing Plaid Cymru, the Welsh nationalist party, argues that for people in Wales the importance of having a 'powerful domestic Parliament with direct links to Europe' would be that it would provide a 'voice in the shaping of Europe tomorrow, and a role in deciding the institutional framework which will guide the EU into the next century' (1996: 47–48). Such sentiments are characteristic of a perception evident across the EU that not only can representatives of sub-state nationalist parties find a 'voice' in the EU, but that they can also exercise a degree of influence over the decision-making process.

As we note in Chapter 8, a significant factor that has given rise to this perception has been the development of EU regional policy. Since the late-1970s, EU regional policy, especially the disbursement of the Structural Funds, has served to stimulate the debate on decentralisation of political power within member states because it is perceived to hold the potential to advance the interests of sub-state nationalist parties. A further factor that has promoted greater involvement of sub-national representatives has been the developments that have centred on the contentious concept of 'subsidiarity'. Since the mid-1970s the discussions of the notion of subsidiarity have been concerned with assessing which tiers of government (EU, national, regional or local) are the most advantageously placed for policy-making and implementation. To a large extent the debate has concentrated on ascertaining the respective areas of competency in policy-making of the EU and national government, yet sub-state nationalist parties have also seized on this concept to argue for greater representation of the interests of sub-state territories.

There is evidence that EU policy is also having an impact on the position of national minorities in the states of central and eastern Europe. A key element of the accession agreements of a number of these states is the treatment of national minorities. In Estonia, for example, a state funded programme on *Integration into Estonian Society, 2000–2007*, along with programmes funded by the EU, the United Nations, and the other Nordic states, have been concerned with promoting training in the Estonian language for speakers of Russian and facilitating dialogue between the Russian and Etonian language groups. In its 1999 report on the 'National Programme for the Adoption of the *Acquis*', the Estonian government declares the need to develop the 'social unification of the society through Estonian language proficiency and acquisition of Estonian citizenship, and, on the other hand, preservation of ethnic differences through acknowledgement of the cultural rights of ethnic minorities and compliance with the constitution.' In Hungary, the government has similarly been concerned with improving its treatment of the Roma, which the European Commission made central to Hungary's accession negotiations. In its 1999 national programme for the adoption of the EU recommendations, the Hungarian government describes the 'improvement of the situation of the Roma as part of the political criteria of membership, is a medium-term priority of the Accession Partnership.'

The European Commission, in its reports on the accession negotiations with the states in this region, continues to be concerned about the protection of the rights of national minorities. In its 1999 composite paper on the progress being made by the candidate countries, the Commission holds that, for example, 'deep-rooted prejudice in many of the candidate countries continues to result in discrimination against the Roma in social and economic life'. More particularly, it maintains that 'some candidate countries continue to face difficulties in finding the right balance between legitimate strengthening of the state language and the protection of minority language rights', highlighting the situations in Latvia and, in particular, Estonia. For the Commission these issues will remain central to its negotiations with these states, just as they will continue to remain priorities if the latter are to accede to the EU. In its 1999 report on the state of its negotiations with the Commission, the Ministry of Foreign Affairs of the Slovak Republic highlights the importance of the Commission's 'positive evaluation' of the former's treatment of the Hungarian minority in Slovakia.

Difficulties will nevertheless remain, as some of these states seek to redefine their new national position after emerging from the shadow of the Soviet era. In such a context, it is likely that national minorities will find it difficult to share in the promotion of the official state national identity. In Estonia, for example, even the section of its response to the Commission's recommendations dealing with the protection of minorities, the government speaks of how policies must be compliant with the 'preservation of the Estonian nation and culture' and of the 'development of a population loyal to the Republic of Estonia.'

The prospect of further fragmentation within the states of central and eastern Europe seems unlikely for the near future. Some states, such as Ukraine, contain what Samuel Huntingdon describes as a 'civilizational fault line' – a demarcation line that divides two cultures with distinctive world-views – but, in spite of nationalist tensions, it is unlikely that will Ukraine will splinter for some time to come. The position of diasporic populations, whether ethnic Hungarians living in Italy, ethnic Poles in Ukraine, or, more troublingly, ethnic Albanians in Yugoslavia, will remain at the fore of political agendas. The Hungarian government, for example, estimates that there are five million ethnic Hungarians living outside the borders of the country, most of them living in Transylvania in Romania. The 1999 declaration of foreign policy of the Republic of Slovenia states that the government:

monitors the position of the members of the Slovenian minority in neighbouring countries and upholds their endeavours to have the countries of their residence respect international obligations relating to their protection. It will assist them in strengthening ties of emigrants and migrant workers with Slovenia and promote their endeavours to preserve a Slovenian identity.

How international disputes involving disaporic populations is resolved among states in this region remains to be seen, in spite of the reassuring language concerning constitutional protection of minority rights. Certainly, past experiences, between, for example, Moldova and Russia, in which the latter supported ethnic Russians in the former, have threatened armed conflict. With regard to those states intent on joining the EU, and where there are significant problems regarding the position of ethnic minorities, the objective of meeting the accession criteria may override national chauvinism. These situations will continue to be dominated by issues of nationalism for some time yet, as the case of Kosovo illustrates.

Summary

- Developments in Europe have been, and continue to be, central to the history of nationalism. During the late nineteenth and early twentieth centuries, the political map of continental Europe was redrawn in line with nationalist demands. As such, the 1919 Versailles peace settlement represented the coming-of-age of the idea that the political and cultural unites should be congruent – as Ernest Gellner (1983) explains, the basic principle of nationalism. Close on a century later, this principle continues to help shape the political agenda in Europe.
- It is important to challenge the perception that nationalism is something that is only experienced in regions undergoing particularly serious social and political change. After Michael Billig (1995), we have argued that the language of nationalism is one of the primary political tools of all forms of government. All governments claim to speak on behalf of 'the people', or 'the nation', no matter whether they are liberal democratic or military regimes. In understanding the role of nationalism in Europe we should direct our attention accordingly, to studying both the more extreme variations of nationalism as well as the policies and rhetoric of national government.

- The relationship between nationalism and European integration is complex. Since the 1980s we have witnessed increasing tension between the EU and its member states, yet, in the same period, governments have also embarked on processes of redefining national interests against the backdrop of formal political integration in Europe. For national governments, there will always be pressure to play the nationalist card, particularly in light of criticism from opposition parties; the advance of integration, as represented by EMU, will only increase the temptations for governments to employ nationalist rhetoric when under pressure. We have, however, explained that many sub-state nationalisms and national identities have thrived in the environment created by EU policies. Among existing member states, the concept of 'subsidiarity' has been employed by secessionist nationalist movements to argue for greater levels of political power to be devolved from the EU and national government down to the sub-state level. Among the states in central and eastern Europe applying to join the EU, constitutional recognition, and government monitoring of minority cultures has been set as one of the political preconditions.
- Nationalism will remain central to the politics of Europe well into the twenty-first century. Indeed, as long as governments are elected by, and accountable to, national citizens, then nationalism will continue to act as a powerful legitimating force and the 'national interest' will continue to be the object of political competition. More worryingly, Europe has not seen the last of conflicts in which nationalism and national identity feature prominently. In central and eastern Europe, for example, the position of diasporic populations, and the relationship between their country of residence and their ethnic 'homeland', will be a source of tension.

Further Reading

Billig, M. (1995), *Banal Nationalism*. London: Sage.

Brubaker, R. (1996), *Nationalism Reframed. Nationhood and the National Question in the New Europe*. Cambridge: Cambridge University Press.

Kupchan C. (ed) (1995), *Nationalism and Nationalities in the New Europe*. Cornell: Cornell University Press.

Özkirimli, U. (2000), *Theories of Nationalism. A Critical Introduction*. London: Macmillan.

Smith, A. D. (1995), *Nations and Nationalism in a Global Era*. Cambridge: Polity.

Wicker, H.-R. (1997), *Rethinking Nationalism & Ethnicity. The Struggle for Meaning and Order in Europe*. Oxford: Berg.

References

Anderson, B. (1983), *Imagined Communities*. London: Verso.

Billig, M. (1995), *Banal Nationalism*. London: Sage.

Blair, T. (1996), *New Britain. My Vision of a Young Country*. London: Fourth Estate.

Breuilly, J. (1983), *Nationalism and the State*. Manchester: Manchester University Press.

Brubaker, R. (1996), *Nationalism Reframed*. Cambridge: Cambridge University Press.

Commission of the European Communities (1996), *The European Union – What's in it for Me?* Luxembourg: Office for Official Publications of the European Communities.

Deutsch, K. (1966), *Nationalism and Social Communication*. New York: MIT Press.

Gellner, E. (1983), *Nationalism*. Cambridge: Cambridge University Press.

Glenny, M. (1993), *The Rebirth of History*. Harmondsworth: Penguin.

Hobsbawm (1995), *Age of Extremes*. London: Abacus.

Hobsbawm, E. (1990), *Nations and Nationalism Since 1780*. Cambridge: Cambridge University Press.

Huntingdon, S. (1997), *The Clash of Civilisations*. London: Simon & Schuster.

Hutchinson, J. (1994), *Modern Nationalism*. London: Fontana.

Kedourie, E. (1960), *Nationalism*. London: Hutchinson.

Kellas, J. (1991), *The Politics of Nationalism and Ethnicity*. London: Macmillan.

Lendvai, P. (1991), "Yugoslavia without Yugoslavs: the roots of the crisis". *International Affairs* 67, 2: 251–261.

Mayall, J. (1990), *Nationalism and International Society*. Cambridge: Cambridge University Press.

Ruane, J. (1994), "Nationalism and European Community integration: the Republic of Ireland". In: **Goddard**, V. A. and J. R. **Llobera** (eds) (1994), *The Anthropology of Europe*. Oxford: Berg.

Schopflin, G. (1995), "Nationhood, communism, and state legitimation". *Nations and Nationalism* 1, 1: 81–92.

Weber, E. (1979), *Peasants into Frenchmen*. London: Chatto and Windus.

Woodward, S. L. (1995), *Balkan Tragedy: Chaos and Dissolution After the Cold War*. Washington: The Brookings Institution.

Wyn Jones, I. (1996), *Europe – the Challenge for Wales*. Talybont: Gwasg Taf Cyf.

Andrew Thompson

People's Europe?:
The Social Dimensions of European Integration

Introduction

Since its inception in the early post-war period, the process of European integration has set in motion changes that have had increasingly important implications for the populations of the Member States (MS) of the EU. Throughout the development of European integration its architects and its participating governments have laudably proclaimed that the objective of this process has been to bring about peace, prosperity and mutual understanding within the European Community, and its successor since 1992, the EU. The creation of a better social environment has always, it is argued, been the underlying rationale for the policies that have been at the core of the mechanics of integration. The preoccupation with market integration, economic growth and global competitiveness, however, has meant that the development of a distinct emphasis on social affairs as an integral and equally important dimension of European integration has not occurred. Only since the late-1980s has attention on the part of policy-makers within national government and the EU, respectively, started to turn more to the importance of the social dimension of European integration. Over the course of the last decade emphasis on the social and political rights of individuals within the EU and concern with levels of popular support for the process of integration have begun to receive greater consideration. As the British government maintained during its presidency of the EU in the first-half of 1998, the development of a 'People's Europe' must be central to the future trajectory of European integration.

Recognising the significance of moving in this direction, the following discussion nevertheless maintains that with regard to policy-making in the EU social issues remain residual concerns. This chapter begins by examining the primary importance of economic integration for the overall process of European integration, before moving on to examine the social dimensions of economic change in the EU. Highlighting the importance of popular support for integration for the overall stability and success of this process, the chapter explores the attempts to strengthen the popular legitimacy of European integration. Central to this discussion is an analysis of the notion of EU citizenship. The final section assesses what role developments at the sub-national tier, in the form of regional and local government, can play in both fostering social integration at the level most immediate to individuals and in generating greater popular awareness of the developments taking place within the EU. The aim here is to consider the strength of the sub-national level in the governance of the EU and the role that it plays in this process of change. Overall, the aim of this article is twofold: to consider the factors which have prevented the development of a strong social dimension to European integration *and* to examine some of the ways in which this issue has, and may be, addressed.

Economics and European integration

In the history of post-war European integration explicit concern with social matters – notably the consequences of the resultant changes engendered by integration for the populations of the MS and the need to give integration a more human dimension – has been persistently overshadowed by the preoccupation with economic and political questions. Since the late-1980s, when the European Commission President Jacques Delors acknowledged the need for a strong social dimension to European integration, there have been moves towards rectifying this shortcoming (most notably in the provisions for a 'Protocol on Social Policy' and a "Citizens' Europe" included in the TEU), although the weakness and ambiguity of these provisions affirm the residual status of this social dimension (Bryant 1991; Lange 1993). The failure as yet to develop a strong social dimension, which might substantially enhance the popular legitimacy of European integration, should not be viewed as a responsibility to be borne solely by the Commission. Certainly, for much of its life the Commission has been a technocratic and rather elitist institution seemingly guided by the principle that the 'Commission-knows-best', but under Delors and, since 1995, Jacques Santer the Commission has actively sought to generate public support for European integration. Part of the responsibility must also be shouldered by the national governments of the Member States (MS), for until recent years they have shown little real interest in producing changes which might serve to generate alternative loyalties to the EU or direct public attention away from the national framework. In addition, the matter of market integration appears to have been categorised as a less 'sensitive' area of governance by the national governments in the sense that while there may be marked differences of opinion as to how this is to be achieved there is a general consensus that change in this area is nevertheless necessary to maintain effective global competition.

Over and above these issues, and the kind of internicine strife which occurs between the supranational Commission and the inter-governmental Council of Ministers, it is the concentration on market integration as the rationale of European integration which has meant that questions of social cohesion have been routinely relegated in the scheme of importance. This is not to say that as the governments of the MS have chased economic growth within the framework created by the European Community (EC), and, since 1992, the EU, that they have not been concerned with their own domestic popularity and the reactions of their national electorates. Rather, it is to suggest that insufficient attention has been given to the social dimensions of integration because the prerogative has been economic growth.

Economic affairs have been central to the post-war history of West European integration. The first European Community – the European Coal and Steel Community, established under the 1952 Treaty of Paris – was concerned with integrating the two industries that had been so pivotal to the war-effort in Western Europe. Thus, while the Treaty of Paris proclaimed that the six founder MS were committed to establishing a "broader and deeper community among peoples long divided by bloody conflicts" (cited in Cockfield 1990), it was nevertheless evident that the motor of political and social harmony would be economic integration. Numerous commentators have pointed out that the belief that public support would follow ameliorative changes in the economic environment was fundamental to the philosophy of some of the principal architects of integration during its early stage (Holland 1993; Featherstone 1994; Wallace and Smith 1995). Subsequent landmarks in European integration, from the founding of the European Economic Community in 1957 to the Single European Act (SEA) in 1987 and, more recently, the 1992 Treaty of the European Union (TEU) and European Monetary Union (EMU), have continued to illustrate that economic matters have provided the axis along which integration revolves. As a European Commission report, *The Single Market and Tomorrow's Europe*, begins "the Single Market is at the core of the European Union', before going on to add that the completion of this borderless trade area 'and its good state of health will be a major contributor to the achievement of the Union's current and future political objectives" (Monti 1996: IX).

After a period during which economic recession and internal disagreements amongst member states had posed questions about the direction – if any – in which the EC was moving, the onset of the '1992 Programme' in the mid-1980s (and entrenched in the SEA) marked a renewed effort by all MS to complete the reforms necessary to remove national barriers to the free movement of labour, commodities, services and capital within the EC. The ongoing construction of the

Single European Market (the '1992 Programme' was a spur to the completion of this project, rather than its actual completion by the 1st January 1993 deadline) has progressively led to the diminution of national controls on a wide range of fronts. To this extent, while national governments participated in the creation of the SEM, the consequences of its creation means that national governments cannot deal with the matters arising from it – although most notably the question of its governance – on an individual basis. By signing up to the SEA, and later to the TEU, MS have relinquished their national controls over key areas of economic life (although these loss of powers have been the accepted price of integration since the formation of the first of the European Communities, the European Coal and Steel in Community, in the 1951 Treaty of Paris). For example, EU legislation is now in place to remove technical barriers to trade which prevent the movement of goods across national borders, while restrictions are also in place to ensure that public sector agencies award contracts on the basis of the most competitive cost rather than simply favour local service providers or local producers. In addition, the legislation associated with the SEM has been concerned with facilitating the free movement of people across borders, a development which is partly oriented towards increasing labour mobility in the EU and which has necessitated moves towards harmonisation of social security policy.

In general terms, the SEM is primarily concerned with progressively removing those barriers which prevent cross-border trade and thus restrict the potential for economic growth across the EU as a whole, although other factors, such as structural reform of national labour markets, are also integral to this programme. In achieving market integration, the primary objective of the SEM legislation, there has been a notable degree of success. A Commission report (Monti 1996) argues that by the early-1990s the SEM programme had contributed directly to increasing levels of inward investment in the EU, generating between 300,000 and 900,000 new jobs and fostering higher levels of intra-EU trade, although it must also be noted that even in key areas the changes have had limited effects on opening up national markets to cross-border competition[i] and state subsidies in key economic sectors continue to remain high in some MS, such as France, Italy and Germany, a phenomenon which flies in the face of the philosophy of the SEM and, should it continue, the principles of EMU.

The social dimensions of economic and political change in the EU

More limited still has been the impact of the key developments in the recent history of the SEM, such as the SEA and the TEU, in promoting social cohesion. In the main such developments, and the legislation which has followed from them, have been of a technical nature, are more directly concerned with erasing impediments to more extensive economic integration. The resultant changes have, as a consequence, had little direct bearing on the lives of much of the general population of the EU; as Mann (1993: 303) has suggested: "Regulations about markets and products rarely reach a mass audience, except for the rampaging of French farmers and for the EC's jokes over who can sell products labelled with words like sherry, champagne or ice-cream". The attendant changes which have accompanied the SEM since the late-1980s have not, for example, produced any significant change in labour mobility; the numbers of EU citizens living in another state increased only by approximately 300,000 in the period 1985–1993 (Monti 1996). Where the SEM touches on the private lives of individual citizens of the EU it is primarily in their capacity as consumers and, to a lesser degree, as workers. In practice, many of the benefits made available to consumers across the EU, such as a wider range of choice of products and services, have arisen as a consequence of legislation which was, at a higher level, intended to facilitate intra-EU trade in these areas. It would be erroneous to view the economic processes in the EU as being bereft of interest in the consequences for, and the response of, private citizens, but the overriding concern has undoubtedly been with the prerequisites necessary for effective market integration. As regards the relationship between individual citizens and the (economic) forces of change in the EU, it is evident that the former are first and foremost addressed as consumers or 'economic citizens' rather than as individuals possessing a broader range of meaningful social and political rights (O'Leary 1995; Laffan 1996).

The two major initiatives with regard to the development of a social dimension to European integration – the notion of EU citizenship and the Protocol on Social Policy contained in the TEU – do not substantially alter the social status of individuals within the EU. For example, since the 1957 Treaty of the European Economic Community the principle of freedom of movement of persons within the Community was part of a programme of 'social' changes which were necessary to establish the structural conditions commensurate with the development of market integration, principally the free movement of workers (as well as their spouses and relatives). In the TEU this right was extended to *all* persons legally defined as nationals of a MS, but there continue to remain impediments to those who cannot support themselves financially and who would, then, become a burden on the host state (O'Leary 1995; see also Fevre 1998). To this end, the principles of freedom of movement and equal treatment for EU citizens continue, in effect, to be limited to those who are self-supporting individuals. The 'free right of abode' is a cornerstone of the attempts to develop an active form of EU citizenship which is not reliant on the relationship between citizenship and nationality; as the Commission states, without this principle "the whole concept of a people's Europe would be devoid of substance" (CEC 1993: 37). Restrictions in this area, then, continue to act as impediments to a more extensive and meaningful notion of EU citizenship. The Protocol on Social Policy, as with the concept of EU citizenship, constitutes a move towards the development of a social dimension to integration, but the new labour market and workplace regulations which it introduces are limited in scope and, in the case of more contentious issues such as collective bargaining, are subject to a unanimous vote in the Council of Ministers (Lange 1993). Other matters, such as the right to strike and wage levels, are exempt from the Protocol. The prospect of bolstering this area is uncertain given the degree of national specificity in the fields of social welfare and industrial relations. Radical changes to the provisions of social welfare, for example, would necessarily involve a fundamental rethinking of the relationship between state and society in MS by virtue of the differing philosophies which have underpinned the evolution of welfare systems and continue to regulate the role of these systems within MS.

Greater emphasis on social policies and the promotion of a more informed public awareness of the changes unfolding above the level of national government (although in which national governments are intimately involved) is nevertheless crucially important for ensuring the long-term stability of European integration. As decision-making in the economic realm increasingly takes on a collective hue and is lifted from the level of national government to the inter-governmental Council of Ministers and the EU more broadly, higher levels of public trust must be invested in these mechanisms of governance. More particularly, as the decisions made at this abstracted level carry greater and greater implications for individual citizens, so it becomes more important that their national representatives secure popular support for their EU initiatives. In the case of EMU, wherein the European Central Bank will assume responsibility for areas of monetary policy vital for economic growth within the EU, popular support for this programme will be a very significant factor in securing its stability (Winkler 1996; Jacquet 1998).

While MS remain part of EMU their participation will mean that they have ceded important monetary tools to an independent supranational institution. Some observers have, however, argued that this participation is not irreversible, pointing out that while national governments remain accountable to their voters any severe economic downturn will test their resolve and commitment to EMU. As *The Economist* has argued: "European governments will still be sovereign... there will be nothing to prevent the government of Spain, say, or France deciding to withdraw from the Euro zone if it calculates such a move to be in the national interest" (*Economist*, 11.10.97). The point here is that there is nothing that commits MS to EMU in perpetuity. The collapse of EMU may have disastrous effects on the economy of the EU as a whole, but nervous governments might be tempted to jump sooner rather later because of the impact on the domestic economy, particularly in the early period of EMU when voters who are still unclear as to what their governments have agreed to continue to adjust to the incipient changes. In the case of the UK, which currently remains outside the 'Eurozone', there is at present a considerable degree of harmony between the Trades Union Council and the Confederation of British Industry with regard to their support for EMU. Should the UK enter EMU in the near-future a serious downturn in the fortunes of EMU would have direct consequences for both employers and workers that would, in turn, undermine confidence in the ability of the ECB to deliver the kind of growth needed for the EU as a whole or its flexibility with regard to regional economic differences across the EU.

Even if EMU produces the desired levels of economic growth this does not diminish the need to both generate greater public understanding of, and support for, the changes which individuals will experience. Nor, indeed, does such a scenario undermine the need for more systematic consideration of the social policy implications of the changes which EMU will produce and the 'safety-nets' (in the form of welfare provision) which will be necessary to catch those who fall through the cracks created by such regulation of monetary policy. As monetary policy is disembedded from its national framework so this alters the framework for thinking about the provision of social welfare, particularly given the potential changes in national labour markets (as a result of regional disparities in economic growth) and the curtailments on public spending which will be imposed on an EU-wide basis by the ECB. Further reductions in public spending, whether in health, education, welfare or state subsidies to agriculture, will have marked consequences for the population of the EU and the domestic fortunes of political parties. It is necessary, under these conditions, that such considerations be to the forefront of thinking about European integration.

Economic integration, therefore, carries important social implications, both with regard to the consequences of this process for individuals in the MS and in terms of the need to encourage greater public awareness of this process and its consequences. The principal reason why the social dimension of European integration has been so poorly developed is because of the emphasis that has, and continues to be, placed on economic affairs. This, however, is only a partial explanation. A more comprehensive understanding of this issue involves a consideration of the tension between the intergovernmental and supranational approaches to European integration. The national governments of the MS have, on the whole, been keen to pursue economic integration, wherein they believe that the losses of sovereignty in this area are made up for by the gains which they make in terms of economic growth, but they have been less enthusiastic about embracing full-blooded political integration (as in the case of common foreign and security policies). Voluntary, indeed enthusiastic, participation in the SEM should not, then, be viewed as a clarion call for wholesale abandonment of all national powers of autonomy. The Thatcher government in the late-1980s had championed the cause of the extension of the free market reforms already underway in the UK to the larger arena of the Community, but simultaneously remained resolutely opposed to any kind of the Commission-led chatter about a 'European identity' and to any increase in the supranational powers of this institution. Rather differently, the Commission actively desires the same kind of economic integration, but because it works to a supranational agenda it seeks to further the kind of political integration that the national governments are generally opposed to.

While integration proceeded at a pace, and in a direction, which suited those national governments opposed to unacceptable losses of political sovereignty, the Commission would be frustrated but the governments of the MS reasonably content. Since the 1980s, and the developments mentioned above, integration has begun to exact a higher price from national governments and, in turn, their constituents. This is particularly the case as far as EMU is concerned. For those individuals living inside the 'Eurozone' created by the eleven MS in 1998, the introduction of the Euro and the attendant withdrawal of their respective national currencies in January 2002 will provide very real reminders of the implications of the changes to which their political leaders have agreed. The result of the developments since the mid-1980s is that European integration has developed to a new stage. As the politics of integration moves to centre stage in the domestic political arena, so governments will be under greater pressure to secure popular legitimacy for their endeavours just as opposition parties will be eager to persuade voters otherwise. To this end, then, national governments must engage in public debate about the implications of European integration in a way in which many have been reluctant to do previously, as the Labour government in the UK, which has promised a referendum on entry into EMU, must do. For the Commission these developments provide it with an opportunity, perhaps even an obligation, to secure the popular support for European integration which will enable this process to transcend divisions of national identity. As Baun (1996) writes, commenting on the future for the EU collectively:

the elitist-technocratic model of European integration – or 'integration from above' – may finally have reached its limits...future integration efforts must consciously inform and involve average Europeans. Doing so, of course, will only make the integration process slower and more politicised and therefore more problematic. As such, the democratic legitimacy problem of the EU and the necessary steps to correct it will pose a major barrier to further integration (Baun 1996: 146).

Demos and 'democratic deficit' in the EU

The growth in the powers and remit of the institutions of the EU, most notably in the wake of the SEA and the TEU, have prompted discussion about levels of accountability of decision-making and questioning of the degree of popular legitimacy for the process of integration. At the heart of this debate lies a concern that a 'democratic deficit' exists in the relations between the institutions of the EU and between the EU and its citizens. For some, terms such as 'democratic deficit' and 'Brussels bureaucracy' signify all that is wrong with the EU, in general, and the Commission, in particular: removed from the concerns of the population whom they govern, elite-dominated and lacking public accountability. Since the TEU extended the reach of EU policy further into the lives its citizens, there have been increasing calls for further democratisation of decision-making processes at the level of the EU. For its part, the Commission acknowledges that decision-making in the EU is perceived by the public as lacking accountability and legitimacy; as it states: "a world of shadowy deals being hammered out behind closed doors is characteristic of many people's perceptions of EU decision-making", adding that "in some ways this image is understandable" (CEC 1996: 8). Similar concerns might, of course, equally be applied to national systems of government, but as an emergent form of governance, and as a source of major political division both within and between MS, the institutions of the EU nevertheless have to work harder to convince *their* public that they are worthy of their support and trust. Resolving this dilemma of governance will not happen by simply giving the European Parliament, the only directly-elected EU institution, more powers in relation to the other institutions of governance or by improving access to information about the decisions made by the Council of Ministers and the Commission.

Changes in the philosophy of these institutions, notably with regard to how they perceive their relationship with the population of the EU, will nevertheless be a crucial step in this direction. The idea of a 'democratic deficit' has much to do with the institutional dynamics of European integration, especially the working relations between the inter-governmental Council of Ministers and the supranational Commission which were touched on above. These problems are not a product of the period since the 1980s. Rather, they can be traced back to the clash of national and supranational interests that underpinned the establishment of the ECSC in the early-1950s. It was the view of Jean Monnet, the principal architect of this initiative, that the ECSC would only be able to function effectively if the High Authority, its trans-national executive, was able to transcend the squabbles between the governments of the MS. That a Council of Ministers, comprising representatives of the six national governments, was added to the institutions of the ECSC was a response to national concerns (particularly among the Benelux states) about the powers of the supranational High Authority; Monnet himself, it has been argued, had been opposed to the creation of such an institution (Holland 1994; Laursen 1996). In addition, there has also been some dispute as to whether or not Monnet was, at least in the early stages of the planning of the ECSC, convinced of the need for further democratic controls in the form of a Common Assembly (the forerunner of the European Parliament before 1962), comprising other nominated representatives of the national parliaments (Neunreither 1995; Laursen 1996; cf. Featherstone 1994). In the High Authority Monnet had envisaged a technocratic body which, in spite of the different forms of institutional checks provided by the Council and the Assembly, would evolve as the main engine of European integration. Monnet's preference for an unelected expert-centred institution independent of national government has prompted one commentator to remark that 'his strategy for the ECSC clearly involved setting his attention firmly on persuading élites, rather than the mass publics, to the European cause' (Featherstone 1994: 161).

Sole blame for the 'democratic deficit' in the EU cannot be attributed to Monnet's plans for the ECSC in the early-1950s, although many of the current criticisms of the role of the Commission do stem, in large part, from his vision of an independent supranational executive. The weakness of the Parliament, for example, may be partly attributed to the institutional dynamics of the ECSC, in particularly the purely advisory role accorded to the Common Assembly, but the reluctance to further extend the powers of the Parliament is better understood in terms of the evolving tension between the intergovernmental and supranational dimensions of integration in the subsequent decades. That is to say, the jockeying for position which occurs between the Commission and the Council of Ministers, and the attempts by each to hold their own power base, has fostered an environment in which granting further powers of accountability to the Parliament is not to the advantage of either. Although relations between the Parliament and the Commission are improving, corresponding relations between the former and the Council are progressing at a much slower pace (Lodge 1996). That the Parliament is still not required to endorse all legislation passed by the Council is a significant example of the 'democratic deficit' that exists beyond those problems which are related to the role of the Commission. Moreover, the term 'democratic deficit' may equally be applied to the role of national governments in the Council of Ministers, especially in the sense that decisions made in the Council of Ministers are frequently not subject to the scrutiny of national parliaments. Judge (1995) has, however, argued that in spite of the limited direct input of national parliaments in the EU legislative process, since the SEA, and particularly after the TEU, national parliaments have shown themselves to be increasingly willing and capable of exercising scrutiny over the actions of their national executives in the Council of Ministers.

The notion of a 'democratic deficit' is, then, neither a recent development, nor one that is restricted to 'Brussels bureaucracy' and a purportedly Machiavellian Commission. It has, however, undoubtedly become a markedly more politically sensitive issue since the mid-1980s. Finding a solution to the travails of the EU must involve an understanding of the complex and mutli-layered form of governance which is emerging, incorporating the institutional pillars of the EU, national parliaments and regional and local government, as a number of writers have recently argued (Bulmer 1994; Caporaso 1996; Goodman 1997; Peterson 1997). Examining the relations between these different mechanisms of governance serves, in turn, to focus attention on the extent to which they serve to legitimise the EU itself (Judge 1995; Obradovic 1996; Chryssochoou 1997). To varying degrees, each of these tiers of governance do constitute important sources of democratic legitimacy for EU policy-making and legislative processes, although the extent to which they can be regarded as delivering public support, and therefore popular legitimacy, for change at the level of the EU is questionable.

The governments of the MS who take part in the EU legislative process in the Council of Ministers are all democratically elected national representatives who, in theory, are accountable to their national parliaments and their electorates. As has already been pointed out, however, questions have been asked about the extent to which national parliaments exercise a satisfactory level of scrutiny over EU legislation (Van Schendelen 1996). In addition, since the increased use of qualified majority voting in the Council of Ministers was introduced by the SEA, in an attempt to speed up the legislative process, national governments unhappy with EU legislation or wishing to deflect blame for 'bad' legislation away from themselves are provided with an opportunity to 'externalise responsibility' (Obradovic 1996). This, of course, does not negate the overall intergovernmental dimension of democratic legitimacy in the EU, but it does help to fuel the claim that decisions are taken at the level of the EU which sometimes conflict with national interests as defined by governments and/or opposition parties. Since 1979, when the first direct elections to the European Parliament, took place, this has provided vital public involvement in the democratic process in the EU and, in doing so, has provided a key source of legitimacy for the EU. Turn-outs for European elections have nevertheless generally been relatively low (although in some MS, such as Belgium and Luxembourg, turn-outs have been dramatically higher than in others, such as the UK) and national political parties have not treated European elections with anything approaching the same degree of importance as their own national elections (Nugent 1994; Lodge 1996). Since 1992, and the creation of the

Committee of the Regions under the TEU, elected representatives of local and regional government from across the EU have formally started to play a role in the decision-making process in the EU. The development of this idea (as will be argued in the following section) represents one of the most potentially significant institutional developments in the EU, yet the COR is still a very weak link in the decision-making chain as it exercises limited powers of scrutiny over a specific range of issues (Christiansen 1997).

Undoubtedly the most significant attempt by the EU to achieve greater popular legitimacy for European integration has been through the promotion of the idea of a 'Citizens' Europe' or a 'Peoples' Europe'. Since the 1970s there has been a gradual recognition on the part of the Commission of the need for a social dimension to accompany, and in a very important way strengthen, the economic and political nuts-and-bolts of integration (Shore and Black 1994; O'Leary 1995). In contrast, then, to the technocratic emphasis on the mechanics of integration which had characterised the developments since the 1950s, the period since the 1970s has seen the Commission progressively promulgate the idea that European integration is 'a profoundly humanistic enterprise' (Commission of the European Communities (CEC) 1993: 6). At the root of this idea is a recognition that the effective functioning of the Community's institutions and, in turn, the long-term survival of the Community, is heavily dependent on its resident population acknowledging the Community as a legitimate locus of political identity. To this end, the official position has been that 'Europe' must become a real and positive presence for its population, rather than being viewed – when considered at all – as a set of distant, and often negative, economic and political forces. To quote the 1975 Tindemans *Report on European Union*, which marked the beginning of this shift in policy, a view which has received growing support both inside and outside the Commission over the last two decades is that "European Union must be experienced by the citizen in his (sic) daily life" (cited in Holland 1994:61).

The idea of a 'Europe close to its citizens', to employ a now widely-cited phrase from the Tindemans *Report*, is therefore an attempt to address the considerable problems of fostering a much-needed source of public legitimacy without being perceived to be forcing individuals to choose between national and supranational forms of loyalty. For the large part, the preferred method of resolving this dilemma has centred on creating the conditions for the emergence of a form of active citizenship beyond the boundaries of the nation-state as a way of encouraging popular attachment to a larger, European polity. As has been suggested already, the advent of the first direct elections to the European Parliament in 1979 may be seen as the first significant steps in this direction. The role of the Parliament as one of the EU's primary sources of public legitimacy has, however, been curtailed by a number of factors, from the relatively low-turn out at European elections to the continued institutional weakness of the Parliament in relation to either the intergovernmental Council of Ministers or the supranational Commission (Nugent 1994).

The most vigorous attempt to address the notion of European citizenship emerged in the late-1980s and early 1990s and culminated in the official birth of the EU citizen under the 1992 TEU. The outcome of this debate is that there was an attempt to move away from the issue of economic rights, which had characterised discussions in the late-1980s (Wiener 1997), towards provisions for political and social rights which would enable citizens to participate more directly in the process of integration. To this end, the TEU may be viewed as a tentative move in the direction of facilitating greater civic participation, with its provisions to allow citizens freedom of movement across the EU, to vote or stand for election in EP and local elections, to enable citizens to appeal to a European ombudsman. The Commission has stated explicitly that EU citizenship should not be viewed as a replacement for the rights to which individuals are entitled by virtue of their citizenship of a member state; as it states, citizenship of the EU "complements national citizenship; it does not replace it. The civic rights granted are simply extra rights" (CEC 1996: 6). In spite of this claim to have granted additional 'civic rights', the TEU has done little to foster the kind of civic participation and public awareness of the European dimension of social life which the Commission believes is necessary to substantially enhance the legitimacy of integration. The EU citizen remains, by and large, a 'consumer citizen' rather than one endowed with a coherent corpus of social, political and economic rights (Jessurun d'Oliveria 1995; O'Leary 1995).

The search to provide the illusive social cement necessary to hold the EU together, and provide a bedrock of popular legitimacy for integration, has sometimes strayed from the path of forging a civic identity and moved more in the direction of talking about a European identity and notions of 'European-ness' which are more resonant of notions of a form of common cultural identity. It would be unnecessarily paranoid to see the introduction of a common EU passport, as occurred in the mid-1980s, as a covert attempt to subvert national identities, yet in talking about the other acquired paraphernalia of the EU the Commission has suggested that part of the importance of having an EU flag and 'anthem' is that they are commonly regarded as the official trappings of government:

Everyone nowadays recognises the sky-blue banner with 12 gold stars symbolising European unification, which we see more and more often flying in front of public buildings. Is there anyone who can fail to be moved on hearing the Ode to Joy from Beethoven's Ninth Symphony, which in some quarters is already being put forward as the future anthem of a united Europe? ... To the sceptic, of course these symbolic measures may seem purely decorative. But because they strike most people's imaginations, and because they come close to the symbols that embody State sovereignty, they testify to the substantial progress made by an idea which has now been transformed from myth into reality. (CEC 1993: 8).

In other documents the Commission speaks of how a "sense of European identity has begun to take shape" (1988:3) and about how a 'common cultural heritage' (1987: 1) is central to this nascent sense of European-ness. Indeed, in one of the key Commission reports in the 1980s, *Television without Frontiers*, it is argued that a European identity is crucial to the larger success of European integration; as it states: "European unification will only be achieved if Europeans want it. Europeans will only want it if there is such a thing as a European identity" (cited in Schlesinger 1994: 29).

In truth, however, this notion of a European identity is an instance of style over substance. Once unpacked, the 'common cultural heritage' amounts to little more than ragbag of concepts and ideas; how they are specifically 'European', as Shore and Black (1994) point out, is rarely subject to consideration. Academics have, largely, given the notion of a common European identity short shrift (Smith 1992; Wilterdink 1993; Morley and Robins 1995). Any attempt to promulgate a notion of a distinctively European identity is fraught with problems, and may create unnecessary difficulties in terms of how 'Europe' deals with neighbouring states or with regard to the expansion of the EU. The search for a common European cultural identity seems to be born more out of desperation to find something (no matter how intangible) which will provide the social cohesion necessary for integration, rather than one which is genuinely concerned with correcting a 'democratic deficit'.

Genuine concerns with building a social dimension into the EU have come late to the process of integration. Since the 1970s the Commission has gradually pushed forward the need for popular legitimacy for European integration, and, arguably, as a mechanism for furthering this process to a level which would force the national governments to embrace political integration rather more enthusiastically. Articulating notions of 'European-ness' is not the solution to this quandary. Rather, the goal should be to create the conditions under which individuals will come to recognise the different political fora within the EU as legitimate channels through which to direct their concerns. Increasing horizontal accountability across the different institutions of the EU and strengthening of the scrutinising role of national parliaments over their executives in the EU legislative process will be important in this respect. Extending and clarifying the rights available to individuals as citizens of the EU, and supporting ways in which individuals can exercise these rights, should be an indispensable element of this process of change. If the idea of a 'Europe close to its citizens' is to mean anything substantial, it is necessary that the involvement of those representatives operating below the level of the state be involved much more intimately in the decision-making processes in the EU. It is to a consideration of this question that the following section turns.

A Europe of the Regions?

Jones (1996), a Plaid Cymru MP, argues that for people living in Wales the importance of having a "powerful domestic Parliament with direct links to Europe" would be that it would provide a "voice in the shaping of Europe tomorrow, and a role in deciding the institutional framework which will guide the EU into the next century" (1996: 47–48). Such sentiments are characteristic of a perception evident across the EU that not only can representatives of regional and local government find a 'voice' in the EU, but that they can also exercise a degree of influence over the decision-making process. Elsewhere in Britain, the Scottish National Party, with its slogan of *Independence in Europe*, has for some time now advocated the position that a *Europe of the Regions* offers the potential for bypassing Westminster and, as with the argument made by Plaid Cymru, gaining access to the channels of power in the EU (Keating and Jones 1995; Roberts 1997). Similar cases have also been made by political parties in, for example, Italy, Spain, Belgium and France (Dessideri and Santantonio 1996; Kerremans & Beyers 1996; Keating 1997; Letamendia 1997). Across the EU representatives from a growing number of sub-national authorities are engaged in establishing links with EU institutions, with other sub-national representatives and seeking to secure EU funding through the European Regional Development Fund. In France, for example, as Smith (1996: 121) explains, 'issues relating to European integration have steadily worked their way onto the agenda of French sub-national actors. References to the European context are now commonplace and European level-funding is now sought after in more systematic fashion'. Indeed, in the case of Belgium (admittedly, since 1988, a fully-fledged federal state) representatives of sub-national parliaments have been able to directly occupy places in the Council of Ministers (Andersen 1996).

Over the course of the post-war period, and particularly since the 1970s, a number of those states now incorporated within the EU have sponsored varying degrees of regionalisation. The federal system of government in the then-Federal Republic of Germany had been established in 1949 as part of the post-war settlement. The governments in Italy and Spain introduced programmes of regional devolution in 1970 and 1978, respectively, while France also initiated similar reforms beginning in 1982. Most recently, in the United Kingdom, formerly one of the most centralised of unitary states in the EU, a devolved Assembly has already been established in Northern Ireland, while Scotland and Wales will also acquire regional forms of government in 1999. In other MS regional and local government have differing forms of relations with central government: Austria, for example, has a form of federalism not unlike that of Germany; Portugal has granted autonomy to Azores and Madeira island groups, but the rest of the country remains strongly centralised; Denmark, Finland and Sweden have strong local government, but have not undergone regionalisation; in Greece, the Republic of Ireland and Luxembourg government remains firmly centralised with little indication of moves towards the introduction of a regional level of administration (Loughlin 1996). Across the MS, then, there are varying degrees of involvement of the sub-national tier of government, although in some states the role of directly elected regional assemblies is considerably stronger than in others. In all MS, however, there have been growing calls for the devolution of political power to sub-national agencies in order to promote regional and local development. What have been the factors promoting this process of change?

Not surprisingly, the regional representatives have themselves been among the most vociferous campaigners for the accentuation of the sub-national dimension within the EU. As MS have initiated internal programmes of decentralisation, representatives of regional and local government have been increasingly active in directing attention and funding towards the areas for which they are responsible. In those MS with strong regional participation in governance, such as Belgium and Spain, some political parties operating at a regional level have sought to use regionalisation within the EU as a way of circumventing central government. In other instances, such as in Italy during the early 1970s, the demand for a more coherent regional policy within the EU was intended to focus attention on endemic regional economic differences across the Community. It was with this issue to the fore that the European Regional Development Fund was established in 1975. A further factor which has promoted greater involvement of sub-national representatives has been the developments which have centred on the contentious concept of 'subsidiarity'. Since the mid-1970s the discussions of the notion of subsidiarity have been concerned with assessing which tiers of government (EU, national, regional or local) are the most advantageously placed for policy-making and implementation. To a large extent the debate has concentrated on ascertaining the respective areas of competency in policy-making of the EU and national government. Scott, Peterson and Millar (1994) cite Article A of the TEU, which emphasises the significance of employing the concept of subsidiarity to ensure that decisions are "taken as closely as possible to the citizen", to argue that 'subsidiarity' involving greater participation by sub-national government in the decision-making procress offers the potential for one possible 'antidote' to the present democratic deficit in the EU. Perhaps the strongest agent of change with regard to the role of the sub-national government in the EU has, however, been the creation of the Committee of the Regions, as established under the TEU.

The COR provides the first formal recognition of the role of sub-national government within the EU decision-making process. The COR comprises 189 members, the membership is roughly divided between representatives of regional and local government, although the respective domestic role of these tiers can have a quite considerable impact on the nomination of members; in the case of some MS (such as Germany and Spain) the overwhelming majority of representatives are drawn from regional government, while in other MS (such as the Republic of Ireland and, at present, the UK) the representatives are taken from local government. Building on the growing regional dimension of EU social and economic policy, and more particularly on the success of other 'informal' regional groupings within the EU (such as the Assembly of European Regions), the creation of the COR was designed to give 'regions' some input in the decision-making process at the level of the EU. This role has, however, been formally restricted to a consultative one through which the COR may be requested by either the Council of Ministers or the Commission to deliver an opinion on legislation and policy initiatives in those specific areas of competence defined within the TEU (such as where issues of education, economic and social cohesion, culture, where specific regional interests are involved, as well as decisions under the ERDF). The COR may, in addition, deliver judgements on issues outside of its specific remit, and although neither of the main EU institutions are therefore obliged to play any attention to these pronouncements the Parliament has used some of recommendations of the COR in these 'extra-curricular' areas in formulating its own amendments to EU legislation (Warleigh 1997).

Assessments of the impact of the COR have been mixed, although many academics have been of the view that its institutional weakness, combined with the differences of opinion between regional and local representatives and other organisational problems, mean that the current role of the COR is relatively limited (Jeffrey 1996; Christiansen 1997). Moreover, while the issues which dominate the integration process, such as EMU, are not specifically 'regional' issues, and while these issues are subject to dispute among representatives of national government in the Council of Ministers, the activities of the COR will not feature prominently on the policy agenda. In carving out a more significant role for itself than at present the COR will face a number of major institutional obstacles, not least from the Council of Ministers where the majority of representatives are not, unsurprisingly, favourably disposed towards granting more influence to a body which would in all likelihood be a thorn in its side. The Commission, while keen to see pressures on national governments from below, might view a beefed-up COR as another source of control on its decision-making powers. Establishing strong relations with the COR may, however, provide the Commission with an indirect source of popular legitimacy, in the sense that links with democratically elected representatives would be beneficial without acting as constraints in a formal manner and there are indications through its dealings with the COR that the Commission is aware of these benefits (Loughlin 1996; Warleigh 1997).

Whatever the reasons for the Commission assuming the role as a surrogate 'parent' for the fledgling COR, a strong sub-national dimension is necessary to strengthen the popular legitimacy of the EU. There are at least four reasons why participation by sub-national representatives, and thus the fostering of an active 'regional' level of governance, should be integral to the programme of establishing a prominent social dimension to European integration. Firstly, the *Idea* of a *Europe of the Regions*, in a period in which issues of decentralisation are gaining growing popular currency, stresses the importance of bringing issues of decision-making towards a more localised level. In a study of popular attitudes towards different tiers of government in Rhone-Alps region of France, for example, Lecomte (1994) argues that there is a growing level of public confidence in the regional level, and that after the *Commune*, the most local form of government, the regional tier attracts the highest level of public support. More recently, in the UK devolution referenda demonstrated high levels of public support in Northern Ireland and Scotland for regional government, while in Wales a comparatively lower level of support has led to the establishment of a regional assembly. As with the idea of a *Citizens' Europe*, although with a greater degree of clarity, the idea of a 'Europe of the Regions' points to the need to involve representatives who may be more sensitive to local needs. A second reason why the involvement of sub-national representatives is important is that it enables the expression of interests that may not be voiced in the EU by national representatives. To take one such case, the 1995 Report of the Welsh Affairs Committee, *Wales in Europe* (Vol. 1), points to the need for the representation of 'Welsh interests' within the Council of Ministers; as it states: "We... believe that there should be greater willingness within the United Kingdom Government for its collective interests to be represented at appropriate Council meetings by a minister from a regional department such as the Welsh Office" (WAC 1995: x). Providing for such measures, whether within the MS or at the level of the EU, would therefore allow for policy-making in the EU to be more responsive to regional interests. Following on from this, a third rationale would be that, working with the principle of subsidiarity, policy could be implemented in such a manner as to make it work for local interest or to enable regional representatives and agencies to develop regional economic specialisations. The involvement of these parties would, in turn, be important in directing information and advice about regional circumstances upwards to the national and EU levels of government. A final reason why the involvement of the sub-national levels of government is so central to the development of public awareness of, and participation in the changes taken place as a consequence of integration is that these levels are crucial for aiding the development of civil society at its most local level. The role which local and regional government plays in bringing together diverse sectoral interests at a level more immediate to the concerns of individual citizens would be an important element of the promotion of social integration (Clarke 1998).

The COR, while an important development, and the larger programme of regionalisation will not alone solve the problem of the 'democratic deficit' or necessarily bolster the popular legitimacy of European integration. Undoubtedly the formal involvement of elected regional and local representatives in the decision-making process at the level of the EU does serve to provide added legitimacy to the EU, but if the significance of the 'regional' dimension is to be extended it is important that the role of regional representatives and the place of these 'regions' within the integration process be more communicated to the individuals whom they represent. The future development of this dimension will depend greatly on both the respective political circumstances within the MS as well as at the level of the EU, but it is important that this dimension, so vital for social integration (both at the regional level and that of the EU more broadly), does not merely become a side-show to the larger performance involving the national governments and the Commission.

Summary

- The development of a social dimension to European integration has been a somewhat haphazard and none too clearly directed process. The claims made by the Commission, that integration is a "profoundly humanistic enterprise" (1993: 6), is not supported by the substance of past and present developments. European integration has primarily been an economically-driven process, characterised by the objective of achieving market integration across the territories of the MS. From its beginnings in the Treaty of Paris in the early-1950s, integration has been about the formation of an economic community, *not* about political union as its guiding rationale.
- As has been suggested throughout the above discussion, this is not to argue that the process of integration has not also been about politics, in the sense of the ongoing calculation of national political interests against the need to sustain economic growth in an increasingly competitive environment, or,

even, that it has been entirely devoid of social calculations. Nevertheless, the concentration on the creation of an EU-wide market economy has been one of the principal reasons for the failure to develop a strong emphasis on social affairs as a distinct dimension of European integration. A second reason has been to do with the institutional dynamics of integration, although principally the tension between the inter-governmental and supranational dimensions of integration. A third main factor in explaining the lack of attention given to the social dimension until recent years has been the reluctance of national governments to authorise significant outside intervention in the relation between state and citizen within the MS. Whether it be in relation to the provision of social welfare, pay bargaining or the exercising of political rights at the national level, the national state remains the dominant force within the EU. While these issues are central to the domestic political strategies of national governments they will not welcome undue EU intervention in social affairs.

- Discussion of the social dimension of European integration will, for a number of reasons, nevertheless become more pronounced in the immediate future. As has been suggested above, the need to 'win hearts and minds' will increasingly figure in the forms of politics within the MS towards European integration as well as continuing to feature prominently in the relations between the Commission, Parliament and the Council of Ministers. As European integration begins to increasingly inform political matters within MS, as in the case of EMU, this will, in turn, foster more extensive public consciousness of this process. Other future developments, such as the expansion of the EU, have already begun to generate concern about the impact of such developments for existing MS in relation to the level of spending on the Common Agricultural Policy and, particularly among the poorer regions of the EU, with regard to the future loss of EU structural funds to the new MS. In light of these future developments, public concern with the consequences of integration is likely to increase. As a result, greater consideration will need to be given to the implications for issues of social cohesion and exclusion within and across MS.

- Moreover, as the public becomes more conscious of the Europeanisation of economic, political and social affairs, so the contest to win popular support will intensify. Developments below the level of national government will also contribute to the promotion of discussion of the social dimension. Within regional assemblies across the EU, some political parties have campaigned on the issue of increased representation of regional interests within the EU. Moreover, non-governmental agencies, such as pressure groups and labour organisations, have also been active in communicating the significance of the changes occurring at the level of the EU for individuals

(Goodman 1997). In the UK, for example, the John Monks, the General Secretary of the Trades Union Congress, has called for the need to develop a 'shared British understanding' of how to address the UK's future in the EU (*Financial Times* 30.10.97).

- The future, successful development of the EU will necessitate growing levels of popular support for this project. The idea that social and political change initiated at the level of the EU would not seriously impact on citizens of its constituent member states can no longer be accepted. Whether for good or bad, changes ushered in by developments taking place as a consequence of European integration are having, and will continue to have, increasingly significant effects on people living throughout the EU. This does not mean that nation-states are becoming redundant, but it does mean that existing channels for securing political legitimacy must be re-evaluated to take account of the changing parameters within which political relations are conducted. In June 1998, for example, Helmut Kohl, then Chancellor of Germany, stated that the 'electors want to be part of a strong European Union but they do feel remote from its institutions and that gap has got be closed if the European Union is to continue to demand support for the decisions that it takes' (*Independent* 16.6.98). Moreover in a letter sent to Tony Blair, during the UK's presidency of the EU, Kohl and President Chirac of France remarked that they both wanted to 'bring Europe as close to the people as possible' (*The Financial Times* 18.5.98). Blair himself has voiced similar concerns, arguing that moves to fundamentally reform the relationship between the EU and its public will be central to its immediate future. A Labour Party local policy forum document on the issue of the EU (Labour Party 1998) makes the point that the creation of a *people's Europe* will be central to the government's vision of the development of the EU.

- Translating such sentiments into real political and social practice will be necessary for the stability of the EU, especially given the changes which will take place within the EU in the very near future. Such vocal support for a social dimension to European integration is uncharacteristic among national leaders in the MS of the EU, most notably because of the challenge that a substantive supranational form of citizenship would present to the idea of national citizenship. That governments of the MS will have to address this issue of 'filling in' the social dimension to European integration is undeniable, but the manner in which they deal with it will, past experiences show, continue to be heavily influenced by domestic political interests.

Further Reading

Andersen, S.S. & K. A. **Eliassen** (eds) (1996), *The European Union: How Democratic is it?* London: Sage.

Baun, M. J. (1996), *An Imperfect Union. The Maastricht Treaty and the New Politics of European Integration.* Boulder, CO: Westview Press.

Gowan, P. & P. **Anderson** (eds) (1997), *The Question of Europe.* London: Verso.

Jones, B. & M. **Keating** (eds) (1995), *The European Union and the Regions.* Oxford: Clarendon Press.

Newman, M. (1997), *Democracy, Sovereignty and the European Union.* London: Hurst and Co.

References

Andersen, C. (1996), "European Union policy-making and national institutions – the case of Belgium". In: **Andersen**, S. S. and K. A. **Eliassen** (eds), *The European Union: How Democratic is it?* London: Sage.

Baun, M. J. (1996), *An Imperfect Union. The Maastricht Treaty and the New Politics of European Integration.* Boulder, CO: Westview Press.

Bryant, C. G. A. (1991), "Europe and the European Community 1992". *Sociology* 25: 189–207.

Bulmer, S. J. (1994), "The governance of the European Union: a new institutionalist approach". *Journal of Public Policy* 13: 351–380.

Caporaso, J. A. (1996), "The European Union and forms of state: Westphalian, regulatory or post-modern?". *Journal of Common Market Studies* 34: 29–52.

Christiansen, T. (1997), "The Committee of the Regions at the 1996 IGC Conference: institutional reform". *Regional and Federal Studies* 7: 51–69.

Chryssochoou, D. N. (1997), "New challenges to the study of European integration: implications for theory building". *Journal of Common Market Studies* 35: 521–542.

Clarke, M. (1998) "Governance and the European Union: a discussion of co-government". *Local Governance* 24: 3–19.

Cockfield, Lord (1990), "The real significance of 1992". Special Issue on 'The Politics of 1992: Beyond the Single European Market'. *The Political Quarterly.* Vol. 1–8.

Commission of the European Communities (1987) *A Fresh Boost for Culture in the European Community.* Luxembourg: Office for Official Publications of the European Communities.

Commission of the European Communities (1988) *A People's Europe.* Luxembourg: Office for Official Publications of the European Communities.

Commission of the European Communities (1993) *A Citizen's Europe.* Luxembourg: Office for Official Publications of the European Communities.

Commission of the European Communities (1996) *The European Union – What's in it for Me?* Luxembourg: Office for Official Publications of the European Communities.

Desideri, C. and V. **Santantonio** (1996), "Building a Third Level in Europe: prospects and difficulties in Italy". *Regional and Federal Studies* 6: 97–116.

Economist (1997), "Europe's Single Currency". 11 October.

Featherstone, K. (1994), "Jean Monnet and the 'democratic deficit' in the European Union". *Journal of Common Market Studies* 32:149–170.

Fevre, R. (1998), "Labour migration and freedom of movement in the European Union: social exclusion and economic development". *International Planning Studies* 3: 75–92.

Goodman, J. (1997), "The European Union: reconstituting democracy beyond the nation-state". In: **McGrew**, A. (ed), *The Transformation of Democracy?* Cambridge: Polity/Open University Press.

Holland, M. (1994), *European Integration. From Community to Union*. London: Pinter.

Jacquet, P. (1998), "EMU:a worthwhile gamble". *International Affairs*. 74: 55–72.

Jeffrey, C. (1996), "Conclusions: sub-national authorities and 'European domestic policy'". *Regional and Federal Studies* 6: 204–219.

Jessurun d'Oliveira, H. U. (1995), "Union citizenship: pie in the sky?". In: **Rosas**, A. and E. **Antola** (eds), *A Citizens' Europe. In Search of a New Order*. London: Sage.

Jones, I. W. (1996), *Europe – the Challange for Wales*. Talybont: Gwasg Taf Cyf.

Judge, D. (1995), "The failure of national parliaments". *West European Politics* 18: 79–100.

Keating, M. and **Jones**, B. (1995), "Nations, regions, and Europe: the UK experience". In: **Jones**, B. and M. **Keating** (eds), *The European Union and the Regions*. Oxford: Clarendon Press.

Keating, M. (1997), "The invention of regions: political restructuring and territorial government in Western Europe". *Environment and Planning C: Government and Policy* 15: 383–398.

Kerremans, B. and **Beyers**, J. (1996), "The Belgian sub-national entities in the European Union: second or third level players?". *Regional and Federal Studies* 6: 41–56.

Laffan, B. (1996), "The politics of identity and political order in Europe". *Journal of Common Market Studies* 24: 81–102.

Lange, P. (1993) "Maastricht and the social protocol: why did they do it?". *Politics and Society* 21: 5–36.

Laursen, F. (1996), "The role of the Commission". In: **Andersen**, S. S. and K. A. **Eliassen** (eds), *The European Union: How Democratic is it?* London: Sage.

Lecomte, P. (1994), "Rhone-Alps citizens in the political system: an emerging regional identity". *Regional Politics and Policy* 4: 132–147.

Letamendia, F. (1997), "Basque nationalism and cross-border co-operation between the southern and northern Basque Countries". *Regional & Federal Studies* 7: 25–41.

Lodge, J. (1996), "The European Parliament". In: **Andersen**, S. S. and K. A. **Eliassen** (eds) *The European Union: How Democratic is it?* London: Sage.

Loughlin, J. (1996), "Representing regions in Europe: The Committee of the Regions". *Regional and Federal Studies* 6: 147–166.

Mann, M. (1993), "Nation-states in Europe and other continents: diversifying, developing, not dying". *Daedalus* 122: 115–140.

Monti, M. (1996), *The Single Market and Tomorrow's Europe*. London: Kogan Page/Office for Official Publications of the European Communities.

Morley, D. and K. **Robins** (1995), *Spaces of Identity. Global Media, Electronic Landscapes and Cultural Boundaries*. London: Routledge.

Neunreither, K. (1995), "Citizens and the exercise of power in the European Union: towards a a new social contract?". In: **Rosas**, A. and E. **Antola** (eds), *A Citizens' Europe. In Search of a New Order*. London: Sage.

Newman, M. (1997), *Democracy, Sovereignty and the European Union*. London: Hurst and Co.

Nugent, N. (1994), *The Government and Politics of the European Union*. London: Macmillan

O'Leary, S. (1995), "The social dimension of Community citizenship". In: **Rosas**, A. and E. **Antola** (eds), *A Citizens' Europe. In Search of a New Order*. London: Sage.

Obradovic, D. (1996), "Policy legitimacy and the European Union". *Journal of Common Market Studies* 34: 191–221.

Peterson, J. (1997), "States, societies and European Union". *West European Politics* 20: 1–23.

Robbins, K. (1998), "Britain and Europe:devolution and foreign policy". *International Affairs* 74: 105–118.

Roberts, P. (1997), "Strategies for the stateless nation: sustainable policies for the regions in Europe". *Regional Studies* 31 (9): 875–882.

Schlesinger, P. (1994), "Europe's contradictory communicative space". *Daedalus* 123: 25–52.

Scott, A., J. **Peterson** and D. **Millar** (1994), "Subsidiarity: A 'Europe of the Regions' *v.* the British Constitution?". *Journal of Common market Studies* 32: 47–67.

Shore, C. and A. **Black** (1994), "Citizens' Europe and the construction of European identity". In: **Goddard**, V. A., J. R. **Llobera** and C. **Shore** (eds), *The Anthropology of Europe*. Oxford: Berg.

Smith, A. D. (1992), "European integration and the problem of identity". *International Affairs* 68: 55–76.

Wallace, W. and J. **Smith** (1995), "Democracy or technocracy? European Integration and the problem of popular consent?". *West European Politics* 18: 137–157.

Warleigh, A. (1997), "A committee of no importance? Assessing the relevance of the Committee of the Regions". *Politics* 17: 101–107.

Welsh Affairs Committee (1995), *Wales in Europe*. Fourth Report. Vol. 1. London: HMSO.

Wiener, A. (1997) "Making sense of the new geography of citizenship: fragmented citizenship in the European Union". *Theory and Society* 26: 529–560.

Wilterdink, N. (1993), "The European ideal: an examination of European and national identity". *European Journal of Sociology* 34: 119–136.

Winkler, B. (1996), "Towards a strategic view on EMU:a critical survey". *Journal of Public Policy* 16: 1–28.

David Dunkerley

The Enlargement of the European Union

> The European Union is on the brink of one of the most
> important decisions in its history. Enlargement to the East
> may be the EU's greatest challenge but I also believe it is
> its greatest opportunity.
>
> (*Tony Blair*, UK Prime Minister, Warsaw, 6 October 2000)

Introduction

The enlargement of the European Union (EU) from its present fifteen members has a certain populist ideology in terms of 'back to Europe' or a 'return to Europe' for many of those states that were either satellites of or actually part of the former Soviet Union. The dramatic events in Eastern Europe over a decade ago almost immediately made many of the newly independent states cast their gaze westwards and to the EU in particular since the EU represented all that these states hoped to achieve with their new-found liberty – stable democracy, economic prosperity, a powerful international voice. And so the long process of seeking membership of the EU commenced with the latter itself welcoming the advances.

This chapter traces this process of application to the present day and beyond. It also examines the EU itself, already institutionally creaking from the last enlargement in 1995 and identifies the key problem areas where reform of present arrangements would appear essential in order to accommodate to new member states. These new member states are, of course, different in many respects from former new members particularly in terms of their low economic base. The likely impact of this on present budgetary and political policies is also detailed. Coupled with this has to be an explanation of how national identity and self-interest among existing EU members has and may influence attitudes and practices towards enlargement.

Enlargement To-Date

Since the original Treaty of Rome in 1957 enlargement has been a constant theme of European politics and economics. The 1957 Treaty created a union of six member countries and since then there have been four successive waves of enlargement:

1. 1973 – the entry of the UK, Ireland and Denmark.
2. 1981 – the accession of Greece.
3. 1986 – the joining of Portugal and Spain.
4. 1995 – Austria, Finland and Sweden acceding.

Other negotiations took place over that period such as the proposed accession of Norway in 1975 and in 1995 – on both occasions the electorate rejected membership.

There has, thus, been no shortage of applicants to join, even from the early days though this is not reflected in the long period between 1957 and the first enlargement wave in 1973. As Croft *et al.* (1999: 58) point out, "...the process of economic integration within the EU had barely begun before it was being courted by prospective new members". In spite of its reputation as a reluctant European even the UK was one of these prospective new members when it formally applied for membership in 1961. It was clear to the UK and other prospective members as far back as the early 1960s that membership brought with it a range of improved economic prospects. This perception became even clearer as the decade moved on as can be seen from the UK's second attempt to accede in 1967. Economically, the original six members seemed to be forging ahead of other European countries outside of the Treaty. Arguably the applicants that were successful in 1973 themselves had strong economic ties between themselves anyway and for one to join it became almost necessary for all three to join simultaneously. This was particularly the case with Ireland. In other words, the idea of a grand vision of a united Europe could well have been secondary to the obvious economic benefits of not lagging behind.

While economics were the main driving force of the first wave, politics came much more to the fore in the second and third waves involving the Mediterranean countries. Each of the countries were recent democracies after periods of fascist or authoritarian rule. The Nine, as they then were, were very sympathetic to these countries, recognising the periods of stagnation and repression each had experienced and demonstrating a genuine desire to help them on the road to democracy. In this sense, there was a political will rather than a desire to embrace the countries for the added-value economic strength their membership would bring. Clearly it would not and did not. Within member countries there was strong resistance especially from the farming lobbies who recognised the economic cost of the potential Mediterranean membership. This actually explains the five-year gap between Greece's accession and that of both Portugal and Spain. The latter two countries' membership was strongly objected to by Italian and French farmers in a vociferous and highly active way.

In the most recent wave of enlargement, the actual negotiation period was much shorter but no less difficult than previous waves. Switzerland did not proceed with its negotiations after a referendum demonstrated rejection of membership of the European Economic Area (EEA) – a pre-requisite for membership of the Union. And, as indicated above, the Norwegian population rejected membership in 1994.

In terms of national identity this brief history of previous enlargements shows that the EU itself has little interest in individual identities. The EU's own identity and its economic and political interests come into play during pre-accession negotiations. Yet, individual members can be highly protective of their own national interests and identity. No better example exists than the attitude of France to the UK's application when its veto effectively prevented the UK application going forward for further consideration.

Equally, the first 40 years after the original Treaty have shown that national economic policies have been highly influential in determining whether a member does advance economically according to the original intention of membership. Ireland, for example has forged ahead as a result of the EU economic aid *and* its domestic economic policies whereas Greece has not.

All new members have imposed on them the *acquis communautaire* that is, in effect, a set of principles that members are expected to abide by. They include the laws, policies and practices of the EU together with laid-down objectives and obligations. Furthermore, all the Treaties, all the laws and judgements of the European Court of Justice and all the ultimate goals (*finalités politiques*) have to be adopted by all member countries. In this sense the EU imposes these upon new members even though they have not been party to their enactment.

Present Enlargement Proposals

Membership negotiations took place with Turkey from 1987 and Cyprus and Malta since 1990 but these have floundered as indicated below. The major post-1995 negotiations have been with a number of former Soviet bloc Central and East European countries (CEECs). During 1994/95 applications for membership were received from Bulgaria, the Czech Republic, Estonia, Hungary, Latvia, Lithuania, Poland, Romania, Slovakia and Slovenia. This was an unprecedented set of applications for membership that, if successful, would increase the size of the EU from fifteen to twenty-five. While that in itself is unique, it needs to be recognised that previous accessions have meant that new members had to adapt to the EU through the *acquis communautaire*; the post-1995 applications suggest a change in emphasis with the EU itself having to adapt in order to accommodate to the countries likely to gain admission. A much larger Union necessarily would involve the EU having to prepare itself for this expansion in the same way that individual applicants have themselves to prepare and adapt both in the past and now. There is, of course, no question of all the ten countries above joining the EU at the same time; indeed, the process could take anything up to twenty years for full accession.

Following the initial approaches from the ten, in 1997 the Commission published its 'Opinions' (*avis*) on each CEEC country alongside a statement on policy intentions entitled *Agenda 2000*. The latter is a major policy statement because it covers not only the enlargement process but also how reforms might take place affecting the Common Agricultural Policy (CAP), the Structural and Cohesion Funds and the whole way in which the EU might be financed in the future. In other words, evidence of the EU adapting in ways it never previously has countenanced.

As far as enlargement is concerned *Agenda 2000* recommended that only five of the ten CEEC applicants should go forward for accession negotiations. These were Hungary, Poland, the Czech Republic, Slovenia and Estonia. The other five's applications were not ruled out completely but they were told that eventually membership might be considered after satisfying certain conditions on both economic and political matters. The five 'first wave' candidates from the CEECs were also joined by Cyprus. The actual statement in *Agenda 2000* reads as follows:

Concerning the countries of Central and Eastern Europe...The Commission considers that none of them fully satisfy all the criteria at the present time. However, nine countries satisfy the political conditions,[1] while certain countries have made sufficient progress towards satisfying the economic conditions and those related to the other obligations of membership.

In the light of its analysis, and in accordance with their respective merits, the Commission considers that Hungary, Poland, Estonia, the Czech Republic and Slovenia could be in a position to satisfy all the conditions of membership in the medium term if they maintain and strongly sustain their efforts of preparation.

(EC Cons Doc 9984/97, Vol. 1, Part Two (VII)

The recommendations were adopted in December 1997 by the Luxembourg European Council. At this time also the Council reaffirmed Turkey's eligibility for membership at some point in the future but its deficient economic and

---

[1] Slovakia was deemed not to have satisfied the political conditions.

political indices ruled it out of the two waves of membership envisaged for the ten CEECs.

The position changed, however, as a result of the deliberations of the EU Helsinki Summit in December 1999. The rather dramatic diplomatic manoeuvring at the Summit led to Turkey achieving candidate status for membership even though talks will not start for some years because of the poor Turkish record on political and human rights behaviour coupled with the territorial disputes with Greece in the Aegean and, of course, the unresolved problem over Cyprus.

The December 1999 Summit also agreed to invite six new countries to start accession negotiations in 2000. These are Bulgaria, Latvia, Lithuania, Malta, Romania and Slovakia. It seems unlikely that none of these would actually join the EU before 2004.

It can now be seen what a lengthy, and at times a tortuous, process has to be undergone. Even if the Council of Ministers accepts an application in *prima facie* form, the Council may later reject an application (the case of Morocco comes to mind) and in the case of the CEECs an *avis* has been sought from the Commission on each application. The *avis* is clearly crucial since the Council normally accepts the Commission's advice.

The criteria for membership that have been identified by the European Council are those concluded at the European Council Meetings in Copenhagen in June 1993.

Accession will take place as soon as an associated country is able to assume the obligations of membership by satisfying the economic and political conditions required. Membership requires:
- that the candidate country has achieved stability of institutions guaranteeing democracy, the rule of law, human rights and respect for and protection of minorities;
- the existence of a functioning market economy, as well as the capacity to cope with competitive pressure and market forces within the Union;
- membership presupposes the candidate's ability to take on the obligations of membership including adherence to the aims of political, economic and monetary union.

The Union's capacity to absorb new members, while maintaining the momentum of European integration, is also an important consideration in the general interest of both the Union and the candidate countries.

(Presidency Conclusions, Copenhagen European Council, June 1993)

The Copenhagen criteria actually go beyond the *acquis communautaire* and, indeed, the actual *acquis* has expanded since the last wave of enlargement in 1995 since it now includes the Maastricht Treaty (The Treaty of the European Union or TEU) covering, *inter alia*, a wide raft of security policies and co-operation in matters of justice and home affairs. Furthermore, new objectives have been added relating to economic, political and monetary union. Clearly, the condition for joining have become more stringent with an obvious increase in the number and the size of the hurdles to jump over.

Agenda 2000 put forward a Reinforced Pre-Accession Strategy (SPAR) direct to all the CEECs who had made application, regardless of whether they were deemed ready for the 'first wave' or not. The Strategy seeks to work in partnership with the CEECs in developing a clear programme for satisfying the Commission's demands. Thus, the individual *avis* on each of the applications identified specific problems and SPAR seeks ways to overcome these problems. There is also some financial assistance in the pre-accession period, largely disbursed through the PHARE programme. *Agenda 2000* recommended a PHARE budget of euro 1.5 billion a year (at 1997 prices). In addition the intention is, from 2000, to provide agricultural development aid (euro 500 million a year) and structural aid of euro 1 billion. Other financial assistance for the CEECs includes the opportunities for them to participate in certain education, training and research programmes, help in harmonising their legislation in line with Community law and assistance with 'institution-building' in areas such as law, customs, public accounts, environment, telecommunications and energy.

Taking 1999 prices, the Commission is now planning to provide between 2000 and 2006 a total of euro 79.9 billion for the CEECs. "This amount represents about 11% of the total payments throughout the period 2000 to 2006 or just over twice the amount that the Commission expects to spend on administration. Of this euro 79.9 billion, euro 61.8 billion will be transferred to the new members, leaving euro 18.1 billion to the other applicants." (House of Commons 98/56, 1998: 5).

The Economics of Enlargement

At the time of writing the most significant differences between the present EU membership of fifteen and the ten CEECs being considered for membership are between GDP per capita and the proportional size of the agricultural workforce. Thus, if the EU15 GDP per capita is rated at 100 then the equivalent for CEEC10 is a mere 30. Indeed, even if the poorest four EU countries' GDP per capita is taken this is nevertheless double that of CEEC10. "The problems of absorbing the CEEC10 into the EU can be indicated by considering that even with an average growth of 2.5% among the EU15 and 4% among applicant countries, it would take about 25 years for the latter to achieve 50% of the 15's average GDP per head" (HL 41, 1997–98).

Agenda 2000 points out that if the 10 CEECs were to accede, then the population of the EU would grow by over 100 million people from 371.6 million to 476.9 million. Furthermore, the geographical area of the EU would increase from 3.236 million km^2 to 4.314 million km^2.

Taking only the five CEECs selected for the first wave of future enlargement there would be dramatic effects on geographical area, population and GDP as indicated in Table 1. Clearly, the deleterious effects of the five first wave candidates is considerably less than if all ten CEECs were to be admitted.

Table 1. Impact of successive enlargements of the EU

1995 data	Increase in area	Increase in population	Increase in total GDP	Change in per capita GDP	Average per capita GDP (EUR6=100)
EU9/EU6	31%	32%	29%	–3%	97
EU12/EU9	48%	22%	15%	–6%	91
EU15/EU12	43%	11%	8%	–3%	89
EU20/EU15	**17%**	**17%**	**6%**	**–9%**	**81**
EU26/EU15	34%	29%	9%	–16%	75

S o u r c e: *Agenda 2000*, COM(97), Vol. II.

In spite of the obvious difficulties indicated by the above, the Commission remains fairly optimistic about the position. The Impact Study produced as part of the *Agenda 2000* report certainly suggests this:

Economic benefits from enlargement are expected to follow from the expansion of the Single Market, from the overall integration process, as well as from the strengthening of the Union's position in global markets. The Union's human potential will be considerably enriched, not least in qualified and highly qualified labour. Acceding countries have significant natural resources (agricultural land, some minerals, biodiversity, etc). Their geographic position will be an asset with respect to transport, energy transit and communications. The integration of these countries into the Union will be a powerful stimulus to their economic development. Major investments related to the radical modernisation of the acceding countries' economies and their catching up with EU living standards will boost demand across the Union and strengthen competitiveness.

(Impact Study (COM (97)2000, Vol. II, p. 97)

Such optimism is, however, not universally felt across the EU largely because the effect of the accession of the CEECs will be differentially felt from one country to another. *Agenda 2000* makes the assumption that the increased spending that would be required would come, in part, from growth within the EU and from revenue from the newly-admitted countries themselves. The question is whether the predicted growth rate of 2.5% p.a. for existing members and 4% for new members is realistic. The other source of extra money would come from reforms of the Common Agricultural Policy (CAP) and of the Cohesion and Structural Funds (CSF). The latter are addressed below. The worry for many countries is that if the predicted growth rate fails to materialise then existing members may be called upon to find the extra funding.

In a sense, the problem is not a new one. The UK complained, as long ago as 1984, about its net contribution to the EU budget and has secured an annual rebate based upon a complicated formula. More recently, the disquiet has spread to Germany, France, The Netherlands, Sweden and Italy. The case of Germany is particularly interesting since it is the largest net contributor to the EU budget – providing a staggering 60% of net contributions. In each case, the main concern lies with the operation of the CAP and in each case there have been calls for the reform of the policy.

As might be expected, of course, those countries benefiting most from the present financial arrangements are the ones least wanting any kind of reform. Greece, Portugal and Spain are thus the most vocal in this respect alongside Ireland and Belgium. The opposition took a dramatic turn in the debate over the 1997 budget where proposals were made to reduce the budgets of both the CAP and CSF. Greece, Portugal, Ireland and Spain were vehemently opposed to cuts in the Objective 1 budget and Italy joined the opposition because of its opposition to cuts in agricultural subsidies. This blocking minority won the day with the outcome that Objective 1 funds were not cut.

The importance of the CAP and CSF to the debate over enlargement can be seen from the fact they consume 46% and 35% of the total EU budget – over 80% of the total. It is to these two core features that the Chapter now turns.

The Common Agricultural Policy

The financial implications of extending the CAP to the new CEEC members cannot be emphasised enough, given as indicated above that the Policy consumes nearly a half of the Union's budget and cost almost euro 40 billion in 1999. As Table 2 shows, agriculture is a far more significant feature of the economies of the CEECs and is certainly less efficient than is found in EU countries.

Within the CEECS, as shown in Table 2, there are major differences in the importance of agriculture with Poland and Romania have very large agricultural sectors compared to the *relatively* smaller proportions to be found in the Czech Republic and Slovenia.

Table 2. Relative importance of agriculture in CEEC10 and EU15, 1995

Country	Agricultural production as % of GDP	Employment in agriculture as % of total
Czech Republic	5.2	6.3
Hungary	6.2	8.0
Poland	7.6	26.9
Slovakia	6.3	9.7
Slovenia	5.0	7.1
Bulgaria	13.9	23.2
Romania	20.5	34.4
Estonia	8.1	13.1
Latvia	9.9	18.5
Lithuania	9.3	23.8
CEEC10 total	8.6	22.5
EU15 total	2.4	5.3

S o u r c e: CEC (1997), Vol. II, p. 68.

Another key fact not shown by the figures above is that the market conditions in the CEECs are very different from those prevailing in EU15. For example, prices are between 40 and 80% of those in EU countries partly because of the high support prices in the EU and partly because of lower quality in the CEECs. Furthermore, efficiency levels are considerably lower and all CEECS with the exception of Hungary are net importers of EU food.

With this background, it is understandable that the net contributors to the EU are alarmed if the existing CAP remains in force. The CAP has been moderately successful in its aims of protecting European agriculture as well as developing it. The set prices and subsidies do appear to engage with deficiencies in the market as well as overcoming instability. But alongside this are the problems of the CAP's increasing cost, the fact that it distorts the market and the contentious issue of over-production. Attempts at reform have been made over the years (for example, in 1970 the CAP consumed over 80% of the community budget) but over the last thirty years the costs of the CAP have grown over eight times.

It is estimated that if the five 'first-wave' countries were to accede to the EU with no change in the current CAP then double the present amount would have to spent on the CAP. Anderson and Tyers (1994) put the actual annual figure at between euro 35–30 billion, a figure considerably higher than that suggested by *Agenda 2000* where the estimate is euro 11 billion a year. The latter does, however, recognise that reform of the CAP will be necessary if the 'first-wave' countries do accede. As a consequence, the Commission has suggested in the first instance that there should be a reduction in basic support prices for beef, milk and cereals. This would be followed by other products such as olive oil and wine. (Grabbe and Hughes 1998: 98).

What should not be forgotten is the strength of the farming lobby in all EU15 countries. For example, although Germany is expressing increased concern over its net contribution to the EU budget, the German agricultural lobby argues that no reform of the CAP should take place. In this sense, when (not if) change does occur it will not be overnight and is most likely to come about as a consequence of external pressure such as the need to reduce export subsidies in the 2000 World Trade Organisation (WTO) negotiations.

Cohesion and Structural Funds

The basic aim of the CSF has been to try to produce a degree of economic harmonisation across EU member states. In this sense, the less developed countries have always benefited at the expense of the more economically prosperous. The budget of the Cohesion Fund stands at around euro 2 billion whist that of the structural funds is about euro 11 billion. The latter cover a broad range of projects including halting industrial decline, high unemployment, education and training, rural areas and the like. The structural funds are separated into regional policy objectives (one having been introduced as an inducement for Sweden and Finland since it covers areas of low population density) with Objective 1 (regions having per capita GDP below 75% of the EU average) swallowing up 70% of the total allocation. In this way, the allocation of funds is highly selective and advantages poorer and smaller countries.

The Cohesion Fund is far more selective in that to qualify under existing arrangements member countries need to have a GDP per head of less than 90% of the EU average which has tended to restrict its allocation to Greece, Portugal, Spain and Ireland.

As far as enlargement is concerned, *Agenda 2000* suggested that only a small addition to the CSF would be needed (though with the proposal that that there should be a ceiling of 4% of GNP on Structural Funds receipts). If that were to be the case then the allocations would be spread much more thinly than at present with EU15 since the CEECs – under existing arrangements – would all qualify for Objective 1 and Cohesion Fund money. In this way many of those regions and, indeed, countries presently benefiting from CSF would lose a considerable amount of their entitlement. In all probability regions such as Northern Ireland, eastern Germany and the whole of Belgium would lose out completely. In these circumstances, there is every reason to suspect that any proposed reforms of the current CSF system would be likely to be met with considerable opposition. The effect, then, on fundamental European principles such as solidarity and cohesion is likely to be immense and very divisive.

Reform of the EU

Much of the above suggests that if enlargement does go ahead – even if with only five new members – the EU's institutions will themselves have to change. The last enlargement to 15 members produced strains in the EU's institutions; the peculiar problems that the CEECs would bring with them could strain the institutions to breaking point. This is not a new observation. There is widespread acceptance that things need to change, that reforms have to be made and that there must be a willingness of the part of existing member countries to expedite change. Where there is not acceptance is in deciding what kinds of changes need to be made, how fundamental they should be and when they should be introduced. The Amsterdam Intergovernmental Conference (IGC) of 1997 opened the debate on such matters but resolved nothing.

The failure of the Amsterdam IGC displayed the strains within the Union itself and the self-interest of individual member countries in protecting the system from which they were benefiting. Furthermore, the Amsterdam failure suggests that the commitment to enlargement on the part of some members is low. By achieving nothing the IGC might possibly have made the enlargement process more difficult. For example, by not even agreeing to changes in qualified majority voting (QMV) (this, in turn, would have placed limits on the number of Commissioners as well as giving larger countries more say and limiting the size of the European Parliament) a major opportunity was missed in starting to address some of the institutional problems that enlargement will inevitably give rise to.

One ray of light from the Amsterdam IGC was a protocol to the Amsterdam Treaty. The protocol does address the issue of the number of Commissioners and suggests only one for each member state when the 'first-wave' of accessions occurs. The caveat to this is that there should be a weighted voting system – this has yet to be agreed.

Overall, then, although institutional reform is an obvious pre-requisite to enlargement the progress so far has been minimal. The Amsterdam Treaty protocol does say that there should be another IGC before the 'first-wave' accession (assuming they all join together) or before the EU expands to a membership of twenty (in the case of them not all joining at the same time).

Another key issue as far as institutional reform is concerned relates to the question of flexibility and the actual introduction of a flexibility clause in the Amsterdam Treaty. Flexibility is, according to Grabbe and Hughes (1998: 104), "a way of dealing with political and economic diversity between member states, especially where 'awkward' member states such as Britain have been seen as a brake on further integration." In the event a highly inflexible flexibility clause was introduced, "it must involve a majority of member states and must not affect the rights and obligations of those member states that do not participate... flexibility must not affect existing Community policies or programmes, impede trade and competition, affect the exclusive competences of the Community, or result in discrimination between member state national" (Grabbe and Hughes 1998: 105).

External Relations

The discussion so far has concentrated on the internal implications of enlargement to the EU itself and how it might cope with the extra member states from central and eastern Europe. It must be stressed, however, that the EU does not operate as if an island; events in recent years (e.g. Kosova) have shown the (growing) importance of the EU as an international player. Clearly if the enlargement with the CEECs does take place then the Union, at a stroke, becomes a more powerful and influential player on the world stage. Furthermore, it will have different eastern borders from those existing now and will be cheek-by-jowl alongside Russia, Ukraine and Turkey. In this sense there will be a redrawing of the geo-political map of Europe with the ensuing questions of European security.

Beyond Europe, there is little doubt that the USA would expect European states and the EU itself to be less dependent on American security support. At the same time the USA would, in all probability, expect the EU to provide greater assistance in global security matters. It is the case, however, that the USA strongly supports an enlarged EU. It is, of course, NATO that the USA uses as the conduit for its influence in Europe and, again, there is strong support for NATO enlarging the number of member states beyond the CEECs that have already joined. It should be noted that Turkey is a keen supporter of NATO as well as being a close ally of the United States – facts that did not go unrecognised in the Helsinki overtures to Turkey in December 1999.

The problem with all this is that the EU has yet to formuiate a clear and realistic foreign or external policy. In the same way, as argued above, that enlargement could prove to be divisive rather than integrative for the EU's institutions so too could the very differences between member states and their very heterogeneity prove to be a major barrier to producing any credible external policy.

As far as the new borders are concerned there have been no objections from Russia or any of the newly independent states (NIS) about the accessions of the CEECs. Some concern has been expressed about trade balances. Geographically, it is worth pointing out that Ukraine could be the most significant of EU20's neighbours given that it could have three of the new member states on its borders – Poland, Hungary and Slovakia.

Discussion

The road to the next wave of EU enlargement was never going to be smooth and this Chapter has briefly discussed the main, though by no means all, difficulties to be overcome before the CEECs accede. It is clear that the process is going to take considerable time given all the institutional, political and financial problems that have been identified. The process is likely to be divisive for the Union itself as the interests of individual member states come to the fore. The enthusiasm with which enlargement was originally greeted has declined. Each of the problem areas discussed in the Chapter are inter-dependent and until each has been solved to the satisfaction of all, the problems will remain. Yet, in all likelihood, the problems will continue to be faced in a piece-meal fashion. These problems could so easily lead to a slowing down of the enlargement process and certainly a slowing down of the process of European integration.

The proposed fast-track entry of the 'first-wave' of CEECs is, in fact, proving divisive and exposing current weaknesses within the EU itself. Unless a systematic programme of institutional and financial reform takes place the enlargement process will become even more complicated and liable to stall. However, it is perfectly understandable why certain member states are objecting to any reform of the current system since the benefits to them are enormous. National identity, rather than the grand European federal vision, becomes paramount for a member state likely to lose the economic advantages it has enjoyed in recent years.

It should also not be forgotten that the enthusiasm for membership among the general populations of the CEECs appears to have dampened as the years have dragged on. This is largely a result of the long drawn-out process of negotiation but also an increasing recognition that whatever budgetary reforms are made within the EU, the CEECs are never going to receive the same positive financial discrimination that the Mediterranean states and Ireland have received.

There is also a growing awareness among those CEECs in the 'second-wave' that they could receive fewer economic benefits than those in the 'first-wave' as successive reforms of the EU's budgetary policies take effect. Rather than an integrated Europe, the future could be a multi-layered Europe with a range of internal conflicts and strains embedded within it.

References

Avery, G. & F. **Cameron** (1998), *The Enlargement of the European Union*. Sheffield: Sheffield Academic Press.

Croft, S., J. **Redmond**, G. **Rees** & M. **Webber** (1999), *The Enlargement of Europe*. Manchester: Manchester University Press.

Grabbe, H & K. **Hughes** (1998), *Enlarging the European Union Eastwards*. London: Royal Institution for International Affairs.

Price, V., A. **Landau** & R. **Whitman** (eds) (1999), *The Enlargement of the European Union: issues and strategies*. London: Routledge.

Henderson, K. (ed) (1999), *Back to Europe – Central and Eastern Europe and the European Union*. London: UCL Press.

Preston, C. (1997), *Enlargement & Integration in the European Union*. London: Routledge.

Tiersky, R. (ed.) (1999), *Europe Today*. Oxford: Rowman and Littlefield.

Andrew Thompson

Regions, Regionalisation and Regionalism in Contemporary Europe

Introduction

Across Europe, in the closing decade of the twentieth century, the 'region' is stepping out of the shadow of the nation-state. While formal systems of regional government are not novel, over the past decade the region, regionalisation, and regionalism (see Fig. 1) have moved squarely on to the policy agenda across

---

Region. This a fairly amorphous concept in practice, although it can be stated that a region is, irreducibly, a territorial unit. For the large part, as used in this chapter region is applied to those territorial units that operate between the levels of local and national government. These are, then, administratively defined territorial units, as in the case of the German *Lander*, the Spanish autonomous communities, or, in the case of the United Kingdom, the devolved administrations in Northern Ireland, Scotland, and Wales. It should be noted that, defined in this way, region is a sub-unit of a state. Usage of the concept of region may vary, however. For example, the regions that are the object of EU regional policy will not always correspond to regions as defined by national government. To take one such example, in the next round of the Structural Funds (2000–2006) only part of Wales will qualify as an Objective One region. For the purpose of British central government, it is the *whole* of Wales that is the object of British government regional policy. Indeed, the matter is complicated further by virtue of the fact that some organisations regard Wales not as a region of Britain, but as a distinct nation in its own right. The meaning of the term region, therefore, lies in the eye of the beholder!

Regionalism. In contrast to the previous term, regionalism refers to the manner in which certain political parties and other organisations have promoted the distinctiveness of the region. Regionalism, therefore, is both a political ideology and strategy, utilised for the purpose of securing advantages for the region. The Lega Nord in northern Italy, for example, promotes the interests of a region, and its demands for a separate region-state should not be viewed as a form of nationalism

Regionalisation. This term refers to the process of devolving, or transferring, powers from central government down to regional administrations. This process, then, involves the recognition of regional units as legitimate territorial entities, which are sufficiently distinct in their cultural, economic, or political conditions to warrant self-government.

Figure 1. Region, Regionalisation, and Regionalism

European countries, as well as at the level of the European Union. It is not just national policy-makers, however, who are exercising their judgements on this matter. Within European countries, pressure has come from politicians elected to regional assemblies, from assorted political parties and organisations representing regional business interests, and from sections of the population living in these regions.

In this chapter we will be addressing two principal issues. Firstly, we will be examining some of the varying forms of regional government in operation across Europe. Secondly, we will be turning our attention towards a consideration of the region within the context of EU policy.

Regions in Europe in the post-war period

As the preceding section highlighted, when employed to analyse empirical conditions at the sub-national level across Europe the concept of 'region' has a chameleon-like quality. There are, for example, considerable differences between the Austrian and German Länder, on the one hand, and the nominal regional entities that are the focus of regional development bodies in Greece or the Republic of Ireland, on the other hand. Indeed, that some regional polities, such as North Rhine-Westphalia in Germany, manage budgets larger than the national state budget of Denmark or Greece underscores the considerable disparities between regions across Europe (see Van Der Knapp, 1994). Even without drawing attention to such extremes of difference, the most cursory evaluation of conditions across Europe reveals that there exist varying levels of administrative, economic, and political decentralisation between countries, as

Table 1. Different Forms of Regional Administration in Europe

Federal System	Regionalised Unitary States	Devolving Unitary States	Classic Unitary States
Austria	Italy	France	Bulgaria
Belgium	Spain	Netherlands	Denmark
Germany	United Kindom	Portugal	Finland
Switzerland			Greece
Yugoslavia			Hungary
			Norway
			Poland
			Sweden
			Republic of Ireland

well as, in a number of cases, within them as well. How, then, can we categorise the differing empirical conditions found across Europe in order that we can develop a more general comparative framework? The four dimensional approach utilised by Bullman (1996) and Loughlin (1996) to categorising differences between regional entities in the EU provides a useful starting-point (see Table 1).

Federal Systems of Government

In the first instance this model distinguishes between federal and non-federal systems in Europe. In the case of the former, countries such as Austria, Belgium, Germany, and Switzerland possess federal structures. In addition, prior to political changes in the 1990s both the former-Czechoslovakia and the former-Yugoslavia were organised on a federal structure, although a depleted Yugoslav federation remains between Serbia and Montenegro. There are nevertheless marked differences in the way in which federalism is, and, in the case of the former-Czechoslovakia and the former-Yugoslavia, was, practised in each of these countries, although there is a greater degree of commonality between the systems operating in Austria and Germany, respectively. Austria's federal system is divided between the *Nationalrat*, to which members are directly elected and the *Bundesrat*, the latter comprising members appointed by the nine, directly elected federal assemblies (*Landtage*). The principle that the political balance should be in favour of the *Landtage*, enshrined in the Austrian constitution, does not bear out under scrutiny. The areas over which the *Landtage* have sole legislative authority are comparatively limited (to topics such as pre-school education, planning regulations, and nature preservation) when viewed in relation to the wide array of areas over which the federal government enjoys a legislative monopoly (see Gruber 1997; Honauer 1999). In Germany, while there remain areas of mutual legislative exclusivity for the governments of the 16 Länder and the federal government, there has nevertheless been a movement towards increased cooperation between the two structures across a wide range of policy areas. A major factor behind this 'co-operative federalism' (Gerstenlauer 1995; Benz 1998) has been the impact of EU policy on legislative areas for which the Länder governments are responsible, and the desire of the Länder to ensure that they can exert an influence over the direction of federal policy in relation to the EU as a compromise.

If the German and, to a lesser degree, the Austrian systems of federalism allow for appropriate modes of contact between the regional and federal levels of government, in Belgium the federal system that was created in 1988, and which was reformed more radically in 1993, tips the balance in favour of the three 'communities' and three 'regions'. Since the reforms initiated in 1988 these sub-national units have accrued an expanding legislative portfolio, and, since 1993, they have been able to undertake international agreements with other states. Moreover, as a result of the 1993 reforms the communities and sub-national entities have been entitled to participate directly in discussions within the EU Council of Ministers in areas where authority is shared with the federal government or where the issues under discussion are exclusively subject to the control of the sub-national units. Thus, as Kerremans and Beyers (1996) argue, the 1993 reforms allowed the regions and communities to legally operate at the 'Second Level', rather than the 'Third Level' at which regional bodies conventionally function.

Regionalised Unitary States

The political situations in the above countries, most notably that in Belgium, are far from the norm across the rest of Europe. There are nevertheless contexts within which regional political bodies exercise varying degrees of legislative and executive competence in other European countries. In the typology outlined by Bullman (1996) countries such as Italy and Spain are characterised as 'regionalised unitary states'. The United Kingdom may also be characterised as a regionalised unitary state, following the constitutional reforms introduced under the Labour government since 1997 (see Fig. 2).

Following referenda held in Scotland and Wales in 1997, and in Northern Ireland in 1998, devolved administrations have now been established in three of the territories of the United Kingdom. Each of these institutions have emerged in response to different kinds of political circumstances. In the case of the Northern Ireland Assembly this is evident from the complex manner in which legislation and voting is conducted to ensure that there is sufficient cross-community cooperation. In addition, there are some significant differences between each of the devolved administrations with regard to their respective powers. Of the three institutions, the Scottish Parliament holds the most extensive range of powers. This 129-member body possesses primary legislative competence (i.e. legislation that does not have its origins in the UK Parliament in London) over a range of policy areas, such as health, education, housing, and most areas of criminal and civil law. The Scottish Parliament also holds tax-varying powers. The 108-member Northern Ireland Assembly holds full legislative and executive authority over the fields of economic development, education, agriculture, the environment, finance and personnel, health and social services. The 60-member National Assembly of Wales possesses secondary legislative powers, meaning that it has, within legal limits, the right to apply the provisions of laws made by the UK legislature in such a way as to suit the specific conditions in Wales. A Joint-Ministerial Committee has also been established to coordinate relations between the British Prime Minister and the heads of each of the devolved administrations.

Figure 2. Devolution in the United Kingdom

Of these three countries, Spain has experienced the most comprehensive regionalisation process. In the 1978 constitution provisions were made for regions to form elected regional governments with varying degrees of legislative and executive authority, although, as is routinely observed, the constitution proclaims the continued 'indissoluble unity of the Spanish nation' (Morata 1996; Luelmo and Williams 1999). The constitutional changes of 1978 nevertheless accorded a greater degree of autonomy to the regions of Catalonia, the Basque Country, Galicia, and Andalusia, in recognition of the cultural distinctiveness of the inhabitants of these territories. Since 1989, however, all 17 devolved regions enjoy 'full autonomy', although the extent of the powers of individual devolved governments varies considerably.

Similarly, in Italy, where the 1948 constitution provided for the establishment of fifteen directly elected 'ordinary' councils and five directly elected 'special' councils, there are differences between the constitutional status of particular regions (including, between the 'special' and 'ordinary' councils, different financial arrangements with central government). Where there exist differing levels of autonomy within regionalised unitary states the process of decentralisation is a complex process, and different constitutional arrangements for particular units leads, almost inevitably, to growing pressures on central government to address the conflicts that arise as a consequence. Thus, central government in Madrid has had to address claims that Catalonia and the Basque Country, for example, are privileged to the disadvantage of other regions. In a similar manner, Plaid Cymru in Wales maintains that the National Assembly of Wales should possess the same legislative powers as Scotland.

In the case of each of these countries, however, central government continues to act as the primary locus of political power, and can claim a constitutional entitlement to oppose legislation passed by regional governments where the latter conflict with the legislation passed by the former. In Italy, for example, the councils do not possess primary legislative powers and therefore must work within the legislative framework established by central government. Morata (1995) has noted that similar conflict exists in Spain, where, in the first decade of the existence of the autonomous communities, more than 800 legal cases had arisen from incidences where central government had blocked decisions taken by the regional governments. This situation does nevertheless highlight how regionalisation, particularly where devolved governments have been established, alters the relations between central government and the regions. Under these changed conditions central government faces greater pressure to establish structures for resolving disputes between regions and the centre, not least because of the need to maintain support for the governing political party among the electorate in the regions.

Devolving Unitary States

The situation in 'devolving unitary states', Bullman's (1996) third category of regional government, generally involves greater restrictions on the autonomy of regional bodies, as well as differences in the form of these bodies. As with the other categories of regional government, however, there are considerable differences between countries. Portugal, as established in the 1976 constitution, is divided into three forms of regions: the 'autonomous regions'; the 'administrative regions'; and, since 1991, the 'metropolitan areas'. Of these categories, only the first has any political significance, where the autonomous regions of the Azores and the Madeira Islands have established formal devolved governments that exercise executive control over regional issues and possess some legislative functions. In contrast, the administrative regions are rather more nebulous entities. Reforms in 1991 advanced the development of regionalisation, creating the new metropolitan regions, but, as Pereira (1995: 272) comments, the administrative regions remain an 'intermediate level of government at a not-yet-attained decentralisation goal'. France represents another example of a devolving unitary state, where directly elected regional assemblies have existed since state reforms in 1982. Moreover, the reforms of 1982 also established a regional assembly in Corsica, with a more extensive range of powers than those held by other French regions. The powers of the 22 regions are tightly circumscribed, being limited to the areas of planning, regional economic development, and post-16 education and training. The evolution of the role of the regions in French political life represents part of a broader strategy of redefining the relations between central government and the various levels of sub-national government, from the regions down to the *communes* (the level closest to the French citizen). If, as a number of commentators argue, the potential of the French region remains unfulfilled, due in large part to the existence of significant alternative modes of sub-national government, the role of regions in the Netherlands is even weaker. The Netherlands is divided into 12 'provinces', each of which are overseen by a directly elected councils. As with the French regions, the Dutch provinces are mainly entitled to be involved in provincial planning issues, but their powers are even more limited than their French counterparts.

Classic Unitary States

The relative degrees of autonomy enjoyed by French regions and Dutch provinces are nevertheless in advance of the powers held by sub-national units in 'classic unitary states', the fourth category of regional government identified by Bullman (1996). This mode of regional government exists in all of the Nordic states, Greece, the Republic of Ireland, and in most central and east European states (see Fig. 3).

The states of central and eastern Europe have each experienced moves towards reform of domestic political structures. In large part this has involved coming to terms with the legacy of the era of communist government, during which sub-national units of government served the interests of national government. For example, the municipal elections that took place in Poland in 1990 were the first such elections for fifty years. The drawing-up of new constitutions in the early-1990s provided the conditions for initiating reforms to the operation of government at all levels. The subsequent period has seen significant legislative developments, mostly directed towards the reform of local government. In the case of Bulgaria, the creation of the new constitution in 1991 was shortly followed in that year by the Local Self-Government and Local Administration Act, and has continued with the 1995 Laws on the Administrative-Territorial Structure of Bulgaria and Local Elections, respectively. Similar developments elsewhere in the region also followed on from constitutional changes. In Estonia the 1992 constitution redefined the role of local government, and a law on local government, adopted in 1993, outlined the new relations between the former and the national government. In the Czech Republic, too, the adoption of a new constitution following the break-up of the former-Czechoslovakia, led to a complete reorganisation of local and regional government. The 1993 constitution of the Czech Republic provided for a three tier structure of government below that of central government: the region (*vyssi uzemne samospravny celek*); the district (*okres*); and the municipality (*obec*). Of these three, the first has yet to be established in practice, the second acts as a sub-central unit of national government, while the latter is a directly-elected local administration that performs a range of independent activities as well as a range of activities transferred from central government. As in the Czech Republic, much of the momentum behind the reforms to regional and local government in central and eastern Europe has been directed towards establishing strong municipal government. Both the constitutions of Hungary and Slovakia, for example, furnish municipal government with a broad range of powers. The near future will undoubtedly witness further moves towards reform of local and regional government, especially for those central and east European states that will be the next wave of new entrants to the EU.

Figure 3. Sub-National Administration in Central and Eastern Europe

Within these contexts, regional tiers of government do exist, although these are largely for administrative purposes, while central government remains the dominant source of political power. As with the other categories of regional government, the situation in classic unitary states is far from static, and in each of the countries identified there have been recent moves towards identifying and clarifying the role of regional bodies. In Finland, Norway, and Sweden, while central government is the dominant locus of political power, there is nevertheless a tradition of strong local government. The states of central and eastern Europe, with the exception of the federal structures in the former-Yugoslavia and the former-Czechoslovakia, have been controlled from the centre, especially during the Communist era. Changes in political organisation are now taking place, albeit at different speeds. In Poland, for example, state reforms in 1999 have led to the creation of 16 self-governing authorities, to replace the former system of 49 centrally administered regions.

The pressures to reform political structures within a number of classic unitary states is gaining momentum. In Greece, one of the most resolutely centrally administered states in the EU, since the mid-1980s there have been growing internal demands for state reform. To date this has led to the establishment of elected councils in the 52 prefectures, a development which was legislated for in 1986 but which did not transpire until 1994 when the first elections to these councils took place. For the future there is the potential for further reform of regional government, in the form of an elected level of government above that of the prefecture (Christopolous 1999).

As these latter examples illustrate, even within the most centralised of unitary states there are pressures for momentum in the direction of enhanced regional involvement in legislative and executive processes. Indeed, the changes in the UK that have occurred since 1997 highlight how the political relations between the national and regional levels of government can change dramatically in a relatively short space of time. Movements in this direction can arise for a number of reasons. Firstly, regionalisation may occur as a consequence of a top-down rationalisation of sub-national tiers of government. This is a factor that has gained increasing significance because of developments unfolding at the level of the EU, as is the case in the reforms in the different cases of the Netherlands and Greece, for example. In addition, the countries of central and eastern Europe are presently witnessing moves to restructure or create a regional level of government after the demise of communist centralised planning. In each of these countries there had existed differing forms of sub-national spatial organisation, but, as Horváth (1995) suggests, the generic three tier module applied in each of these countries was based on the Soviet model and was used to implement central government strategies. As a consequence, the reorganisation of regional government in central and eastern Europe involves coming to terms with the manner in which these units operated under the communist regimes in the past and recognising the necessity for a new role for regional units with a degree of self-governing authority. Secondly, regionalisation is implemented to address disparities in economic circumstances. In France deteriorating economic circumstances in a number of regions, along with demographic changes in others, provided a good deal of the impetus for the state reforms of the early-1980s, and serve to partly explain why the regions have come to be responsible for measures concerning regional economic development and training. Thirdly, regionalisation may arise as a response to regionalism. This is most evident in the privileged position of the Basque Country, Catalonia, Andalucia, and Galicia in the 1978 Spanish constitution, in the special statute relating to Corsica in the French reforms of 1982, as well as in the precarious settlement in Belgium. A final factor, and one that has gained increasing importance since the 1980s, is the political change at the level of the EU. The fostering of the concept of a *Europe of the Regions*, the impact of the structural funds, and the institutionalisation of a regional dimension to the policy-making process at the level of the EU have, together, served to simultaneously generate pressures for regionalisation within existing member states, as well as among those states applying to join the EU, and to create a more fertile environment for the promotion of regionalist objectives. It is to a discussion of the impact of EU policy that this discussion now turns.

European regions and EU policy

Throughout the 1990s, for policy-makers across the EU the place of the region prompts a range of questions. What are the most effective measures for reducing regional social and economic disparities across the EU? How can regional politicians best contribute to policy-making at the level of the EU? What form should the dialogue take between regional and national government with respect to national positions on EU business? What is the potential impact of the widening membership of the EU for regions, especially those with more serious economic and social difficulties, within existing member states? These are policy matters about which there is a great deal of dispute and which, due in part to the specificity of national arrangements over regional government, it is impossible to speak of uniform regional or national responses (see Keating 1998). What is clear, however, is that the trajectory of European integration over the past two decades has pushed issues relating to the role of regions in this larger process and, in turn, its impact on regions, increasingly on to the political agenda. In drawing attention to some of the key dimensions of this changing climate we settle on three issues: firstly, the evolution of an EU regional policy since the late-1980s; secondly, the implications of the Structural Funds; and finally the role of regional politicians and organisations within the policy-making processes at the level of the EU.

The Evolution of EU Regional Policy

Taking the first of these dimensions, there is some debate as to the origins of an EU regional policy. Armstrong (1995), for example, traces the genesis of EU regional policy to the establishment of the European Regional Development Fund (ERDF) in 1975. Hall and van der Wee (1995), however, argue that the 1988 reforms of the Structural Funds (see below) mark the start of a 'genuine regional policy since interventions in this field prior to then were essentially actions by the Community in support of nationally-determined regional policy' (1995: 9). There is nevertheless a common ground between these two positions. It *is* the case that the creation ERDF, to assist social and economic disadvantaged regions, marks the origins of an EU regional policy, but it is also evident that the member states exerted a great deal of control over the dispersal of the funds and largely opposed the transfer of regional development powers to the level of the EU. Since 1975, subsequent reforms to the ERDF, and the Structural Funds more broadly – in 1979, 1988, 1993, and 1998 – have, however, involved a shift in the balance in the relationship between the member states, on the one hand, and the EU (and, in particular, the European Commission), on the other hand. The key point in this shift was the reforms that were introduced in 1988, which saw the creation of a new set of objectives for tackling social and economic problems across the EU.

Evidence of the new balance in this relationship is apparent in that after 1989 it was the EC that defined the areas that would be eligible for assistance. Whereas previously it was the member states who drew up the maps defining eligible areas, this change was indicative of the growing authority of the EU in the field of regional policy. Aside from the changing political currents, there is also a qualitative change in the form of EU regional policy that distinguishes the objectives up to the mid-1980s from those of the subsequent period. From the creation of the ERDF, EU regional policy has involved assisting socially and economically disadvantaged regions, but in the period after the mid-1980s there has been a growing emphasis on economic and social cohesion across the EU. Crucial to this redirection of regional policy objectives was the new momentum given to the completion of the Single European Market (SEM), enshrined within the 1986 Single European Act, especially the necessity of ensuring the gradual elimination of impediments to the functioning of the SEM. In order to realise this larger objective, since 1988 the goal of working towards economic and social cohesion has been channelled through three broad regional objectives: to assist those regions where GDP is less than 75% of the EU average; to aid the restructuring of declining industrial regions; and to address the conditions in particularly problematic rural regions. Following the 1992 Treaty of the

European Union (TEU), in the negotiations on which there was a broad acknowledgement among member states about the desirability of further promoting economic and social cohesion, the funding for this goal has been increased by 40% between 1993–1999, from 21 billion ecu to 30 billion ecu. The most recent radical changes to EU regional policy have been implemented in accordance with the planned expansion of the membership of the EU to include some of the states of central and eastern Europe.

The EU Structural Funds

Central to the plans for widening the membership of the EU to some of the states of central and eastern Europe are the Structural Funds. As we have already noted, for the EU the Structural Funds represent a key device in the efforts to bring about an ameliorative change in the economic and social conditions across the member states. Together, the Structural Funds is the collective title for four funds: the European Regional Development Fund (RDF); the European Social Fund (ESF); the European Agricultural Guidance and Guarantee Fund (EAGGF); and, since 1993, the Financial Instrument for Fisheries (FIFG). The reforms of 1988 led to a reorganisation of the way in which these funds would be dispersed by creating a common set of seven objectives for their utlisation, three of which were specifically marked for particular kinds of regions: Objective 1, dedicated to the structural adjustment of the poorest regions in the EU; Objective 2, for declining industrial regions; and Objective 5b for enabling the development of rural areas. In 1993 the Structural Funds were, again, subject to reform, principally due to the increased emphasis on economic and social cohesion, and regional policy more especially, within the TEU. Among the changes to the Structural Funds were: the establishment of the FIFG; the addition of an Objective 6 programme for the development of extremely under-population regions; the broadening of Objective 3, previously for addressing the problem of long-term unemployment, to include actions designed to tackle youth unemployment; and the creation of a new Objective 4 now targeting the adaptation of workers to industrial change.

From 1999 onwards, the Structural Funds will have been reformed even more radically, with the reorganisation of the previous seven objectives into three broad objectives. (for a discussion of the evolution of the Structural Funds up to 1999, see Michie and Fitzgerald 1997; see Morgan and Price 1998, for a discussion of the post-1999 reforms to the Structural Funds). This most recent shake-up in the role and dispersal of the Structural Funds is largely concerned with improving the efficiency of the structural funds and with altering the relations involved in the management of the Structural Funds. Thus, with regard to the former, the proportion of the EU population covered by the Structural Funds will be reduced from 51% to 35–40% in order to maximise the impact in especially disadvantaged regions, and, with respect to the latter, in future there will be a greater involvement of regional governments and local authorities in the dispersal and management of funding. Another substantial development in the recent reforms is the increase in the level of funding available under the three redefined Objectives. The amount available for the phase to run 2000–2006 will be increased by 38% from the funding for the previous phase, 1993–1999. Built into the 2000–2006 budget is a separate allowance for the planned new entrants, such as the Czech Republic, Hungary, Poland, and Slovenia, amounting to approximately one sixth (ECU 45 billion) of the total ECU 275 billion.

The decision to reduce the percentage of the EU population covered by the Structural Funds has been driven by a recognition that funds too widely distributed will not have a sufficient impact on the most seriously disadvantaged regions and by the attendant costs of enlargement. Questions of funding – from how it should be raised to how it should be dispersed – are politically sensitive issues, with disputes revolving around further increases in the financial contributions to the Structural Funds to the efforts of some members states to exert increased national control over regional policy, as well as over the general effectiveness of the Structural Funds in realising their intended objectives (Bachtler 1998). Referring to the case of Wales, for example, Thomas (1996) argues that the significance of the Structural Funds with regard to economic conditions in Wales must be 'qualified with respect to both its scale and nature' (1996: 213). In particular, Thomas points out that much of the funding in Wales has gone to 'hard infrastructure' projects (such as roads), while not enough has gone to projects designed to foster indigenous economic development (such as business support and training initiatives). Other commentators have been generally more commendatory with respect to the impact of the Structural Funds in reducing regional disparities across the EU, but hold that if further substantial increases in the levels of funding available do not transpire this will inevitably have a negative impact on the success of regional policy (Armstrong and de Kervenoael 1997; Bachtler 1998). This question becomes all the more pressing when the matter of enlargement of the EU is taken into consideration. In spite of the statements from the European Commission about the political and economic imperatives for ensuring cohesion within future member states, the subject of enlargement is often reduced by some regional and national players to the issue of cost. The specific implications of the impact of enlargement for EU regional policy are difficult to project, but there is little doubt that this development will ensure that spending on regions within existing members states will have to be more focused than at present, even with an increase in the budget of the

Structural Funds. In this changed political environment compromises will be necessary to ensure that the most disadvantaged regions in existing member states continue to benefit from targeted funding, while also contributing to the development of the new member states. The form of this compromise will impact on much more than EU regional policy: due to the considerable significance of this policy to the broader objective of enlargement, it will have a bearing on the relations within an expanded EU.

Regional Involvement in the EU

The 1998 reforms to the Structural Funds, in particular the changes to the management of their deployment, highlights the issue of the role of regional and local authorities in the planning and implementation of EU regional policy. As we have already noted, across Europe the specific arrangements between the national and sub-national levels of government vary from national context to another, but it is nevertheless possible to speak of an increased regional participation in structures of governance in many European countries throughout the 1990s. In the context of the EU, the regional level has been given an added boost with the establishment of the Committee of the Regions, a 186-member body comprising representatives of regional and local government from across the EU. Indeed, the nature of its membership id a reflection of the differing national arrangements for regional government that was the subject of our discussion in the previous section. Created by the 1992 TEU, the Committee of the Regions acts as an advisory body to the main EU institutions on regional policy matters. The impact of the Committee of the Regions on policy formation has been the subject of considerable dispute, especially given that the main institutions are not formally obliged to accept the former's recommendations (Kennedy 1997; Warleigh 1997). The Committee of the Regions lacks political clout in its own right, but it is evident that both the European Parliament and, more particularly, the European Commission have made good use of the work of the former. Notably, the European Commission, in its relations with the Committee of the Regions, has often accorded it a *de facto* status that exceeds its *de jure* remit.

Clearly the Committee of the Regions provides a channel through which regional or local government politicians can take direct part in the policy-making process in the EU. Some of its members are nevertheless already entitled to take part in the business of the Council of Ministers by virtue of the specific arrangements made between national and regional government in some member states. Thus, elected representatives of regional government in Belgium and

Germany can, in certain policy fields, be involved in negotiations in the Council of Ministers. These are, however, the exceptions to the general practice across the EU. In Spain and Italy plans to move towards more formal institutional processes for involving the regions in the drawing up of national responses to EU policy matters has not yet borne significant fruit (Mazey 1995). In the UK, the importance of the Joint Ministerial Council, which will bring together the heads of the devolved governments and the British Prime Minister, will be judged in time. If formal institutional arrangements for a regional input to national policy responses is, at present, absent in most EU members states, regional players nevertheless pursue their objectives through informal lobbying. Differences in levels of organisation are, again, present with respect to lobbying. A growing number of regional and local authorities are establishing their own offices in Brussels in order to be better placed to monitor developments and lobby relevant EU politicians. The Scottish Office, for example, although part of the domestic infrastructure of the British government, established an office in Brussels in 1999. In addition, regional interests are lobbied via commercial offices based in Brussels, such as Breizh Europe, an organisation funded by Breton small- and medium-sized companies to promote Breton exports, or the Wales European Centre, which performs a similar task for Welsh business interests. As successful as some of these ventures are, they are nevertheless not an alternative to formal structures for a regional input to the formulation of national policy. As numerous commentators maintain, the increasing regional dimension to EU policy has not led to a uniform improvement in the standing of regional players in relation to national planning, although some regions have prospered rather better than others (Martin 1997; Smith 1998).

Future trajectories

The plans for improving communication and collaboration between national, regional and local government under the 1998 reforms to the Structural Funds are intended to facilitate greater participation from sub-national actors in directing EU regional policy. The extent to which this will be successful, will become clearer early in the next century, as the mid-way point of the next phase of the Structural Funds will require holders of funding to account for how Objectives are being met. By way of a conclusion, we shall briefly identify two matters that will be crucial to the future of regions across Europe.

Firstly, the progression of regionalisation programmes across the EU member states and other European countries. There has been a general move in this direction, but there exist considerable disparities in the levels of regional political autonomy. The process of European integration has acted as a powerful pressure on national governments to reform state structures, and the moves towards greater regional and local government involvement in the management of EU funding programmes post-1999 should continue the momentum in this direction. Significant reforms to political structures within European countries are rather more difficult to predict, as the case of the changes in the United Kingdom illustrate. It is, however, likely that further reforms to local government, although not the establishment of devolved regional assemblies, will occur within the Czech Republic, Estonia, Poland, and Hungary as they continue to prepare for entry into the EU.

Following on from the above point, a second matter is that it will be necessary to enhance our understanding of the conditions within given regions across Europe. Research highlights that, while prevailing economic conditions are pivotal for the successful development of a region, the ability of regional bodies to create a conducive environment for inward investment and local economic development is also a key factor, as the cases of Baden-Württemberg, Germany and Emilia-Romagna, Italy illustrate (Cooke, Price and Morgan 1995; Garmise 1995). Other commentators, however, are not so convinced on the transferability of lessons from one region to another. Lovering (1999), for example, criticises the application of generic models of regional development, arguing that it is necessary to develop a more contextual understanding of the economic problems that beset individual regions and, therefore, develop models for development that are themselves contextual without being parochial. Increased regional self-government may serve to produce an improvement in the economic and social conditions in regions across Europe, as, indeed, might an emphasis on technological innovation. If, however, we are to experience a significant reduction in the disparities between regions in Europe it is necessary to recognise that a response of this magnitude will require a broader regulatory framework.

Summary

- As a combined consequence of political reforms that have taken place in a number of European countries, demands from sub-national organisations and political parties, and EU policy, the region has become an increasingly significant aspect of European politics over the past decade.
- There are currently significant variations between the different modes of sub-national administration across Europe. It is nevertheless possible to distinguish between four principal modes: federal systems of government; regionalised unitary states; devolving unitary states; classic unitary states.

- Pressures for strengthening regional involvement in legislative and executive processes can occur for a number of reasons. These include: central government-led political reforms; to address regional disparities in economic and social development; as a consequence of demands from sub-national organisations and political parties; and as a result of EU policy initiatives.
- European integration has had a considerable impact on regions, both directly and indirectly. Directly, EU policy initiatives, especially the Structural Funds, have directed attention towards regional disparities across the EU and have served to galvanise regional mobilisation on the part of political parties and business, among other groups. Indirectly, the growing discussions about the most appropriate levels of decision-making for the implementation of EU policy, as well as about the need to take such decision-making closer to EU citizens, have raised questions about the necessity of a 'third level' of governance below the transnational and national levels, respectively.

Further Reading

Bachtler, J. and I. **Turok** (eds) (1997), *The Coherence of EU Regional Policy. Contrasting Perspectives on the Structural Funds.* London: Jessica Kingsley Publishers.

Le Gales, P. and C. **Lequesne** (eds) (1998), *Regions in Europe.* London: Routledge.

Loughlin, J. *et al.* (1999), *Regional and Local Democracy in the European Union.* Luxembourg: Office for Official Publications of the European Communities.

Wagstaff, P. (ed) (1999), *Regionalism in the European Union.* Exeter: Intellect.

References

Armstrong, H. W. (1995), "The role and evolution of European Community regional policy". In: **Jones**, B. and M. **Keating** (eds), *The European Union and the Regions.* Oxford: Clarendon Press.

Armstrong, H. W. and R. de **Kervenoael** (1997), "Regional economic change in the European Union". In: **Bachtler**, J. and I. **Turok** (eds), *The Coherence of EU Regional Policy. Contrasting Perspectives on the Structural Funds.* London: Jessica Kingsley Publishers.

Bachtler, J. (1998), "Reforming the Structural Funds: challenges for EU regional policy". *European Planning Studies* 6 (6): 645–664.

Benz, A. (1998), "German Regions in the European Union: from joint policy-making to multi-level governance". In: **Le Galès**, P. and C. **Lequesne** (eds), *Regions in Europe*. London: Routledge.

Bullman, U (1996), "The politics of the third level". *Regional and Federal Studies*. Special Issue on The Politics of the Third Level.

Cooke, P., A. **Price** and K. **Morgan** (1995), "Regulating regional economies: Wales and Baden-Würrtemberg in transition". In: **Rhodes**, M. (ed), *The Regions and the New Europe. Patterns in Core and Periphery Development*. Manchester: Manchester University Press.

Christopolous, D. (1999), "Regionalism in Greece". In: **Wagstaff**, P. (ed), *Regionalism in the European Union*. Exeter: Intellect.

Garmise, S. O. (1995), "Economic development strategies in Emilia-Romagna". In: **Rhodes**, M. (ed), *The Regions and the New Europe. Patterns in Core and Periphery Development*. Manchester: Manchester University Press.

Gerstenlauer, H.-G. (1995), "German Länder and the European Community". In: **Jones**, B. and M. **Keating** (eds), *The European Union and the Regions*. Oxford: Clarendon Press.

Gruber, M. (1997), "Perspectives on EU regional policy from a new Member State: Austria". In: **Bachtler**, J. and I. **Turok** (eds), *The Coherence of EU Regional Policy. Contrasting Perspectives on the Structural Funds*. London: Jessica Kingsley Publishers.

Hall, R. and M. **van der Wee** (1995), "The regions in an enlarged Europe". In: **Hardy**, S., M. **Hart**, L. **Albrechts** and A. **Katos** (eds), *An Enlarged Europe. Regions in Competition?* London: Jessica Kingsley Publishers.

Honauer, J. (1999), "Federalism in Austria". In: **Wagstaff**, P. (ed), *Regionalism in the European Union*. Exeter: Intellect.

Horváth, G. (1995), "Economic reforms in east-central Europe". In: **Hardy**, S., M. **Hart**, L. **Albrechts** and A. **Katos** (eds), *An Enlarged Europe. Regions in Competition?* London: Jessica Kingsley Publishers.

Keating, M. (1998), "Is there a regional level of government in Europe?". In: **Le Galès**, P. and C. **Lequesne** (eds), *Regions in Europe*. London: Routledge.

Kennedy, D. (1997), "The Committee of the Regions: an asessment". *Regional and Federal Studies* 7 (1): 1–4.

Kerremans, J. and A. **Beyers** (1996), "The Belgian sub-national entities in the European Union: Second or Third Level players?". *Regional and Federal Studies*. Special Issue on The Politics of the Third Level.

Loughlin, J. (1996), "Representing regions in Europe: the Committee of the Regions". *Regional and Federal Studies*. Special Issue on The Politics of the Third Level.

Lovering, J. (1999), "Theory led by policy: the inadequacies of the "new regionalism"", *International Journal of Urban and Regional Research*.

Luelmo, J. **del Rio** & A. **Williams** (1999), "Regionalism in Iberia". In: **Wagstaff**, P. (ed), *Regionalism in the European Union*. Exeter: Intellect.

Martin, S. (1997), "The effects of EU regional policy on local institutional structures and policies". In: **Bachtler**, J. and I. **Turok** (eds), *The Coherence of EU Regional*

Policy. Contrasting Perspectives on the Structural Funds. London: Jessica Kingsley Publishers.

Mazey, S. (1995), "Regional lobbying in the new Europe". In: **Rhodes**, M. (ed), *The Regions and the New Europe. Patterns in Core and Periphery Development.* Manchester: Manchester University Press.

Michie, R. and R. **Fitzgerald** (1997), "The evolution of the Structural Funds". In: **Bachtler**, J. and I. **Turok** (eds), *The Coherence of EU Regional Policy. Contrasting Perspectives on the Structural Funds*. London: Jessica Kingsley Publishers.

Morata, F. (1995), "Spanish regions in the European Community". In: **Jones**, B. and M. **Keating** (eds), *The European Union and the Regions*. Oxford: Clarendon Press.

Morgan, K. and A. **Price** (1998), *The Other Wales. The Case for Objective 1 Funding Post 1999*. Cardiff: Institute of Welsh Affairs.

Pereira, A. (1995), "Regionalism in Portugal". In: **Jones**, B. and M. **Keating** (eds), *The European Union and the Regions*. Oxford: Clarendon Press.

Smith, A. (1998), "The sub-regional level: key battleground for the Structural Funds?". In: **Le Galès**, P. and C. **Lequesne** (eds), *Regions in Europe*. London: Routledge.

Thomas, D. (1996), "Winner or Loser in the new Europe? Regional funding, inward investment and prospects for the Welsh economy". *European Urban and Regional Studies* 3 (3): 225–240.

Van Der Knapp, P. (1994), "The Committee of the Regions: the outset of a 'Europe of the Regions'?", *Regional Politics and Policy* 4 (2): 86–100.

Warleigh, A. (1997), "A committee of no importance? Assessing the relevance of the Committee of the Regions". *Politics* 17 (2): 101–107.

David Dunkerley

Race and Immigration in Europe

Background

For many, issues of race and immigration in Europe have been a post-Second World War phenomenon hastened by labour shortages in the more highly industrialised countries such as the former West Germany, France and the UK. In fact, as shown in Chapter 3 European countries had for centuries been involved in exploration, colonialisation and imperialism. A by-product of this was to instil in the psyches of many European populations notions of racial superiority and inferiority as well, of course, to generate legislation in many countries that today would be regarded as blatant racism. Furthermore such attitudes and enactments extended not simply to colonialised people but also to indigenous minorities within many of the colonial and imperial powers themselves. 'Race' and 'nation' became synonymous in the 19th century – an idea that still prevails amongst many right wing ideologies.

Arguably, the slave trade was one of the first examples of racism in practice and theory. Certainly as far as Britain is concerned much of its 19th century wealth can be associated with the direct and indirect economic benefits of the importation of millions of slaves from Africa to the Americas. The trade in slaves, in raw materials and finished manufactured goods was fundamental to the wealth and prosperity experienced by British entrepreneurs. Whilst certainly true for Britain the proposition holds for other European colonial powers such as The Netherlands, Spain, Portugal and France. The justification for the slave trade came from ideas about the biological inferiority of black people to the extent of them being dehumanised in the public mind.

Yet at the same time the conditions for much of the population in the industrialising societies were little better than for African slaves regardless of whether they were factory workers or agricultural workers and particularly so for minority groups. German attitudes to and treatment of Slavs and Poles, Austrian attitudes towards Serbs and Czechs, French attitudes towards Algerians or British attitudes towards the Irish all illustrate this form of internal racism.

Colonial populations associated with all European powers were systematically marginalised and excluded during the 19th century. Even in the case of France where the policy was to provide the potential for the colonised population to obtain French citizenship this rarely happened in practice. Similarly, the *assimilado* policy of the Portuguese had little impact. This exclusion again reinforced stereotypes and further generated racist attitudes towards minorities whether they were actually 'foreign' or non-Christian as in the case of the Jews. The overwhelming attitude developed of such people being 'alien' and 'aliens' and not like Europeans regardless of country.

The early decades of the 20th century provides evidence of racism becoming more formalised. In Britain, for example, the Aliens Act of 1919 led to the deportation of over 30,000 'enemy aliens' many of whom were Jews and originally from countries such as Russia, Hungary, Turkey, Austria and Germany. In the same year the race riots at many British ports led to the repatriation of 600 black men. By the 1930s in Britain a virtual total 'colour bar' was operating. In practice this meant that black people were denied accommodation, service in cafes and restaurants and even entry to places of entertainment. The idea that black people and Jews were somehow inferior took deep root at this time even in communities where a black population had been well-established. In Cardiff, for example, in 1935 there existed something like 3,000 non-European seamen and yet the local police made the assumption that all of them were aliens even if proof could be shown of British citizenship.

In France immigration had been encouraged after the 1st World War in the face of labour shortages but by the 1930s during the period of economic slump repatriation and deportation became common-place.

In Germany a similar policy was adopted to the extent that the numbers of foreign workers were reduced by at least three quarters of a million between 1907 and 1932, the principal target being the Jewish population. The consequences of the Weimar Republic and the rise and dominance of Nazism as far as race and immigration are concerned are well-documented. Of great consequence was the eugenics policy aimed at destroying the weakest and supporting the strongest followed by the euthanasia policy affecting not just racial minorities but also the mentally ill, homosexuals and the 'asocial'. By 1935 it became illegal for Jews, gypsies and black people to marry Germans and a certificate of 'marriage fitness' had to be produced. The impact of Nazi racism during the 2nd World War needs no elaboration.

Although it might be thought that the ultimate racism displayed by the Nazi regime would act as a warning, racism remained rife in the years following the 2nd World War. Anti-Semitism was as much a feature of British cultural life as in the pre-War period. In many European countries migrants were perceived of and defined as simply guest workers. Nowhere was this more the case than in the former West Germany. The times of labour shortages in the 1950s and early 1960s almost encouraged this attitude.

Even though the period to the present day from the early 1970s has been one of degrees of economic uncertainty, Western Europe has experienced huge amounts of in-migration whether it be from the West Indies, Western and Southern Asia, the Mahgreb, parts of Latin America, Western and Eastern Africa or more recently from Eastern Europe. As immigration expanded so individual European nations introduced restrictions on immigration and continue so to do to the present. This was the case regardless of how liberal or otherwise the nation. Immigration was unrestricted to Sweden until the late 1960s; Italy had no restrictions until the 1970s. West Germany officially had a 'no-immigration' policy prior to 1978 as applied by The Foreigner Law in 1965. The collapse of the Soviet Union and the reunification of Germany generated a vast influx of a variety of East European ethnic groups whose presence was most felt in the eastern part of Germany where there appears to have been a propensity for outbreaks of fascist violence directed at immigrants. The revised Foreigner Law of 1990 made for more open immigration although the Kohl administration did subsequently re-impose some controls.

The actual nature of immigration and of immigrants themselves varies considerably across the EU. In the first instance is the question of what is meant by the term 'immigrant' and who should it include. In the former colonial powers such as Britain, France, Portugal, Belgium or The Netherlands the previous open-door policies of the 1950s have been altered and become more restrictive. A discussion of the situation prevailing in a selection of EU countries will make this clearer.

France

The case of France is an interesting one not merely because of its former colonial interests that involved mass immigration, people who technically were French subjects from South East Asia, the West Indies, West Africa and, of course, the Mahgreb. The combination of the economic difficulties of the 1970s and changing political attitudes had the effect on immigration experienced elsewhere in other European countries. Mitterand's election in 1983 certainly generated a more tolerant attitude and in 1984 immigrants were, by law, allowed rights of permanent residence. Immigrants were, however, mobilised to seek further political and human rights (see, for example, the work of *Fédération des associations de solidarité aux travailleurs immigrés* or the *Conseil des associations immigrées en France*). It was the pressure groups, then, not so much the political parties that fought for greater rights for immigrants. During Mitterand's re-election campaign in 1988 he was remarkably quiet on the issue of immigration although the harsh *loi Pasqua* was replaced in 1989 by *la loi Joxe*, effectively getting rid of the residence card regime.

By the 1990s the immigration 'problem' had become one relating to the non-integration of Islamic groups coupled with the increasing political militancy of a number of immigrant groups. Muslim identity and militancy came to the fore especially amongst Algerians and other Mahgrebian groups and most particularly amongst second-generation individuals within such groups. Muslims were in a sense forced into a minority ethnic identity situation by the legal expectations pertaining at the time.

In France, then, there appears not to have been too much consistency in policies relating to immigrants. But even where public policy has prevailed institutional and individual racism remain common in France. France has long advocated the need for a strong relationship between nationality and citizenship even though at times the advocacy has perhaps been stronger than the reality. This is an issue returned to later in the chapter when the broader European position is discussed since – in principle – the Treaty of Maastricht brought together social, civil and political rights.

United Kingdom

As indicated earlier immigration to the UK has a long history with some seaports (e.g. Cardiff, Liverpool and Glasgow) having been home to black people for over a century. In the post-War period the first significant piece of legislation was in 1948 when Commonwealth Citizenship was granted to all those from Commonwealth countries. The following year the political rights of Irish immigrants was guaranteed (Ireland had recently withdrawn from the Commonwealth). During the 1950s immigration was encouraged in order to make up the shortfall in the labour market particularly in unskilled, male (typically precarious) occupations. By 1962 limits were placed on immigration by the Conservative government and the 1964 election was characterised by overt anti-racist speeches. Such anti-racism in the public arena continued into the early 1970s as witnessed by the outpourings about "rivers of blood" from Enoch Powell and the apparent support he received from members of his own (Conservative) Party.

During the 1970s a different form of racism became apparent that emphasised cultural rather than biological differences. In this way debates about citizenship and national identity have incorporated race and racism. Cultural differences have included religion, language, customs and ethnicity and as such have had a deep influence on social institutions in the legal, educational and political spheres.

A series of immigration laws placed progressively greater restrictions on the right to migrate to the UK. The 1981 and 1988 Acts very significantly reduced the rights of Commonwealth citizens to settle in the UK and more recent legislation has made the position even more difficult for refugees from any country.

Given the relatively long history of immigration to the UK it is perhaps surprising how the generic term 'immigrant' is still applied to second or third or even fourth generation individuals given their full British citizenship and their identity with things 'British'. Indeed, the very term 'British' has been the subject of some debate. Well over 3 million British inhabitants are non-white, belonging to 'ethnic minorities'. Interestingly around 80 per cent of this population is aged under 25 years.

Germany

Germany presents an interesting case largely because of it having been a divided nation and the impact previously of *Heimatvertriebenen, die Mauer* and latterly *Ossis* and *Wessis*. But arguably the key issue since the 1950s in West Germany (FDR) was the issue of the 'guest workers' (*Gastarbeitern*). These were individuals mainly from South-Eastern Europe and North Africa whose status was always insecure and highly precarious. These workers, often in the FDR for decades, had little entitlement to German citizenship nor to enfranchisement. During periods of labour shortage, as seen elsewhere, guest workers were welcome but by the recessions of the early 1970s onwards their position became even more marginal with public opinion urging a forcible return to the countries of origin. The government position was somewhat unrealistic and bound up with a legacy from the Third Reich in the notion of a 'peoples' community (*Volksgemeinschaft*).

Before reunification the position of the two Germanys provides an interesting contrast. East Germany was host to thousands of migrant or 'contract' workers (some estimates go as high as 200,000) from around sixty different countries by 1989 (for example, an estimated 60,000 Vietnamese, 52,000 Poles and 8,000 Cubans) who were almost completely segregated from the indigenous population except at work. For the majority, accommodation comprised separate hostels thus ghettoising these workers. When reunification occurred overt nationalistic hostility towards these migrant groups quickly surfaced.

In West Germany the position was different since the basic law suggested an ethnic definition of citizenship so making it hard, if not impossible in practice, for immigrants to gain such citizenship. In spite of this, following the collapse of the Berlin Wall, Germany became a haven for political refugees. Something like a million refugees seeking political asylum have fled to Germany since 1989 either from Eastern Europe or from the disintegration of the former Yugoslavia, Bosnia, Herzegovinia and from northern (Kurdish) Turkey.

Racist incidents towards migrants, particularly in the eastern part of Germany, have been widely reported in recent years with arson attacks on hostels for asylum seekers, defenestrations from trains of Africans and physical attacks on Polish commuters near the border. Although those directly responsible appear to come from extreme right wing allegiances, opinion polls show middle class support for such actions.

Sweden

Swedish neutrality during the Second World War and, indeed, its very strong economy before the war meant that in the immediate post-war period Sweden was able to capitalise on its position through several big export-led industries such as Volvo, Ericsson, ASEA and SKF. What was required was not capital as in many post-war economies but labour and during the 1950s cheap labour from Italy and Yugoslavia in particular was imported in abundance. The Swedish welfare model, argued by some to be a form of conscience compensation for the guilt felt for the war, that developed at that time attempted to be completely inclusive, overtly protecting the interests of the disadvantaged and the weak in society. Coupled with the welfare state were the liberal industrial relations policies obviating the need for industrial strife and promoting wealth for all. The 'common good, the 'state' and the 'public interest' prevailed over and above the 'individual'.

By the 1960s the industrial migrants from Mediterranean areas were followed by African and Asian refugees who tended not to stay for long periods. The late 1960s and 1970s witnessed political refugees from Spain, the Middle East, Eastern Europe and Latin America. The relative lack of restrictions on immigrants and refugees led in the 1980s to an influx of migrants from all over the world and this continued through to the early 1990s when, for example, 60,000 Bosnian refugees were granted asylum.

By the 1990s, however, the Swedish bubble had begun to burst with large-scale unemployment and macro-financial difficulties. For the first time, Sweden imposed limits on immigration and even repatriated long-term resident immigrants.

The question is raised of the extent to which immigrants have actually been integrated into Swedish society in spite of the long period of an open-door policy. The metropolitan areas, perhaps inevitably, have the largest concentration of immigrant groups and within such areas are to be found distinct districts for different groups. Possibly the most famous (infamous?) of these is *Hammarkullen* in Gothenberg with its dominant ethnic groups from Turkey, Iran and East Africa. *Hammarkullen* became a no-go police area, was frequently the scene of street fighting and where the local authority seemed unable to find a solution to the often conflicting interests and demands of its multi-ethnic population. This has not been a unique situation. In many Swedish urban communities there has been a growing consciousness and awareness amongst immigrant groups – a consciousness and awareness that racism and discrimination are rife in Swedish society and that the Social Democratic Party had perhaps lost its way in terms of encouraging a multicultural society. There is also evidence that a growing identification with black culture (with its concomitant potential for exclusion and discrimination) amongst some immigrant groups is contributing to greater segregation. This is evident in areas such as Uddevalla (north of Gothenberg) where violence and counter-culture elements have come to the fore. Equally, in many of Gothenberg's suburbs all the classic indicators of an underclass have emerged amongst young people of Turkish, Vietnamese, Lebanese and Latin American origin and, indeed, even amongst some elements of Swedish youth.

The very liberal policy relating to immigration to Sweden and for acquiring citizenship (originally simply a residence qualification of seven years and often less) has now been adjusted following the huge numbers of refugees arriving from Bosnia, Kosova and Somalia. The model to which many European countries might have aspired has moved to one remarkably similar to that prevailing in such countries.

Lessons from Europe

The above brief review of the position in four European countries demonstrates that there is no unitary approach to handling matters of immigration and race. On the contrary, each country pursues its own policies and these policies appear to derive from history, pragmatism and political ideology. Although it might be argued that some convergence has occurred between European countries, harmonisation of policies has certainly not occurred. EU policies themselves, as indicated below, have led to some convergence but immigration and citizenship are two of the most crucial areas where it is clear that national interests and national identity seem to be stronger motivators than international governance.

As far as labour immigration is concerned, the influence of macro-economic factors cannot be over-emphasised. In each of the countries examined the immediate post-war period was one of labour shortage and, as a consequence, the flow of immigrants into these countries was welcomed. What actually happened to immigrants upon arrival and during their sojourn differs significantly. In France, for example, the idea was that immigrants should be given the right to permanent residence. In the case of France it should be recalled that a large proportion of immigrants came from countries previously under French colonial rule and could be easily assimilated culturally into French society. Germany, as seen blatantly in the use of the word *gasterbeiter*, clearly saw labour immigrants as temporary residents who were 'guests' who could over-stay their welcome. In the UK the first waves of post-war immigrants were fairly easily assimilated coming as with French immigrants, from former colonies of the host country. Furthermore, the demand for labour and the decline in the fertility of the indigenous population ensured the need for labour immigration. Again in Sweden the buoyant economy in the immediate post-war period and the emphasis on exporting industries created the demand for immigrant labour for a sparely populated country.

In each case, the change in fortunes of national and international economies from the early 1970s onwards produced changes in demand for labour and, in turn, changes in public and political attitudes towards immigrants. Nevertheless the actual numbers of immigrants continued to rise but the nature of the immigration differed. Instead of being driven by the prospect of immediate work for many the motivator was the desire to join extended family members or – increasingly – escape from political oppression. At this point, for each of the countries analysed and for most other West European countries immigration became a problem. The problem was a major social one for immigrants themselves but also for governments as conflict arose and as, in some eyes, the social cultural fabric of a particular nation was under-going fundamental change.

However, as seen, different countries have addressed 'the problem' in different way. The underlying French policy of assimilation continued, the German policy of separation was, if anything, strengthened following reunification and the UK policy of subordination through pluralism each show different solutions to the same fundamental 'problem'.

Asylum Seekers

Most EU countries have had to cope in more recent years with the issue of asylum seekers whose reasons for seeking residence are obviously different from those of labour migrants and who do not necessarily derive from source countries displaying similar cultural features. It is to this issue of asylum policy to which the discussion can now turn.

All EU member states are bound to certain obligations under the 1951 Geneva Convention and the Universal Declaration of Human Rights (UDHR). In both cases the obligations were made and accepted before movements of refugees reached current levels. Two factors in particular have significantly increased the numbers of those seeking asylum in EU member countries – the collapse of the Soviet Union and the collapse of and subsequent conflict in the former Yugoslavia. This was particularly noticeable in the early 1990s. For example the number of asylum applications to Germany rose from 57,000 in 1987 to a staggering 438,000 in 1992; the respective figures in The Netherlands were 13,000 in 1987 to 52,000 in 1994 and in the UK from 6,000 in 1987 to 73,000 in 1991. Since then numbers have continued to increase significantly.

Such increases led to a more co-ordinated approach among West European countries especially since it looked as though some countries (Germany and Sweden in particular) appeared to be more popular choices of destination for asylum-seekers and such countries were on the brink of being overwhelmed by the sheer numbers. The European Commission had tried to introduce a policy document on the integration of third state nationals but a ruling by the European Court made clear that this went beyond the Community's jurisdiction. The Maastricht Treaty introduced intergovermental decision-making and within that context the Commission has sought to produce EU-wide proposals. Thus, member states have tried to develop common policies and done so in the absence of European legislation. The Treaty of Amsterdam did introduce a new Article 6a to the EC Treaty:

Without prejudice to the other provisions of this Treaty and within the limits of the powers conferred by it upon the Community, the Council, acting unanimously on a proposal from the Commission and after consulting the European Parliament, may take appropriate action to combat discrimination based on sex, racial or ethnic origin, religion or belief, disability, age or sexual orientation.

In spite of such a bold statement the EU policy of asylum remains very incoherent because what policies do exist have been made intergovernmentally and largely designed on the basis of national considerations. The best hope lies in the Intergovernmental Conference.

Racism

In spite of the amendment proposed by the Treaty of Amsterdam there remains a lack of effective measures to confront and curtail racism in EU countries. Again, the Intergovernmental Conference appears to be the place where such policy changes might be introduced even though some member countries (the UK in particular) are very much opposed to EU-wide policies.

It has already been suggested above that national policies in different EU countries provide the stumbling block for a concerted effort to tackle racism.

Although there remain stringent restrictions on immigration into the UK, the legislation relating to racism is itself quite stringent and certainly compared to some other European examples. Black immigrants to the UK have, in the main, been Commonwealth citizens with a right to settlement and, importantly, with a political franchise. In many other EU countries there has not been any right of citizenship, residence or franchise.

Although there is international law there is a glaring absence of Community law on the issue of racism. The UDHR or the UN International Convention on the Elimination of All Forms of Discrimination have been signed up to by all EU member states. The Convention is quite clear that parties to it should seek to introduce policies to remove and eradicate incitement to discrimination and to acts of discrimination. Parties to the Convention are required biennially to submit reports on what they have done to meet the conditions of the Convention. However, the UN General Assembly to whom these reports eventually arrive for consideration has very little power. For example, it can only look into complaints when the country against whom there is a complaint agrees to an investigation.

Discussion

As far as the question of European identity is concerned, issues relating to race and immigration provide an interesting example of the continued strength of national policies rather than European policy. This chapter has clearly shown that the position of ethnic minorities and immigration policies have been held to be the concern of the individual nation-state. The examples discussed show the different ways in which different countries have addressed these matters. Each country, in the post-Second World War period, passed its own legislation and dealt with issues such as border controls in their own way. However, things are changing and the genesis of this change can be seen over the last fifteen years or so – such change is a good example of an increasing European integration.

As common European law has been enacted and as European political institutions have become stronger so the power of the individual nation-state to impose its own policy on, say, immigration, has been reduced. Coupled with this has been the strengthening of human rights and within them of citizenship rights (see Chapter 11 for more a detailed exegesis of this).

A big part of the reason for this move towards a European position rather than a collection of individual national positions has been the changing nature of (would-be) immigrants themselves. From the end of the Second World War through to the 1970s immigrants to the different countries were broadly, but not exclusively, from former colonies or were guest workers. The changes in Central and Eastern Europe from 1989 onwards produced new types of potential and actual immigrants. As seen above there has been a dramatic increase in the numbers of political refugees who, in turn, have claimed political asylum status. Similarly, the increased opportunities for would-be immigrants to travel more easily has increased their numbers and from parts of the world previously not sourced. Conflicts and wars have also significantly increased the numbers of those seeking refuge within the borders of the EU.

The EU itself has, of course, found itself in a confused position here. On the one hand, the numbers and types of immigrants seeking to settle in EU countries has changed and on the other hand EU policies, as part of the move towards greater integration and common identity, have almost deliberately provoked the diminution of cultural and national barriers and differences. In an attempt to overcome this confusion the EU has adopted a series of policy measures that are strictly 'European' in nature and go beyond anything that the nation-states themselves have generated.

The Schengen Agreement (agreed by all EU states with the exception of the UK, Ireland and Denmark) arrived at a co-operative position resulting in free internal borders throughout the EU but with external immigration control. Thus, citizens of EU countries are free to go as they please throughout the countries of the Union and, at the same time, non-EU nationals are subject to quite strict control. Similarly the Dublin Convention holds that if one EU country rejects an individual as an asylum seeker then that individual is rejected by all and returned to the country of origin. Furthermore, the Schengen Agreement is part of the *acquis* for those countries currently seeking to join the EU.

The position of those non-EU migrants who have gained admission to Europe but who do not yet have citizenship in their country of residence raises some interesting questions as a result of Schengen. These so-called 'third country nationals' are, under existing convention, inferiors compared to EU nationals since they do not appear to have the right of free movement throughout the EU. It also raises the vexed question of how citizenship may be harmonised within the EU.

This chapter has shown how different EU states have, through legislation, dealt with immigration matters with each country arriving at different positions as a result of history, economics, culture or political persuasion. Until the EU has common laws relating to anti-discrimination, nationality, immigration and the like the over-arching aim of improving human rights and protecting minority status is unlikely to be achieved.

The Treaty of Amsterdam in 1997 certainly went some way towards addressing such issues especially clarifying immigration and asylum matters within the 'third pillar'. But to argue that there now exists a clear policy of immigration within the European Union would be an exaggeration. The implementation of the Treaty of Nice (December 2000) may clarify matters. Overall, though, race and immigration are unresolved questions in spite of the extensive rhetoric and posturing on the part of the Commission and the IGC. Symbolic acts such as pronouncing 1997 as the European Year Against Racism and Xenophobia remain just that – symbolic. Until there is a clear and forceful position taken by the EU on these matters national policies and prejudices will prevail often to the cost of immigrants and ethnic minorities themselves.

Further Reading

Carr, F. & A. **Massey** (1999), *Public Policy in the New Europe*. Cheltenham: Edward Elgar.

Gundara, J. & S. **Jacobs** (2000), *Intercultural Europe*. Aldershot: Ashgate.

Joppke, C. (1999), *Immigration and the Nation-State*. Oxford: Oxford University Press.

Konstadinidis, S. (1999), *A People's Europe: turning a concept into content*. Aldershot: Ashgate.

Sykes, R. & P. **Alcock** (1998), *Developments in European Social Policy*. Bristol: Policy Press.

Lesley Hodgson

Human Rights – the European Experience

Introduction

This chapter concerns itself with the development of human rights initiatives. It argues that human rights have traditionally been bound up with national sovereignty and that moves to internationalise rights have largely been hampered by a lack of commitment and implementation at nation state level. Within the field of international relations human rights hold "no sacrosanct quality" but rather are "proclaimed or ignored in accord with the interests" of the individual nation states (Mansell 1999: 71). In following this line of argument, the chapter will outline the development of various human rights documents and suggests than rather than adding to this array of documentation, the time has come to ensure that existing treaties are put into practice in a more consistent way than at present.

Rights were once seen as primarily the concern of the nation state; indeed until the end of the second world war a general principle within international affairs was that of sovereign determination which, with regard to human rights, propounds that how a state treats its own citizens is an internal matter and not the legitimate concern of 'outsiders'. This principle is still invoked today (although to a much lesser degree than previously). The last fifty years however, have seen the development of the view that human rights need to be internationally protected (Brown 1997; Sieghart 1986). It is now widely accepted that we not only have rights as citizens of a particular state, but also within a much wider context, human rights: rights by virtue of the fact that we belong to the wider global community of humankind.

This view has led, over the intervening years, to a mushrooming of human rights documents, treaties and conventions (with added options and protocols) that affect almost all aspects of our lives; political, social and cultural. The enforcement of these rights however rests, for the most part, on the shoulders of the nation state.

Fifty years on from the setting up of the Universal Declaration on Human Rights (UDHR), inhumane treatment and human rights violations continue.

Amnesty International recently reported that a third of the world's governments still torture their prisoners, and half imprison people solely because of their belief, race, gender or ethnic origin (Amnesty in Action 1998/99). Recent events in Rwanda, Bosnia, and Kosovo have been highlighted by the media, alongside cases of abuse in Palestine, Israel, the Congo and Sierra Leone. Added to this are accounts of trafficking in women and children, police use of torture in Turkey, the rise of sweatshop working practices throughout the world and the abuses by transnational corporations. Consequently, although we have a plethora of international human rights legislation, there are serious issues to be raised regarding the enactment of this legislation, not only in the ratification and interpretation of treaties (which is outside the remit of this work) but also in the wider political context of non-intervention.

The first section of this chapter investigates the role of the nation state in the implementation of human rights treaties and traces the development of rights alongside the rise of the nation state. Issues surrounding the first explorations of the globe (arguably the beginnings of globalization), the Enlightenment period, and the Industrial Revolution are investigated in light of the influence these phenomena had in the internationalising of rights issues. The discussion then moves on to the development of post WWII rights processes, including the Nuremberg International Tribunal and the setting up of the League and United Nations. The latter section deals with the development of more recent rights documents and supranational organs, both in the United States and Europe. All of the above issues are addressed in the light of the dichotomy between national sovereignty and international human rights.

A discussion of these issues will help to develop a clearer picture as to how human rights can be implemented in the future. There is a need to take rights out of the realm of the 'ideal' and develop a feasible and practical agenda, moving away from debates concerning nationalism and universalism and moving toward the implementation of policy agendas that carry with then enforcement measures (Ishay 1997: XXXIX).

Throughout, this chapter invokes what has been termed the, "western construct of rights" (Pollis & Schwab 1979). Some have argued that these rights are a new form of imperialism however Kofi Annan, the UN Secretary General, rejects this idea, asking, "Do not African mothers weep when their sons or daughters are killed or maimed by agents of repressive rule? Are not African fathers saddened when their children are unjustly jailed or tortured?" (Annan quoted by FCO 2000). Whilst recognising cultural differences, it has been suggested that, the formulations of the UN Declaration and it's European equivalent have, "the best-known formulations and (have) instituted the most effective systems of implementation – both nationally and internationally."

(bracket inserted, Robertson & Merrills 1993: 9) and for this reason I have concentrated on these.

Human Rights and the Nation State
– the Historical Development

In order to be able to assess the direction human rights should take in the future it is necessary to investigate their historical development. Human rights programmes have been moulded by history: in response to periods of persecution and oppression, as an outcome of war and social conflict, and as a result of the rise of the nation state. This section equates the evolution of human rights alongside the emergence of the nation state, and investigates this changing relationship. It should be noted that it is not the intention of this narrative to look at the history behind every human rights document, there are volumes of such work to be found (Lauterpacht 1950; Sieghart 1983; Meron 1984; Robertson & Merrils 1989; Steiner & Alston 2000).

Historically there have been those who have fought against oppression and stood up for what they believed to be 'right'. Most religious texts, ranging from the Bible to the Koran, to Buddhist writings, outline a series of moral principles and normative concepts by which humans 'ought' to live. The ancient philosophers, of which Plato and Aristotle are but two, spent centuries debating issues affecting human rights.

This overview of human rights developments makes it's start in medieval times, with arguably the beginnings of the first written charter on human rights; the Magna Carta of 1215. The importance of the Magna Carta was emphasised by Eleanor Roosevelt, in her famous address to the UN at the launch of the Universal Declaration on Human Rights when she stated, "This Universal Declaration of Human Rights may well become the International Magna Carta of all men everywhere" (BBC Archives 1998).

It is fitting therefore, that we use the Magna Carta as a starting point for this analysis.

Medieval Times

Medieval society was feudal in nature, the economy being based on agriculture. There was a growing tension between the newly developing towns and the well-established rural communities, with constant changes in the pattern of rulership and in the plethora of kingdoms, principalities and duchies that existed. No one ruler or state sovereign was supreme over a given area and population. There was tension too between the rulers of the time (who we will call Princes) and the Church. The Church saw itself as the main tool in uniting feudal society under a theocracy, although it never fully succeeded in holding secular power. The individual had a dual loyalty, on one hand to obey ecclesiastical laws, and on the other, as a subject of the Prince, to obey the law as it was administered in their area. Poggi suggests therefore, that the political system of the time was distinguished by "a network of interlocking ties and obligations, with systems of rule fragmented into small autonomous parts". (Poggi 1978: 27). Two distinct features concerning rights can be established during this time; the doctrine of natural law, and the practice of extracting charters of liberties (Baylis & Smith 1997: 473).

The central tenant of natural law is based on the premise that a common universal moral standard exists among humans; that humans as sentient and intelligent beings have the innate ability to make moral judgements, and a duty to adhere to those standards (Robertson & Merrills 1993: 3). In practice, however, the politics of the medieval world meant that rights were not always upheld as power struggles dominated any leaders political agenda. As attempts to undermine the power of feudal nobles continued, the practice of charters, specifying systems of rule became increasingly commonplace. Nobles of the time came to realise that if they subsumed their differences and presented a united front against the King they would be in a better position to fight for their interests. The Magna Carta was a result of this struggle, and although it was probably extracted for personal and economic gain, it did secure certain rudimentary rights and liberties from King John that were to have an impact for the future. Although its applicability at first was limited to nobles and landowners, these liberties not applying to the 'common people', that was to change with time. (For a fuller discussion of the limited applicability of the Magna Carta, see Sellar & Yeatman 1930). Most notable among the rights gained were, freedom from imprisonment, exile or from dispossession of his property, "unless by the *lawful judgement of his peers* or by *the law of the land*" and a crude form of a right to fair trial in the words "To none will we sell, deny or delay *right of justice.*" When King Edward reaffirmed the charter in 1354 he undertook that no man, "of whatever estate or condition should be harmed without *'per due process de ley'* "(due process of law) (Sieghart 1986: 24). This was to become one of the foundations upon which human rights were to grow.

The Charter played an important role in the development of ensuing rights documents; succeeding rulers reissued it at least thirty-eight times in the centuries that followed. *The Petition of Rights* (1628), the *Habeas Corpus Acts* (1679), and *The Bill of Rights* (1689) all refer directly to the Charter, as do the national and state constitutions of the United States (Ishay 1997: XVIII).

It has been suggested (Held 1995) that medieval politics saw the very beginnings of a change in rulership, and the emergence of the nation state. Throughout Europe, in some small way sovereignty was beginning to pass from the ruler to the ruled as new ideas flourished, so it was that in 1581 a group of Netherlands subjects of King Philip II of Spain proposed, "that God did not create the subjects for the benefit of the Prince… but the Prince for the benefit of the subjects, *without which he is no prince*" (italics inserted, Sieghart 1986: 24).

This time period also saw the beginnings of global exploration, with such people as Dom Enrique (Henry the Navigator) and Vasco de Gama, at the forefront. Europeans were developing a concept of the world as an "accessible and attainable whole". New ideas concerning the 'individual' and their place in the larger world began to develop and concepts of 'humanity' changed as fresh images of the shape of the globe and different ways of living were discovered and use of the Gregorian calendar became widespread (Robertson 1994: 58). Nation states, as they began to develop, were however still supremely insular, focusing primarily on issues surrounding territorial boundaries and internal order, with little interest in what went on elsewhere (Waters 1995: 36).

Some have dated the crisis in feudalism as early as 1300 (Held 1995: 34). Whether this is substantiated or not it is true that this period of time saw great unrest in political terms, and yet out of that unrest was to rise a human rights document that was to have far reaching affects: the Magna Carta.

The Enlightenment and Industrial Revolution

The Enlightenment saw a period in history in which the authority of the church was openly challenged and rights became increasingly secularised. Spurred on by advances in the natural sciences and the liberation from traditional religious dogma, there emerged an increasingly marked shift in the balance of power away from the religious toward the political. This phenomenon has been linked to the development of the modern state system (Fukyama 1992). It was recognised that in order to rest power away from the Catholic Church, former groups and factions needed to consolidate power so that, by the end of the 17th century Europe was no longer a "mosaic of states" (Held 1995: 36). Individuals within those states came to realise that they were 'citizens' of a new political order. People began to develop a sense of national identity and to realise that they had rights and duties as citizens of their state. This is not to suggest that the newly formed nation states welcomed the notion of citizenship, but those in government realised that to have any form of legitimacy, at a time when traditional forms of legitimacy were being undermined, they needed to develop a 'reciprocal relationship' between governors and those governed. The latter would have a duty to respect the authority of the state and it's laws, whilst the former would have the duty to "act fairly in accordance with the mandate of the people" (Held 1995: 69).

Prominent European writers and philosophers of the time such as, John Locke (1632–1704), Hugo Grotius (1583–1646), Jean-Jacques Rousseau (1712–1778), and Charles Montesquieu (1689–1755) were influential in changing political and legal attitudes in regard to the role of the state. The French (1789–99) and American (1775–83) Revolutions established the use of written constitutions which outlined the role of government and also enumerated the rights of the individual within the state system (*Declaration des droits de l'homme et du citoyen* 1789 & *Bill of Rights* 1791 respectively). These two documents were fundamentally different from the *Magna Carta* in that they were not concessions extracted from a King or Prince but were coherent catalogues of fundamental rights and freedoms. For the first time in history there were written documents outlining *universal* rights that no one could give or take away. Over time, rights became enshrined within the legal paraphernalia of various nation states and so we see the development of national human rights law: a synthesis of the notion of universal rights with the practice of governance, so that human rights were, "...universal in principle but particularistic in application...cosmopolitan in moral but not in institutional terms" (Baylis & Smith 1997: 474).

The responsibility for upholding human rights was now placed firmly on the shoulders of the nation state and the legislature within that state. As these fundamental catalogues of rights were adapted to suit local national circumstances, certain rights were being upheld in individual countries, but domestic governments had no interest in securing the rights of individuals outside their territory. The development of the nation state in the C19[th] was accompanied by the doctrine of national sovereignty, the principle that states have sole jurisdiction over the physical domain (territorial sovereignty) and over its citizens within or outside its domain (personal sovereignty). Problems were to arise when an individual's rights were violated by their own state; the individual had no recourse to any outside body.

The Industrial Revolution fuelled calls for change. States were obliged to establish and consolidate links with each other to facilitate trade. Transport and communication systems were implemented that nourished the globalization process that had begun earlier. A system of international relations developed (Waters 1995: 37). There were attempts to take human rights out of the hands of government and set up international bodies to secure rights. For example, the First (1864) and Second International (1889), which were concerned with the rights of workers; and the various treaties drawn up to abolish slavery, most of the latter were however, bi-lateral agreements between states (such as the Berlin Conference [1845] between Germany, UK, France, Portugal and Belgium). One of the first major *international* pieces of legislation was the anti-slavery Act of 1890 which was signed by 18 states at a conference held in Brussels. The League of Nations was later to incorporate this Act.

Steps to further internationalise human rights, taking rights out of the realm of the nation state, were hampered as nationalist discontent rose up throughout Europe and national interests took supremacy over human rights issues as the threat of war emerged.

International Treaties and Declarations

The League of Nations
The massacre of World War I led to a new search for peace and the setting up of the League of Nations in 1919. Although it had no direct human rights provision it was assumed that its members would be states that would respect human rights: respect what lawyers term an "international standard of justice" (Vincent 1988: 44). The fact that the United States refused to join and that the League had no power to enforce decisions however meant that it was largely ineffectual. The League did develop the Minorities Treaties, placing international obligations on particular states in regard to the treatment of minority groups within their territory, but it was often a long and arduous task to bring complaints to the League and very few complaints were passed on to the Permanent Court of International Justice. (For a fuller discussion see Robertson & Merrills 1992; Vincent 1995). Human rights were still firmly held in the domain of the nation state and it's legislature, and the non-interventionist attitude of states meant that human rights could be abused as they were in the 1930s under Stalin's soviet rule when around 10,000,000 are thought to have been killed in the Great Purge 1936–38. The League also failed to stop yet another war (Falk 1995: 248; Held 1995: 84).

The atrocities of World War II are well documented and do not need to be reiterated here. Nevertheless, it is interesting to note that both Hitler and Stalin were "supreme legal positivists: the only rights that existed were those they allowed to be enforced in their own countries" (Sieghart 1986: 37). They used the doctrine of national sovereignty to stop outsiders from meddling in the internal affairs of their countries. When Hitler came to power he initiated legislation that made it easier for him to treat those he considered undesirable in the way he did, and international law at that time meant that no outside state could infringe their territorial or personal sovereignty even though the vast majority of these laws violated human rights. Hitler's inhuman treatment of others was legal in the sense that laws had been put in place to uphold his actions. However, "...even the most hardened positivist could not readily qualify (these laws) as just" (brackets inserted, Cranston 1983: 5). National human rights laws to date had failed.

The Nuremberg Trials

The post-war International Tribunal at Nuremberg, and its equivalent Tribunal in Tokyo, decreed for the first time in history, that international rules protecting human rights take precedence over state laws. The Trials rejected the defence of obedience to superior authorities in matters of responsibility for war crimes (Held 1995: 102). The principles established at Nuremberg have however proven difficult to apply impartially and consistently throughout the world. Nevertheless, there developed a major shift in attitudes toward the principle of non-intervention as the international community, albeit in the shape of the victorious powers, became involved with the rights of the individual within another nation state. There was now for the first time, "...international concern with and action to denounce, expose and prevent human rights abuses" (Zalman & Siegel 1997).

The UN Charter

The setting up of the United Nations (1945) was the chrysalis for the globalization of human rights. There was a growing acknowledgement that nations were becoming more interconnected and interdependent, and that if the lessons from two world wars were to be learnt, a new form of international governance needed to be set up, especially after the failure of the League. The UN Charter (drawn up at the San Francisco Conference 1945) forms the constituent Statute of the United Nations as an inter-governmental organisation and proposes to promote 'respect for human rights and fundamental freedoms'. Article 56 states that 'all members pledge to take joint and separate action' to achieve this purpose. The UN Charter recognised that states are "jealously sovereign", but linked together and "under pressure to resolve disagreements by peaceful means and according to legal criteria... and constrained to observe certain standards" (Cassese 1991: 265). The Charter does not specify however, what *are* the human rights and fundamental freedoms that are to be protected and, Article 2 of the Charter espouses the principle of state sovereignty. It was within this framework that the Universal Declaration of Human Rights (UDHR) was drawn up in 1948.

The Universal Declaration of Human Rights

The Universal Declaration of Human Rights (UDHR) was adopted, by vote, on 10 November 1948. It sets out in its 30 articles the fundamental freedoms that are to be promoted including civil, political, and economic rights. The Declaration however, reflects the fact that the UN was dominated by Western powers and although 48 nations voted for the Declaration, 8 abstained. South Africa, whose policy on apartheid meant that it could not accept Articles 1 and 2, objected on the grounds that the declaration violated the protection of the 'domestic jurisdiction' of states. Saudi Arabia objected to Article 18, again asserting that state law (in this case the forbidding the practice of religions other than Islam) was supreme. The Soviet Union and five other Soviet Bloc countries abstained because of a lack of attention to economic and social rights.

It should be noted that the UDHR is a 'declaration' of rights, which has considerable moral force but is *not* a treaty and therefore *not* a legally binding document. As stated earlier the UN regards any violations of human rights as its proper concern, but this is at variance with Article 2 of the UN Charter prohibiting the interference in the domestic affairs of nation states. There was therefore a need to transform the UDHR into a legal document; this was accomplished through the adoption of the *International Covenants on Human Rights* (1966). The two covenants: one focusing on civil and political rights and the other on social and economic rights, are legally binding on states that ratify them, so that these matters no longer come under the sole jurisdiction of the nation state. Whereas it had only taken three years to adopt the Universal declaration it took twenty years to adopt the treaty texts and another ten years before the required 35 states ratified both of them (1976). By 1994, some 130 states had ratified them including the United States, who signed in 1992 'with reservations'. It has been suggested (Falk 1995) that the reason for this tardiness on the part of states stem from the fact that they value their sovereignty above all else. Western states recognising that the declaration was not a treaty (and therefore not legally binding) argued that, democratic countries by their very nature conformed to human rights standards and that any differences in how they measured up to those standards could be attributed to differences in ideology (Falk 1995: 183). This viewpoint however, was open to abuse.

The Covenant on Civil and Political Rights (which entered into force in 1976) paved the way for the setting up of the Human Rights Committee (HRC), the principle organ for implementing the Covenant and for receiving complaints. *The Covenant on Economic, Social and Cultural Rights* had no such committee, reports being made to the Economic and Social Council. In practice, the bureaucracy involved in solving disputes and ensuring implementation of principles is a tedious and long-winded procedure one that ultimately lacks teeth and therefore hampers both covenants. At first, the Human Rights Committee (HRC) only heard complaints brought before it by states concerning states, the possibility of considering complaints by non-governmental organisations or individuals was rejected (Sohn 1968: 143–4). The HRC is not like a domestic court, issuing and handing down judgements and enforcing them, rather, it puts forward it's views to the individual or government concerned, and publicises and pressurises the state to conform. The Conventions offer no means of collective enforcement and therefore states are able to violate the principles therein.

The Covenant on Civil and Political Rights has had two Optional Protocols added: one enables private individuals to file complaints of abuses against a state (having exhausted domestic remedies), and the other has as it's aim the abolition of the death penalty. As with the Covenants however, these only apply to countries that ratify them and the majority of UN member nations have not accepted the Protocols. The US and the UK for example have refused to ratify the first Optional Protocol and the US refuses to ratify the second – indeed less than half of the parties to the Covenant have done so.

International Treaties and Declarations – the European Experience

The European Convention for the Protection of Human Rights and Fundamental Freedoms

Foreign Ministers of the member states of the Council of Europe met on 4 November 1950 to sign the *European Convention for the Protection of Human Rights and Fundamental Freedoms* (ECHR), "an organisation within the Council of Europe to ensure the collective guarantee of human rights" (Teitgen, Maxwell Fyfe *et al.* 1949). The Council of Europe is an intergovernmental organisation that has, as one of its aims, the protection of human rights. It should not be confused with the European Union. Any European state can become a member of the Council of Europe subject to their acceptance of the principle of the rule of law and the guarantee to uphold human rights. The member states of the EU are all members of the Council of Europe.

When drawing up the Convention the members of the Council were able to refer to the statement of rights as outlined in the UDHR. The European Convention entered into force in September 1953. At first the Council was concerned with the upholding of civil and political rights, but recognised that social rights would be addressed at some future date (Teitgen PH, Official Report 7.09.1949). This was to be remedied with the adoption of the Social Charter in 1961, which came into force in 1965.

The Statute of the Council of Europe specifies that the preservation of human rights is not just an objective of the Council but a, "condition of membership," the violation of which can lead to suspension or expulsion from the Council (see Articles 1, 3 and 8 of the Statute). The Convention deals with a wide range of issues including: the right to life, the right not to suffer torture or inhumane treatment, the right to a fair trial and many others. This does not mean that these rights are guaranteed without limit, some are, but others take into consideration such things as national security, public safety, the prevention of crime and so forth. It has been suggested, that the ECHR has proven to be the, "most fully developed and best observed of all regional human rights treaties" (Robertson & Merrills 1993: 286).

Europeans had a special interest in human rights, for it was in the heart of Europe that the Nazi atrocities had taken place, and those experiences were still fresh in the minds of many. It was recognised that,

Democracies do not become Nazi countries in one day... One by one freedoms are suppressed...It is necessary to intervene (and)... warn them of the peril and to show them that they are progressing down a long road which leads...to (a) Buchenwald or even a Dachau (brackets inserted, Teitgen P.H. Official Reports 1949: 1158)

In an effort to implement the collective enforcement of human rights, the Convention created two main institutions: the European Commission of Human Rights (1954) and the European Court of Human Rights (1959). These institutions along with the Committee of Ministers of the Council of Europe (this organ being composed of the Ministers of Foreign Affairs of the Members States or their representatives) were to ensure the collective enforcement of human rights obligations that contracting states entered into.

Member states or individuals (the right of individual petition came into being in 1955 and has been described as the, "cornerstone of the Convention", See Robertson & Merrills 1996: 13) could bring any alleged violation of the Convention to the attention of the Commission. The Commission played a filtering role; investigating the alleged breach of the Convention and if possible arrange a friendly settlement. If conciliation failed, a report was made and sent to the Committee of Ministers. The Commission or a State, but not in this case an individual, could refer the matter to the Court, if the Court ruled that a breach of the convention had been made the matter was passed back to the Committee of Ministers of the Council of Europe for 'appropriate action'. This was to change with the adoption of the 9th Protocol that came into force in 1994 amending Article 44, giving individuals the right to bring a case before the Court. Individuals and associations had to first try to settle the matter through the domestic courts, only after this had been exhausted could a matter be brought to the attention of the Commission. An individual could only make a complaint, "if the respondent country had recognised the right of individual petition" (Ewing 1999: 83). There was no provision for the Court to demand that a State take remedial action or to force them to repeal their acts. The Court could however, award damages to the injured party/parties.

The Committee of Ministers (set up before the Convention) like the Court, had no power to invalidate or overrule a national decision or to specify what remedial action should be taken on the part of the violators of rights (see Article 32 of the Convention). It was, and still is, the responsibility of the individual government concerned to decide what measures should be taken. The Committee could however, prescribe a time period in which these measures should take place, and impose 'sanctions' if this was not done. These 'sanctions' took the form of published reports on the abuse, the states and/or the individuals involved. This was an unusual and effective device at the time, as reports would not normally have been published. Today with the proliferation of reporting of all cases before the court this no longer acts as a credible deterrent. The Committee does however, have the power to suspend or expel a member state if they "seriously" violate Article 3 of the Statute of the Council of Europe; this Article makes respect for the law and the "enjoyment of all persons within it's jurisdiction of human rights and fundamental freedoms", a condition of membership. To date this has never been used (Robertson & Merrills 1996: 328). The European Convention unlike the International Covenants allows a state party to denounce them; that is, to announce to other state parties that they will no longer be bound by them. This has happened once when Greece withdrew from the Council of Europe before it was effectively expelled in 1969, after a *coup d'etat* in 1967. Democracy was restored in 1974 and Greece rejoined the Council and ratified the Convention.

Through the 1980s and 90s the number of cases brought before the European institutions rose significantly (registered applications rose from 404 in 1981 to 4750 in 1997), this was in part, due to the accession of new Contracting States (to date some 41 states have ratified the Convention and various optional Protocols, including most of the states of central and eastern Europe) (http:/www.echr.coe.int). The increased workload and pressure on the various institutions meant that reform of the human rights mechanisms was needed, and on November 1 1998 the new European Court of Human Rights came into being in line with Protocol 11 (a decision taken at the Vienna Summit in 1993 and confirmed at the Strasbourg Summit in 1997). This Protocol, concerned with the restructuring of the human rights machinery was initially opposed by the UK who objected to the fact that the right to petition by the individual should be allowed to remain open for periodic review. The UK finally agreed only after it was made clear that the whole procedure could not go ahead without unanimous support (Spencer 1995). The old Court ceased to function on October 31, 1998 and the Commission was dissolved in November 1999.

The new European Court of Human Rights comprises a number of judges equal to the number of Contracting States (41 to date). Judges sit as individuals and not as representatives of their country. The court is divided into four

Sections, each Section being presided over by a President. Each Section has a Committee of three judges that carry out the filtering work previously carried out by the Commission, and a Chambers of seven members. A Grand Chamber of seventeen judges presides over difficult cases or cases where there is no previous set precedent.

States or individuals that claim to be a victim of a breach of a Convention right, can now lodge complaints directly with the Court; in the case of individuals, after they have taken the matter before a domestic court. Each application is assigned to a Section, and after some investigation a decision is made as to whether a settlement can be made, or if not, to determine the appropriate level at which the complaint should be dealt with (Committee, Chamber or in exceptional cases Grand Chamber). Proceedings, except in exceptional cases, are public and the Court's decisions are binding on respondent states even when contrary to national legislation. The state also has jurisdiction over inter-State affairs. The Committee of Ministers of the Council of Europe no longer has a role to play in the hearing of cases but monitors the execution of judgements and decides whether states have taken 'adequate' remedial measures to apply the Courts recommendations.

There is little doubt that the European Court of Human Rights is a powerful force for challenging the authority of an individual State. It has the, "broadest application" of any rights document: applying to "all persons within the jurisdiction of the signatory states" (Bahbha 1999: 117). Judgements of the Court are binding on signatory states.

An analysis of the system however, does raise some concerns. In the past the Commission was responsible for admissibility, securing an early friendly settlement, drafting a final report to the Court and acting as assistant to the Court, whilst the Court made the final judgement. The Court itself now has to take on the work of the Commission, engaging in its own 'fact finding' both of the alleged events and of the individual national law of the States involved. This has led some commentators to question whether the Court system will become too bureaucratic and officious and whether ultimately this will have an effect on the timing of proceedings (March, Hunnings 1996).

Another factor to be mindful of is that, although individuals can make an application directly to the Court, they can only do so after having "tried all remedied in the State concerned" making "correct use of the available remedies" (ECHR 22/05/2000:1) and having fulfilled a number of other criteria (see Betten & Grief 1998: 36). This means that individuals are for the most part involved in an often time consuming, complex, legal process at an international level that is largely out of their control. Many of the cases coming before the Court are declared inadmissible because of not fulfilling procedural requirements. This is not surprising as Betten & Grief argue (1998:37) "many of the complaints sent to the ECHR are made by individuals who have not consulted a lawyer".

Another area of concern relates to the enforcement of individuals' rights at the nation state level. While it is true that many of the Courts judgements are adhered to, "the doctrine of 'the margin of appreciation'" developed by the ECHR means that in practice "states are accorded considerable discretion and leeway, particularly in 'sensitive' areas" (for example, public security and immigration) (Bhabha 1999: 117). In the light of these issues, it is clear that the European Court of Human Rights only partially limits the role of the state and for the most part the state is still the main forum for the implementation of rights.

The Conference on Security and Cooperation in Europe

Within the European system another strand in upholding human rights can be viewed through the work of the Conference on Security and Cooperation in Europe (CSCE), now known as the Organisation for Security and Cooperation in Europe (OSCE). In 1997 the OSCE comprised 55 member states.

The CSCE initially convened in Helsinki on 3 July 1973. The 35 participating states included all the sovereign states of eastern and western Europe (with the exception of Albania who became a member in 1991), the USA and Canada: one of its main purposes was to put pressure on the USSR. It was decided that one of the most effective ways to accomplish this was to try and secure political commitment from the USSR to act on human rights issues. It thus, at that time, became fashionable and politically expedient for politicians to speak about human rights issues in a way they had not done before.

As the name suggests the CSCE is concerned mainly with international security and relations between states, within the 'Final Act' (otherwise known as the Helsinki Accords signed on August 1 1975) however, there are a number of Principles specifying human rights issues. Principle VII for example states that participating states will " respect human rights and fundamental freedoms" and that they will "fulfil their obligations as set forth in the international declarations and agreements in this field...by which they may be bound." In practice however, when a participating state accuses another of failing to comply with Principle VII the other can invoke Principle VI , "The participating states will refrain from *any* intervention...in the internal or external affairs falling within the domestic jurisdiction of another participating state" (OSCE docs. 2000): again the invoking of the principle of national sovereignty. What has come to be called the 'Helsinki Agreement' is not a treaty and is therefore not legally binding. Nonetheless the CSCE process did, in 1989 at the Vienna Conference feature a number of key human rights features including, an agreement to develop law in the area of human rights, a commitment to freedom of religion and also provisions for dealing with national minorities. A monitoring procedure was also set up, which has become known as the Human Dimension mechanism (for a full discussion see Bloed & van Dijk (1991: 74). This monitoring procedure is not a legal procedure but rather a political one. It consists mainly of naming and shaming states involved in human rights abuses. Reading through the proceedings of one of the review meetings one could be forgiven for thinking that this mechanism is used as a 'tit for tat' exercise with states condemning each other in such a way as to negate the whole procedure (Pentikainen 1997). This is not to suggest that it has not been used effectively, for example the UK used the procedure against Czechoslovakia that ultimately led to the release of the playwright Vaclav Havel, and the process was used to implement sanctions against South Africa to protest against apartheid. However it is ultimately a politically subjective process leading to inconsistencies in the issues raised and responses to those issues. For example, Yugoslavia has been suspended as a member because of human rights abuses whilst Bosnia and Hercegovina have been admitted despite findings of human rights abuses by Council of Europe monitors (see Nowak 1999)

At the end of the cold war, the member states of the CSCE met once again at Helsinki. It could be argued that one of the most significant challenges to state sovereignty came about in this 1992 Declaration of the Helsinki Conference. The Declaration addresses the need for states to become increasingly accountable to one another with regard to human rights issues. It states in part,

...the (human rights) commitments undertaken... are matters of direct and legitimate concern to all participating states and do not belong exclusively to the internal affairs to the state concerned. The protection and promotion of human rights... continue to be a vital basis for our... security (brackets inserted, CSCE 1992: 2 para 8).

It has been suggested that this declaration signals a new approach to the concept of legitimate political power within an international context (Held 1995: 105). Whilst the CSCE (now the OSCE) undoubtedly has a role to play in international affairs and human rights it is necessary to keep in mind that the Declaration is a statement of intent and not a legally binding document and as such is open to misuse and abuse. Indeed it can justifiably be argued that many CSCE states are themselves guilty of human rights abuses: Ex-Yugoslavian states have been guilty of hampering the movement of refugees; Turkey for its treatment of minority groups; Albania, Bulgaria, Slovakia, the Czech Republic and Romania for their treatment of the Roma and the US for its capital punishments agenda.

The EU and Human Rights

The events leading up to the establishment of the European Union, the role of the various institutions and the enlargement process are documented elsewhere in this volume (see The Nation State and European Institutions and European Enlargement), this section will look at these processes in the light of the impact they have had on the human rights agenda. The 1957 Treaty of Rome (TOR) establishing the European Community was primarily used as a means of promoting closer economic integration within Europe. Earlier in the 1950s the drawing up of a bill of rights was proposed but "none of the subsequent treaties contained such a bill or a list of enumerated rights" (Steiner & Alston 2000: 790). The TOR was more concerned with the protection of the rights of states from EC interference than with the rights of the individual. Protections for individual rights were deemed to be the domain of the nation state. The Preamble to the TOR did however, outline the need for the EC to function in, "accordance with the principles of the Charter of the United Nations (recall at this point that the Charter indicates one of its aims as the promotion of the 'respect for human rights and fundamental freedoms'). No codification of human rights was provided however, which in effect nullified the statement.

The 1992 Treaty on European Union (commonly referred to as the Maastricht Treaty), did make provision for human rights in Article F (s) which states,

The Union shall respect fundamental rights, as guaranteed by the European Convention for the Protection of Human Rights and Fundamental Freedoms signed in Rome on 4 November 1950 and as they resulted from the constitutional traditions common to the member states, as general principles of Community law (TEU 1992).

The use of the word 'respect' however does not carry any enforcement mechanism. These words were reiterated later in the amendment to the TEU (which was provided for by the Treaty of Amsterdam 199/), Article 6 1&2 provide that:

(1) The Union is founded on the principles of liberty, democracy, respect for human rights and fundamental freedoms…principles which are common to the member states.
(2) The Union shall respect fundamental rights as guaranteed by the [ECHR]….

Article 7 does however allow for the suspension of membership rights in the EU if, a 'serious and persistent breach' of human rights is considered to have occurred within a member state.

The approach to human rights taken by the EU has been criticised for being, "splintered… (without necessary) leadership and profile… and marginalised in policy-making" (brackets inserted, EC Report 1999). Back in 1996 Amnesty International in a proposal put forward to the EU Intergovernmental Conference suggested that greater 'respect' would be shown to human rights if the EU itself were to accede to the ECHR, four years on this still has not been done. So the dichotomous arrangement exists whereby nation states within the EU are bound by the ECHR whereas the EU itself is not.

The European Court of Justice

Based in Luxembourg, the judicial arm of the EU, the Court of Justice (ECJ) is primarily concerned with "ensuring that the law is observed in the interpretation ₊and applications of the Treaties establishing the European Communities" (Europa downloaded 28/09/00). Way back in 1969 however, the ECJ (in the Stauder case no: 61969J0029) used the consideration of human rights within its deliberations. For the most part however, human rights within the ECJ have been applied to the actions of the European Community itself and not to the actions of specific nation states. The Amsterdam Treaty, mentioned earlier, did however increase the Courts jurisprudence within Articles 6 (1&2). The involvement of the ECJ into the human rights domain although specifically in a limited way (concerns for the implementation of EU legislation in a human rights 'friendly' way) has meant that it some cases there is an overlapping of roles between the ECJ and the European Court of Human Rights. The ECJ being part of the EU has not acceded to the ECHR and although there are arrangements to facilitate consultation and co-ordination between the various organs of the EU and Council of Europe, they are separate entities with separate concerns and operating in different arenas.

A Charter of Fundamental Rights?

In recent years, there has been a call to embed human rights within the European Community itself by means of a Charter of Human Rights. The Helsinki European Council in December 1999 allowed for the setting up of a working group that would draw up a draft Charter, which would be ready for submission to the European Council by December 2000.

This has largely come about because of the overlapping of the roles of the European Court of Justice (ECJ) and the European Court of Human Rights. It has been suggested (Miller V 2000) that the inclusion of new states into

Europe especially from Central and Eastern Europe might necessitate the inclusion of stronger human rights guarantees within the EU legal system and a Charter would be a means of doing this. The Charter would incorporate elements from the existing charters and international rights declarations and treaties especially the European Convention on Human Rights. Discussions are ongoing as to whether the European Communities would benefit from becoming signatories to the European Convention on Human Rights and acceding to the Convention, which in turn could mean that the European Court of Human Rights might take precedence over the ECJ in human rights matters, although this is not certain.

Some basic issues can be raised however, one cause for concern is raised by Weiler (1996: 79–81) who suggests that yet another human rights mechanism could lead to, "rights saturation rather than rights deprivation." This is linked to questions, as yet unanswered, as to whether the proposed Charter would be a proclamation or a legally binding document and concerns as to the problems of having two courts ruling on similar issues, or if we take into account the national state legislature, three court systems and the controversy over the exercise of powers at different levels. (Canor 2000: 3) Looking practically at these issues the potential extra work involved for whichever Court took responsibility for these issues within the context of the EU, might lead to a slowing down of procedures and it would necessitate the setting up of yet more institutions for filtering and admissibility considerations.

Discussion

Human rights agreements can reinforce democracy but they cannot guarantee freedom from abuse when powerful forces violate democracy, as in the case of Greece in 1967. A recent survey of the Democratic Audit, a project based at the Human Rights Centre at the University of Essex, investigating the United Kingdom's "compliance of British law with (the country's) international human rights obligations", identifies forty-two separate violations of international human rights standards. (brackets inserted, Klug, Starmer & Weir 1996). So even when conventions and treaties are in place these do not necessarily ensure rights will be respected. This may be due, in part, to the view that seems to dominate many major states, including the USA and the UK, that, "(ratified) human rights treaties are instruments of foreign policy rather than domestic" (brackets inserted, Falk 1997: 179). Falk (1997) suggests this may be why the Foreign Office in the UK is the main department with responsibility for overseeing the UK's obligations under the ECHR and the UNIC, and why the

USA takes umbrage when domestic abuses are brought to it's attention, yet often leads international HR crusades itself. An example of this can be found in the recent visit by Madelaine Albright to China. Both countries condemned each other for carrying out HR abuses, both citing AI reports concerning the other country and led Tang Jiaxuan, the Chinese Foreign Minister to suggest that, "...human rights was no excuse for...interfering in other countries affairs" (see Gitting J. *The Guardian* 2/3/99).

Where monitoring procedures *are* put in place, action is not standard but arbitrary. For example, South Africa suffered sanctions because of apartheid whereas China, who has signed up to the legally binding Covenants of the UDHR (even though they are in breach of almost every article therein), has been allowed to maintain friendly relations with the West, being visited recently by both President Clinton and Prime Minister Tony Blair.

Conclusion

This historical perspective has equated the rise of the human rights process alongside the rise of the nation state. It has become evident through this analysis that over the intervening years a dichotomy has arisen between nation state sovereignty, with it's non-interventionist approach, and movements to internationalise human rights. Gradually, incremental gains *have* been made, gains that often cannot be recognised without the benefit of hindsight. A plethora of treaties, covenants and declarations have developed throughout the years since the time of the Magna Carta. The European Convention and the two UN International Covenants have been hailed as landmarks in the human rights process (Robertson & Merrills 1993: 287).

The criterion for success however must *not* be based on how many of such documents can be drawn up but rather, the extent to which they are ratified. If the treaties already established were accepted more widely then human rights legislation would become stronger. Where the implementation of human rights procedures are optional however, states often do not incorporate them. Whilst the nation state, for the most part, is still the focal point for implementing human rights legislation it is still the place where violations take place.

Recent years have seen major changes within the European system for upholding human rights with the founding of the new European Court of Human Rights and calls for an EU Charter of Fundamental Rights. The conflict between national, international and supranational legal systems still remain however, and the drawing up of new charters, treaties and declarations does not provide us with a clear solution to this problem.

References

Amnesty International (98/99), Amnesty in Action pamphlet. *Amnesty*. Nov/Dec 1998.

Annan, K. (2000), Speech online at: http://hrpd.fco.gvo.uk/home.asp?page= universality

Bhabha, J. (1999), "Enforcing the Human Rights of Citizens and Non-Citizens in the Era of Maastricht: Some Reflections on the Importance of States". In: **Meyer**, P. & H. **Geschiere** (1999), *Globalisation and Identity: Dialects of Flow and Closure*. Insitutue of Social Studies.

Baylis, J. & S. **Smith** (1997), *The Globalization of World Politics*. Oxford: Oxford University Press.

BBC Archives (1998), BBC Human Rights Watch.

Betten, I. & S. **Grief** (1998), *EU Law and Human Rights*. Addison Wesley Longman.

Brown, C. (1997), *Human Rights in The Globalization of World Politics*. Oxford: Oxford University Press.

Bloed, A. & D. **van Dijk** (1991), *The Human Dimension of the Helsinki Process*. Dordrecht.

Cassese, A.(1991), "Violence, war and the rule of was in the international community". In: **Held**, D. (ed.), *Political Theory Today*. Cambridge: Polity Press.

Canor, I. (2000), *"Primus inter pares*. Who is the ultimate guardian of fundamental rights in Europe?" *European Legal Review*. Feb 2000.

Cranston. M. (1983), "Are There Any Human Rights?". *Daedalus*. Vol. 112: 1–17.

CSCE (1992), Conference on Security and Cooperation in Europe. *Helsinki Declaration*. Helsinki 1992.

European Court Justice (1969), Stauder case no: 61969J0029
http://europa.eu.int/smartapi/cgi/sga_doc?smartapi!celexplus!prod!CELEXnumdoc
&lg=en&numdoc=61969J0029

Europa (2000), *What is the European Community?*
http://europa.eu.int/cj/en/pres.comp.htm

European Commission (1999), *Affirming Fundamental Rights in the European Union*. Report of the Expert Group on Fundamental Rights 1999.

Ewing, E. (1999), "The Human Rights Act and Parliamentary Democracy". *The Modern Law Review*. Vol. 62, No. 1.

Falk, R. (1995), *On Humane Governance Toward a New Global Politics*. Cambridge: Polity Press.

Fukyama, F. (1990), *The End of History and the Last Man*. London: Penguin Books.

Gitting, J., *The Guardian* 2/3/99.

Held, D. (1995), *Democracy and the Global Order: From the Modern State to Cosmopolitan Governance*. Cambridge: Polity Press.

Ishay, M. (ed.) (1997), *The Human Rights Reader*. London: Routledge.

Klug, I., M. **Starmer** & S. **Weir** (1996), *The Three Pillars of Liberty*. London: Routledge.

Lauterpacht, H. (1950), *International Law and Human Rights*. London.

Mansell, W. (1999), "Fundamental Human Rights Premises". In: **Bell**, C., *Teaching Human Rights*. National Centre for Legal Education. Warwick.

March, H. (1996), *The European Courts*. London. Cantermill Int. Ltd.

Meron, T. (ed.) (1984), *Human Rights in International Law:Legal & Policy Issues*. Oxford: Claredon Press.

Miller, V. (2000), "Human Rights in the EU: The Charter of Fundamental Rights". House of Commons Research Paper 00/32. International affairs and Defence Section. House of Commons Library. Available online at: http://www.parliament.uk

Nowak, N. (1999), "The case of Bosnia Herzegovina". *Human Rights Law Journal* HRLJ 30th November 1999 Vol. 20, No. 7–11.

OSCE docs (2000), Final Act – Helsinki Summit 1975, available online at: http://www/osce.org/docs/english/1990–1999/summits/helfa75e.htm

Pentikainen, M. (1997), "The Human Dimension of the OSCE in the 1996 Vienna Review Meeting". *Helsinki Monitor*. Vol. 8, No. 1. Netherlands Helsinki Committee and the International Helsinki Federation for Human Rights.

Poggi, G.(1978), *The Development of the Modern State*. London: Hutchinson.

Pollis, I. & M. **Schwab** (1979), "Human Rights a Western Construct". In: **Pollis**, I. (ed.), *Human Rights: Cultural and Ideological Perspectives*. London: Praeger.

Robertson, R.(1994), *Globalization*. London: Sage.

Robertson, A. & J. **Merrils** (1989, 1993), *Human Rights in the World*. Manchester: Manchester University Press.

Robertson, A. & J. **Merrills** (1996), *Human Rights in Europe*. Manchester: Manchester University Press.

Sieghart, P. (1983), *The International Law of Human Rights*. Oxford: Clarendon Press.

Sieghart, P. (1986), *The Lawful Rights of Mankind*. Oxford: Oxford University Press.

Sellar, D. & M. **Yeatman** (1930), *1066 and All That: A Memorable History of England*. London: Methuen.

Sohn, L.(1968), "A short history of United Nations documents on Human Rights". *The United Nations and Human Rights*. Commission to Study the Organization of Peace. New York.

Spencer, M. (1995), *States of Injustice: A Guide to Human Rights and Civil Liberties in the EU*. Pluto Press

Steiner, H. & P. **Alston** (2000), *International Human Rights in Context: Law, Politics, Morals*. Oxford: Oxford University Press.

Teitgen, Maxwell Fyfe (1949), *Official Reports*. September 1949.

Teitgen, P. H. (1949), *Official Reports*. Dordrecht.

Vincent, R. J. (1988), *Human Rights and International Relations*. Cambridge: Cambridge University Press.

Waters, M.(1995), *Globalisation*. London: Routledge.

Weiler, J. (1996), "European Citizenship and Human Rights". In: **Winter**, G. (1996), *Reforming the Treaty on European Union: The Legal Debate*. London: Routledge.

Zalman, N. & S. **Seigel** (1997), *Criminal Procedure: Constitution and Society*. 2nd ed. West. St Paul. MN.

Stanisław Konopacki

Citizenship: the Concept and its Development

The concept of citizenship

The question of citizenship has been especially salient since the end of the 1980s. According to Jürgen Habermas three political developments have rendered this term very problematical. First, the issue of the future of the nation state has unexpectedly become topical in the wake of German unification, the liberation of the East Central European States and the nationality conflicts that are breaking out throughout Eastern Europe. Second, the fact that the states of the European Community are gradually growing together, especially with the impending *caesura* which was created by the introduction of a common market in 1993, sheds some light on the relation between nation state and democracy. For the democratic processes that have gone hand in hand with the nation state lag hopelessly behind the supranational form taken by economic integration. Third, the tremendous influx of immigration from the poor regions of the East and South with which Europe will be increasingly confronted in the coming years lend the problem of asylum seekers a new significance and urgency. This process exacerbates the conflict between the universalistic principles of constitutional democracies on the one hand and the particularistic claims of communities to preserve the integrity of their habitual ways of life on the other (see Habermas 1995: 255–256).

These three universal/European phenomena are accompanied by some internal (visible on national level) developments which somehow undermine the traditional idea of citizenship. Here, mass unemployment provides the most gloomy perspective for millions of people, excluding them from a sense of full participation in the civic society. Another question is an increasing gap between individuals and their governments. This regards the question of "rights of citizens" in the light of overwhelming power of the contemporary state and private corporations. This includes: the rights to privacy in the context of accumulation of electronic data on individuals; rights to employment in the situation when ever growing number of sectors of economy is dependent on international financial markets. The interest in citizenship is also promoted by the "new social movements" like ethnic minorities, feminism, gay rights movement which put under question the problem of identity and rights within traditional political settings. It seems that national citizenship is being undermined by globalising developments as well as by local forces. These two opposing pressures, however, are intertwined. Local groups express their identity most forcefully as global developments tend to threaten them. It is not coincidence that the European integration process is accompanied by a growth of nationalistic movements being against any idea of unification (for example Le Pen's National Front). The two developments undermine the stability of the state and by this the civic dimension it determines.

What is the meaning of the term 'citizenship'? In general, it describes relations among citizens and between citizens and state. Therefore, it represents a concept of participation in public life being broader than the range of political life. The second aspect of the concept discussed is that a citizen is an individual who both governs and is governed. That includes values such as autonomy, judgement and loyalty which any person claiming to be a citizen should meet. Another aspect of this term is that it refers on one side to obligations and duties and to rights and entitlements on the other. In an ideal situation 'citizenship' includes activity of a person ready to subject his/her private interest to the general benefit of the community. That differs him from burgeois or economic citizen who normally is not inclined to sacrifice his/her interest on the altar of public life (see Van Steenbergen 1994: 2). In the words of Derek Heater, citizenship embraces status, a sense of loyalty, the discharge of duties and rights in relation, first of all, to an abstract idea of state (Heater 1990: 2).

The classical tradition

It is worth to mention that the concept of citizenship, being mostly of European origin, is also present in Judaic and Babylonian tradition but is completely unknown to the political culture of China, Islam and India. The first thorough expression it found in Athens in the 5th and 4th centuries BC. Aristotle wrote in *Politics* that man as a political animal could realise his life and personal identity only by taking part in the events of *polis* (city-state). This statement has two implications. First, the status of belonging to the Athenian community was strictly linked to the role the citizen played in it. That is why the word "state" itself is so important for that tradition. It was to be a small enough in order for the citizens "to know one another's characters". It should be noticed that for this type of citizenship a small tightly-knit community was assumed. *State* was perceived as "commonwealth", "republic", "constitution" and seems to be different from its modern meaning as independent, formal institution being detached if not even contradictory to its citizens. In the ancient Greece these two ideas – *citizenship* and *state* – were tightly interrelated. Actually, the *polis* – state – denoted its citizens. Manville notices that for that reason literary sources never make reference to the Athenian *polis* as "Athens". It is only the name of place. What is meant by state was in fact represented by "the Athenians" as political community of citizens (Manville 1990: 6). For Aristotle, "it is men who are the *polis*". "The *polis* is a compound made up of citizens". It means that in order to understand the nature of the Greek city-state one should first grasp the essence of citizenship.

The second aspect of Aristotelian definition concerns the fact that an active participation in political life was linked to the possession of certain intellectual qualities which the old, the young and workers were seen not to have. Thus, a good citizen "must posses the knowledge and the capacity requisite for ruling as well as for being ruled, and the excellence of a citizen may be defined as consisting in a knowledge of rule over free men from both points of view" (Aristotle, 1946: 105). Citizens in fact took part in the judicial process, public debate and were really responsible for the decision taking policy. Those neglecting their duties were named as "idiots". Citizenship in the Greek state was an inherited privilege understood not as a right to be demanded nor a status to be enjoyed by anybody and especially by those outside the privileged class. It was rather a responsibility borne by the chosen group from which slaves, peasantry, women, and foreigners were excluded. The privileged group in the Greek *polis* was allowed to own property and was expected to play the role of jurors, judges, administrators, politicians and soldiers. Responsibility and sense of obligation towards the community was the highest virtue of a true citizen. That is why Socrates drank the hemlock without any doubts because he knew that he had to obey the laws, even unjust, even to the ultimate limits. He was ready to sacrifice his life which was understood as an act of selfless citizenship. The other virtues of the good citizen praised by the *polis* were: courage in battle; love of beauty and wisdom; discretion in private dealings with neighbours; prosperity; grace and versatility; respect for order and authority – human and divine (Manville 1990: 14, 15).

In comparison with the Greek citizenship which was practical and exclusive, the Roman idea was more complex and open. Citizenship was no longer a matter of tradition and ethnicity but rather of legalistic arrangements. It was Servius Tullius (c. 500 BC) who conferred citizenship upon aliens, merchants and traders who in the Greek city state would be deprived of these rights. Full citizenship was associated with six privileges: public rights (military service, voting in the assembly, eligibility to public office, right to legal action and appeal) and private rights (trade and intermarriage with other Roman citizens). In the next century, facing territorial expansion and need to control its whole empire, Rome conferred full citizenship on its free male inhabitants. It should be mentioned that the Roman system offered a second-class type of citizenship of *civitas sine suffragio* (citizenship without franchise). It was meant to provide some public rights but not political ones. Also, the office of dual citizenship was introduced which allowed inhabitants to enjoy simultaneously the membership of their own city and of Rome. Annexation of new territories was accompanied with granting the privilege of citizenship to conquered tribes. It was a means of power through integration. Roman citizenship however provided total equality before the law; "neither race nor religion nor riches were determinants for acceptance" (Heater 1990: 17).

It was commonly understood that the citizen's performance should be in line with his status. There were expectations from a citizen to cultivate the 'civic virtues'. This ideal of citizenship as 'virtue', often called 'civic republicanism', was sustained by the educational system. During the Republic era the typical Roman civic virtues were provided by the family. Fathers were due to equipped their sons with such qualities like: courage, firmness, self-restraint, dignity, prudence, justice. Young boys were also taught by an experienced friend of the family some elements of law, government and oratory. For Romans, as a practical-minded people, citizenship and supporting it the educational system were instrument to expand its leadership in the world. In the words of Hémery, the Romans by doing this "spread positive law and individualism which are two core notions of modern definitions of citizenship" (Hémery 1997: 2).

The collapse of the Roman Empire led to the situation in which citizenship as a political concept for a long time was not present in the language of political thought. The main feature of the Medieval pattern of political power was a multi-faceted loyalty. Both Prince and Church expected allegiance. As a *Christian* the individual was obliged to follow the orders of the ecclesiastical authorities; as a *subject* of a Prince he had to adjust his conduct to the administrative and legal power. In the Middle Ages the term 'citizen' (as etymologically expressing its urban roots) was limited to the relationship of freely exercised rights and obligations in a city (or a town) and was based on the rules of freedom and fraternity (Heater 1990: 21). Features of citizenship varied greatly from city to city. The development of city-states led to the revival of classical political ideas and Aristotle's concept of citizenship which was introduced by St Thomas. He stressed Aristotelian statement that "it is possible to be a good citizen without possessing the qualities of the good man". It enabled the political man to be judged according to the standards different from those used in evaluation of the Christian. Of course, as a devoted priest he could not eliminate completely God from the political activity. That is why, in St Thoma's mind, the citizen realising human laws is guided by the light of divine reason containing universal natural law. The next step towards a more secular idea of citizenship was made by Marsilius of Padua for whom the state was a self-sufficient entity. According to him the citizens performing their political activities were not limited by divine judgements.

The revival of the ancient concept of citizenship in the thirteenth and fourteenth centuries was followed by the extensive study of Roman law and history in the Renaissance. Italian political thinkers shared the view that the people as a whole have the right to hold the sovereign power and only within the state the people were truly free. Florence provided the spectacular example of a city where the status of the citizen was enjoyed by all its inhabitants exept the representatives of the lesser guilds and labourers. Leonardo Bruni in his *Funeral Oration* from 1428 devoted to the Florentine constitution expressed a new concept of citizenship which appeared to be a break from an idea of hierarchical community to a more egalitarian entity. According to him:

Equal liberty exists for all… the hope of winning public honours and ascending is the same for all, provided they possess industry and natural gifts and lead a serious-minded and respected way of life; for our commonwealth requires *virtus* and *probitas* in its citizens. Whoever has these qualifications is thought to be of sufficiently noble birth to participate in the government of the republic. [...] This, then is true liberty, this equality in a commonwealth: not to have to fear violence or wrong-doing from anybody, and to enjoy equality among citizens before the law and in the participation in public office (Heater 1990: 24).

The most ardent defender of the republican state was Machiavelli. He understood "republic" as a form of government characterised by a share of power preventing arbitrary and totalitarian rule. In *Discourses on The First Decade of Titus Livius* he argued that the people equipped with virtues work for the benefit of the state. By "virtue" he meant qualities needed to defend the state from internal disorder and external threat. They referred to such characteristics like public-mindeness and patriotism. People should be made into citizens through education, religion, and recognition of duty. The essence of real citizenship was also associated with a citizen-army. That is why Machiavelli thought that the decline of ideal of the republican citizenship was responsible for the collapse of the Roman Empire. It made him aware of a gloomy perspective for Italy drawn into corruption and political war between different political factions.

Overcoming of internal unrest and quarrel within domestic political scene and consolidation of the political power was the main prerequisite of Jean Bodin's concept of citizenship expressed in *Six Books of the Commonwealth* in 1576. Citizenship for him was a special type of relationship between a subject and the sovereign defined as "the mutual obligation between subject and sovereign by which, in return for the faith and obedience rendered to him, the sovereign must do justice and give counsel, assistance, encouragement, and protection to the subject" (Bodin 1967: 21). It should be stressed that this relationship was different from that one of the vassal and his lord as "a citizen cannot be the subject of more than one sovereign". Received by birth, adoption or enfranchisement the status of citizenship, although not providing equal rights and privileges, served to cement the fractured state: "the whole body of the citizens...when subjected to a single sovereign power of one or more rulers, constitutes a commonwealth, even there is a diversity of laws, language, customs, religion and race" (Bodin 1967: 20).

Modern citizenship

The modern, more egalitarian concept of citizenship was a result of new political developments which dominated Europe from XVII century onwards. In other words, the situation which determined modernity by the same determined citizenship. According to Max Weber, the dominant feature of modernity is rationality manifesting itself in technical calculation, purposeful action, legitimisation of judgements, rapid development of scientific knowledge, arising of organisations, diminishing role of traditional loyalties, religious feelings. Citizenship is the institutional expression of rationality – "crystallisation of rationality in a social role" (Dahrendorf 1974: 677). Thus, there were some developments of European rationality which radically changed the pre-modern social conditions. Heater argues that the most important question was the consolidation of the concept of state and state sovereignty as a rational and legal entity being the main reference for citizenship. The second issue was the determination of allegiance and rights enabling the distinction between inhabitants and aliens. The next factor refers to the decline of the authority of the prince and hierarchical structures of power in favour of more egalitarian relationships between persons. The fourth change is linked to the right of people themselves to make decisions regarding their laws and forms of government. The fifth element concerns a religious freedom enjoyed by Protestants and Puritans. Another development is a process of secularisation associated with growing freedom of belief and choice. In general, the new modern idea of citizenship presupposes a some degree of equality, recognition of universalistic criteria and secular standards to strengthen obligations and rights.

The 18th century was a witness of a further development of the modern idea of citizenship and its binding up with a concept of state. The French Revolution was an important step towards the rationalisation of social life and transformation of subject into citizen. In this context two intellectual traditions which occurred afterwards are significant: the first is connected with Rousseau and the second with Burke. In Rousseau's opinion the state is a sort of political community where its ties with the individual are close and direct (Nisbet 1974: 618). The legitimacy of the government is rooted in the General Will and there is no need for any other form of associations. The state replaces the family in education activities to such a degree that the father will not mind as "he would only be changing his title, and would have in common, under the name of *citizen*, the same authority over his children, as he was exercising separately under the name of *father*..." (Rousseau: 269). The very existence of Rousseau's state excludes any form of hierarchy and loyalty. Inequality has its source in personal interdependencies and that is why a state seems to be a mean of liberalisation and protection against all forms of such dependency. Out of two forms of links – *among individuals* and those *between individual and state* – the second are to be as important as possible. In his mind: "each citizen would then be perfectly independent of all the rest, and at the same time very dependent on /the state/; which is brought about always by the same means, as the strength of the State can alone secure the liberty of its members" (Rousseau: 48). The work of Rousseau gave the rise to the tradition associated with the conviction of superiority of the *public* sphere over the *private*, the individual one. Later on it assumed a form of reasoning that regarded *central* or national government as a superior over *regional* and local one.

The opposite view on the relation between citizen and state represents Burke. In his *Reflection on the Revolution in France* he rejects the whole practise of revolutionary laws and decrees which rationalised, "geometrised" the idea of citizenship upon which the society was raised. He is an advocate of decentralisation, localism, regionalism and radical pluralism of the social order freed from the centralised power. In his understanding of citizenship he argues that

we begin our public affections in our families. No cold relation is the zealous citizen. We pass on to our neighbourhoods, and our habitual provincial connections. These are our inns and resting places. Such divisions of our country as have been formed by habit and not a sudden jerk of authority are so many little images of the great country in which the heart has found something which it could fill (Burke: 543).

In the decades that followed, Burke's concepts gave the way to conservative, liberal and even radical tradition of political thought.

Marshall's concept of citizenship

The best known account of the development of modern citizenship was given by the English sociologist T.H. Marshall in *Citizenship and Social Class,* published in 1950. Citizenship, according to his theory, is linked to the development of three sets of rights accompanied by the creation of appropriate institutions. Civil rights developed in the eighteenth century involve individual freedom and justice provided by the courts and judiciary system. Political citizenship was established in the 19th century and relates to participation in politics and communal decision-taking procedures. The 20th century is marked by an emergence of social citizenship understood as proper level of life linked to education and welfare services. Marshall argued that "the modern drive towards social equality is the latest phase of an evolution of citizenship which has been in continuous progress for some 250 years" (Marshall 1950: 7).

In Marshall's opinion, the development of capitalism was supported by the establishment of civil rights because individual freedom manifested itself as economic freedom. Yet, the satisfaction of social rights possible only by increased taxation worked against the principles of capitalist market. In a famous phrase Marshall said that: "in the twentieth century, citizenship and the capitalist system have been at war" (Oliver, Heater 1994: 34). This question reflects two features of his idea of citizenship: its relationship to the notion of class and its integrative character. As far as the relation to class is concerned, citizenship involves equality of rights and duties whereas class is a structure of social inequality. Therefore, the growth of citizenship seems to be contradictory to the development of capitalism. The rise of the class system enhanced by the development of capitalism took place in 19th century when political rights were still poor. The increasing importance of social rights on the other hand work against perpetuation of inequality although there are limits to "how far the egalitarian movement may be pushed. In particular, citizenship and the economic system operate with different standards as to what inequalities may be regarded as legitimate" (Hindess 1994: 21).

In his later works Marshall tries to find the compromise between class and citizenship and introducing the model of the "hyphenated society" of democratic-welfare-capitalism. It was an alternative project of organisation of social life to the society developed around the single idea like citizenship. "The hyphenated society can succeed only if it is recognised that both the welfare sector and the mixed economy are contributing to the creation of welfare. [...] it is hardly possible to maintain democratic freedom in a society which does not contain a large area of economic freedom" (Hindess 1994: 21).

Discussing the question of the integrative effect of citizenship Marshall says that it generates "a direct sense of community membership based on loyalty to a civilisation that is a common possession. It is a loyalty of free men endowed with rights and protected by a common law" (Marshall 1950: 40–41). The concept of civilisation as a common possession denotes ability of its members to participate in the political and social life of the community they belong to. Here "equality of status is more important than equality of income". The first provides conditions in which other inequalities might be accepted. Marshall argues that "status differences can receive the stamp of legitimacy in terms of democratic citizenship provided they are not an expression of hereditary privilege" (Marshall 1950: 75–76). Within this concept class inequalities are not legitimated but the idea of citizenship does not exclude other form of inequalities.

Marshall's thought might be conceived as a possible answer, relying upon British experience, to solve the problem of the relationship between capitalism and democracy, that is how to reconcile formal equality with the reality of class division. In his opinion the welfare state providing some social benefits for a citizen would limit negative consequences imposed by the market. The role of social rights guaranteed by the social services would be to ensure participation of all citizens in the social and political life of the community. They found their full realisation within the British welfare politics. According to Turner this body of relatively simple ideas appeared to be very influential not only in Britain but also in American political science.

Four models of citizenship

Liberalism

According to classical liberalism human beings are atomistic, rational individuals, whose existence, needs, feelings are prior to society. The individual is "unencumbered self" completely separated and detached from history, community and tradition. The most expressive picture of "liberal individual" resembling Stirner's *man* was portrayed by Sandel:

"no role or commitment could define me so completely that I could not understand myself without it. [...] For the unencumbered self, what matters above all, what is most essential to our personhood, are not the ends we choose but our capacity to choose them. [...] What is denied to unencumbered self is the possibility of membership in any community bound by moral ties [...] Freed from the dictates of nature and the sanction of social roles, the human subject is installed as sovereign, cast as the author of the only meanings there are [...] We are free to construct principles of justice unconstrained by an order of value antecedently given. And as actual, individual selves, we are free to choose our purposes and ends unbound by such an order, or by custom or tradition or inherited status (Sandel 1992: 18–20).

Individual therefore, is perceived as competitive being pursuing its own interests calculated on the base of the recognition of the others' rights. Its liberty is to be protected as long as it is compatible with a similar liberty for others. Government is a result of rational activity of individuals searching for protection of their subjective rights and liberties. The institution of state and citizenship are legitimised as instruments for realisation of non-political goals. The rationale of political activity is to establish a legal framework necessary for individuals in order to pursue their own interests. That is why for Hayek the main concern was the protection of the right to be left alone ("negative liberty") and the protection of individuals' activity being unobstructed by others.

In later versions of liberalism a real freedom is not conceived merely as a lack of compulsion and restraint but as the maximum of power for all members of the community alike to their benefit (Axtmann 1996: 39). Here the state was understood not as opposed to liberty of individuals but as a mean of freedom. The goal of liberalism is the benefit of the individual which might be achieved only with a support of "welfare state". Therefore, according to Axtmann, liberalism developed a notion of citizenship entailing three ways of relationship between a citizen and the state. Firstly, the citizens were the ultimate source of state authority and legitimacy. Secondly, citizens were the "subjects" of state power, restrained by collective political will. They also enjoyed civil rights and liberties constituting "private space" which was free from the state's interference. Thirdly, citizens were the "clients" of the state securing their welfare and well-being (Axtmann 1996: 43).

The role of the liberal welfare state was to overcome material inequalities that limited individual freedom depriving a formal legal equality of a real value. On the other hand the paternalistic welfare state is inclined to infringe a freedom of individual by making it its client. It is important therefore to combine freedom and equality. Apart from its variations, the main concern of liberalism was to put right before politics. Realisation of rights obliges the state not to interfere with or actively to promote the citizen's liberties. The problem occurs when rights appear to be contradictory, when realisation of one is possible only by an infringement of the other. Some academics support the idea that rights should be linked to specific concept of human community or its vital interests and conditions of well-being. Gray argues in this context that "in political and moral philosophy, the good is always prior to the right: we make judgements about the rights that people have, only on the basis of our judgements of the interests central to their well-being"(Gray 1993: 102). In the conditions of the pluralistic society such judgements are a very complex task. Therefore, according to Bellamy, we have an obligation to participate in politics in order to define the type of our community and to enjoy liberties (Axtmann 1996: 46). Dahl argued that in order to make democracy work there is a need for consensus on basic norms.

Republicanism

In the republican tradition a single community, the public community plays the crucial role in social life. Political activity is a condition for self-fulfilment; the liberty of the person can be realised only within the republican community. Citizenship is conceived as an office and responsibility, not as a status enabling the person a passive enjoyment of rights as envisaged in the liberal tradition. In the words of Walzer: "the first makes citizenship the core of our life, the second makes it its outer frame. The first assumes a closely-knit body of citizens, its members committed to one another; the second assumes a diverse and loosely connected body, its members committed elsewhere" (Walzer 1989: 216).

There is no freedom outside of political and social context. Freedom is a political freedom only to be achieved within the republic community. According to Taylor, freedom does not belong to human beings as such; as political freedom it is integral feature of the citizen. In the perspective of republican tradition, rooted in Aristotle's thought, the political entity is a common project; it is a community of people having a common purpose. Its end is the "good life"; and the "good" in politics is justice meaning in fact the common interest. Aristotle suggests in his statement – "man is by nature a political animal" – that we can develop our virtues and excellences only through participation in the political community. Citizenship denotes a self-governing participation in a self-governed community. Human beings as moral beings can realise their moral selves in sharing their lives with each other in a political community aiming at the achievement of the good both for the community as a whole and for each individual.

Machiavelli supported the classical ideal of citizens' participation in the political community but he did not perceived the *republica* as moral community "bound together by an objective conceptualisation of the common good and particular manifestations of personal morality. His analysis of republicanism was couched predominantly in terms of military powers and imperial glory" (Axtmann 1996: 50).

In 20th century the most devoted representative of the republican tradition was Hannah Arendt who claimed that politics was not a natural part of the human nature. As an artificial phenomenon it is a result of human activity performed to express their plurality. The citizens are united not by the common values but by the institutions they built together, social space they share and recognition of rules upon which these institutions and space were founded. It is worth to mention that Arendt argues that human beings do not need to be good as persons in order to create a common world. The experience of Stalinism and fascism made her believe that personal morality could possibly prevent individuals from supporting totalitarianism, but could not prevent it from happening.

Political activity, according to Arendt, involves participation in discussion, debate on public matters. Politics seems to be the area of "no rule", where human beings face one another as equals and where persuasion, rather than force or violence, "rule" (Arendt 1958: 25–28). By the means of common speech citizens create a public space that brings them together and makes them aware of their plurality. This public space of debate presupposes a common culture on the basis of which everyone can freely articulate their views that are constantly challenged by the diversity and plurality of different perspectives.

Communitarianism

Within communitarian perspective citizenship denotes membership in a historically developed community. The character of the individual is determined by the type of the group it belongs. Its behaviour proceeds within the standards developed by the community. Loyalty seems to be the precondition of successful community and individual. According to van Gunsteren this idea of citizenship avoids the problems typical for the liberal concept.

Individuals are formed by the community. If they conform to the codes of behaviour that have been taught to them, they will ensure the continued existence of the community and each other. They simply repeat the successful formula that enabled the community to grow and survive. Deviation from the code is considered to be corruption and must be resisted. A community that is declining can be saved by fighting corruption and returning to its origins, its beginnings (van Gunsteren 1994: 41).

The second feature of the communitarian citizenship refers to the fact that individual identity cannot be realised outside the community of like-minded and peers and their support. The person with the solid and strong *ego* is immune from changing conditions. The majority of people, however, depend on "the continued existence and membership of a community of roughly like-minded and similarly acting mates, of shared life-styles. Research and historical experience prove time and again that the parties involved, including ourselves, systematically underestimate this dependence" (van Gunsteren 1994: 41). The people who are aware of this dependence would support and esteem the community that defines their character.

The first vice of the communitarian concept found by some scholars concerns the fact that the consciousness of the role and significance of the community is not in itself a guarantee of its maintenance and the will to belong to it. In modern societies characterised by a variety and richness of social groups and an overlapping type of membership it is not possible to take a single community for granted. The second weakness of the idea discussed is its constraint imposed upon freedom. "Emancipation often has been achieved through liberation from the compelling and unfair ties of a community. The emphasis on "right thinking", which easily emerges in communities that cultivate their own existence, is petrifying" (van Gunsteren 1998: 20). There are also doubts concerning the role of modern state which was supposed to protect its citizens against communities. The state's policies are likely to violate its neutrality regarding communities, but also risk to fail protection of citizens against the communities. Gunteren argues that communities are indispensable and dangerous, but it is the task for the state that manages them to constrain their excesses.

Neo-republicanism

The neo-republican idea of citizenship is a combination of the liberal, republican and communitarian perspectives. According to this view the citizen is characterised by membership in the republic which play for him a crucial role. Virtues – similarly to the republic tradition – are also required from the citizen. However these are not qualities of military character but debating, reasonableness, democracy, choice, plurality. It is a matter of sensible, competent and responsible treatment of authority, situations and positions of power. This cannot be exhaustively laid down in rules. Such competence is essential for the effectuation of citizenship.

The citizen in the neo-republican concept is an autonomous and loyal person capable of governing and of being governed as well as of sound judgement. His autonomy is provided by the republic that is also the subject of his/her loyalty. In order to "reproduce citizens" as autonomous individuals the crucial role is played by the government. It establishes certain norms and introduces them into the public sphere realising the task of organising pluralism. The public is to link all the elements together whose interrelations lead to citizenship. In Gunsteren's words, "citizenship is learned and confirmed primarily by its exercising, and in the organisation of plurality. Family, church, school and other connections are important and possibly indispensable contributions, but in a plural society they can never be the officially designated sites where citizenship is defined and the citizen is formed" (van Gunsteren 1994: 47).

Another feature of neo-republican citizenship is that it does not presupposes social equality. A crucial point here is that it advocates political equality. The concept contradictory to it is not inequality but slavery – conceived as a mixture of humiliation, powerlessness and petrification in relationships. Inequalities might be accepted as long as they do not lead to servility and are not the barrier to citizenship. It is also said that citizenship is an *office*. In other words, it does not refer to the ordinary person; its exercise requires of competence; it can modify performance of other offices. Citizenship, considered from the perspective of public domain, plays the role of normative and informative viewpoint. In the situation of loyalty conflict it attributes responsibility to the citizen who is mostly capable of governing and being governed.

In the "creation of citizens" the government plays an important role. Its task considers arranging such conditions within society which prompt mature citizenship. Other institutions like church, family and school are also involved in the process.

Conclusion

There are several reasons for the growing interest in citizenship at the present time. Kymlicka argues that it is a natural consequence of political discourse as the idea of citizenship seems to combine the questions of justice and membership in a community; individual rights and anchorage to a particular social group (Kymlicka 1995: 283). The events mentioned at the beginning of this chapter that caused the revival of the concept are a token of a need for a new "theory of citizenship" – a theory which would reflect the issue of identity, and conduct of citizens together with their loyalties, responsibilities and roles. Moreover, there is a need for the new idea of citizenship that would be able to exploit the achievements of four traditions in order to face the challenges of contemporary Europe concerning the issues of globalisation, post-modernisation and integration.

Further Reading

Gunsteren van, H. (1994), "Four Conceptions of Citizenship". In: **van Steenbergen**, B. (ed.), *The Condition of Citizenship*. London: Sage.

Habermas, J. (1995), "Citizenship and National Identity: Some Reflections on the Future of Europe". In: **Beiner**, R. (ed.), *Theorizing Citizenship*. New York: State University of New York Press.

Heater, D. (1990), *Citizenship: The Civic Ideal in World History, Politics and Education*. London: Longman.

Oliver, D. & D. **Heater** (1994), *The Foundations of Citizenship*. London: Harvester Wheatsheat.

Steenbergen van, B. (1994), *The Condition of Citizenship*. London: Sage Publications.

References

Arendt, H. (1958), *The Human Condition*. Chicago: University of Chicago.

Aristotle (1946), *Politics*, (ed. E. Barker). Oxford: Clarendon Press.

Axtmann, R. (1996), *Liberal democracy into the twenty first century. Globalization, integration and the nation-state*. Manchester: Manchester University Press.

Bodin, J. (1967), *Six Books of the Commonwealth*. London: Blackwell.

Burke, E. (1910), *Reflections on the Revolution in France*. (ed. Dent).

Dahrendorf, R. (1974), "Citizenship and Beyond: The Social Dynamics of an Idea". *Social Research*. Vol. 41, No. 4.

Gray, J. (1993), *Beyond the New Right. Markets, Government and the Common Environment*. London: Routledge

Gunsteren van, H. (1994), "Four Conceptions of Citizenship". In: **van Steenbergen**, B. (ed.), *The Condition of Citizenship*. London: Sage.

Gunsteren van, H. (1998), *A Theory of Citizenship. Organizing Plurality in Contemporary Democracies*. Oxford: Westview Press.

Habermas, J. (1995), "Citizenship and National Identity: Some Reflections on the Future of Europe". In: **Beiner**, R. (ed.), *Theorizing Citizenship*. New York: State University of New York Press.

Heater, D. (1990), *Citizenship: The Civic Ideal in World History, Politics and Education*. London.

Hémery, D. (1997), *European Citizenship* (ms.).

Hindess, B. (1994), "Citizenship in the Modern West". In: **Turner**, B. S. (ed.) *Citizenship and Social Theory*. London: Sage.

Kymlicka, W. **Norman**, W. (1995), "Return of the Citizen: A Survey of Recent Work on Citizenship Theory". In: **Beiner**, R. (ed.), *Theorizing Citizenship*. New York: State University of New York Press.

Manville, P. B. (1990), *The Origins of Citizenship in Ancient Athens*. Princeton.

Marshall, T. H. (1950), *Citizenship and Social Class*. London.

Nisbet, R. (1974), "Citizenship: Two Traditions". *Social Research*. Vol. 41, No. 4.

Oliver, D., **Heater**, D. (1994), *The Foundations of Citizenship*. London.

Rousseau, J. J. (1968), *The Social Contract* (ed. M. Cranston). Harmondsworth: Penguin.

Sandel, M. (1992), "The Procedural Republic and the Unencumbered Self". In: **Avineri**, S. & A. **De-Shalit** (eds), *Communitarianism and Individualism*. Oxford: Oxford University Press.

Steenbergen van, B. (1994), *The Condition of Citizenship*. London: Sage.

Walzer, M. (1989), "Citizenship". In: **Ball**, T. *et al.* (ed.), *Political Innovation and Conceptual Change*. Cambridge: Cambridge University Press.

Stanisław Konopacki

European Citizenship – Maastricht and After

Introduction

In the context of Western Europe the growing interest in the idea of citizenship over the last ten years is mainly a result of three political developments. Firstly, the liberation of East-Central Europe and German re-unification; secondly, the issue of European integration marked by the Maastricht Treaty, Single Market in 1992, the Amsterdam Treaty and finally the challenge of further enlargement. The third reason has its roots in the increasing number of immigrants coming to Europe from different parts of the world and puts under the question the universal values and principles of constitutional democracies. The accession negotiations with the East European countries which started in 1998 shows that the perspective of their membership in the European Union, with all the consequences resulting from that fact, poses the most important challenge for the privileges of Western societies acquired and preserved so far within the concept of European citizenship. The issue becomes more and more important and sensitive especially in the context of the latest developments in Western Europe after the establishment in Austria of the coalition government with the Liberty Party of Jörg Haider. This political grouping, as is commonly known, is not in favour of enlargement and the accession of eastern workers to western labour markets. In fact it is against the future free movement of persons which as the very fundamental right of the EU (one of its four freedoms) is enjoyed by European citizens.

The origins of Union citizenship

Citizenship, in general, denotes a special kind of direct relationship (usually characterised by certain rights and obligations) between an individual and a political community. The Greek word denoting the citizen *polity* comes from the term *polis* and means the rule of an individual (*polity*) subjection to community (*polis*), i.e. city state. In the Roman tradition, on the other hand, relationship between a citizen (*civis*) and the group (*civitas*) denotes a situation in which an individual plays a superior role over the state. In this sense, therefore, one might expect that European citizenship is to denote a specific kind of direct relationship between the European Union and its citizens.

For a long time in the European integration context the term "workers" was used rather than "citizens". The first reference to European citizenship was made at the meeting of heads of state in Paris in December 1974 where they proposed that "a working group be instructed to study the conditions and the timing under which the citizens of the nine Member States could be given special rights as Members of the Community" (see Bulletin EC 1974: point 111). It was a question of certain civil and political rights, especially the right to vote and accession to public office. Later on several initiatives by the Commission and the European Parliament were undertaken in order to develop these special rights. In 1979 the Commission presented a Directive concerning a right of residence for nationals of Member states in the territory of another Member state regardless of the performance of an economic activity. The precondition of this proposal was awareness that free movement of persons could not be completely realised without a permanent right of residence for all Member state nationals. This right was regarded as a first phase in the process of creation of European citizenship.

In 1984 the European Council established an *ad hoc* committee chaired by Pietro Adonnino which presented two reports. The first one tackled a sensitive issue of border controls and formalities as well as the right of residence proposed in 1979. The second report drew attention to some special rights of citizens covering the issues of culture, education, communication and symbols of Community identity like flags, passports, etc. (Bulletin EC Suppl., 85: 18).

In 1986 the Commission issued the report *Voting Rights in Local Elections for Community Nationals*. According to this document free movement denotes that the fact of being a citizen in one Member state results in accession the same rights in another Member state. So far, Member state nationals could not enjoy their political rights in most Member states where they were resident as they were not nationals there; at the same time they could not exercise their electoral rights in their state of origin as they were no longer resident there (O'Leary 1996: 36). The Commission initiated a proposal for a Council Directive on voting rights for Community nationals which was a result of a desire to establish a *Citizen's Europe*.

The discussion on a union citizenship took a clearer form during the Intergovernmental Conference (IGC) preparing the Maastricht Treaty. The establishment of Union citizenship within this treaty was seen as a further step towards a deepening of the integration process. The provisions of the second part of the Treaty develop these values which in the preamble refer to the rule of freedom, democracy, recognition of human rights and basic freedoms as well as to the rule of law.

Objectives of Union citizenship according to the Maastricht Treaty

1. Free movement of persons and economically active persons is a precondition of an effective internal market. For this purpose it was necessary to remove all obstacles and introduce new rights (political rights) which would make the free movement more attractive. In this context the idea of Union citizenship was to improve the status of nationals who reside in a Member state other than their own behind the position of privileged aliens. It is stated in Article B of the Maastricht Treaty that one of the objectives of the European Union is to "strengthen the protection of the rights and interests of the nationals of the Member states through the introduction of a citizenship of the Union". According to the European Parliament's Imbeni Report "the process of making citizenship of the Union a reality must be understood by citizens of the Member States as a better guarantee that they will effectively enjoy the right to work, a decent standard of living (minimum wages, health care, right to housing etc.) and environmental protection" (Document A3 1993: 5).

2. To reduce the democratic deficit resulting from several following reasons (Boyle 1993: 459–477; Neunreihter 1994: 300–314):

a) the decision-making process and sovereignty were transferred to the Community level where decisions are taken in secret and often by the unaccountable Council;

b) the still rather minor role of the European Parliament, the only Community institution directly and democratically elected which does not play a greater role in the legislative process;

c) the executive power of the community lies exclusively with the Commission and Council – institutions which are not directly elected by citizens of the Member States.

3. Building a European identity that refers to the social legitimacy of the European integration programme. Successful internal market and economic and monetary union need some public consent and the establishment of European citizenship is perceived as a means of achieving this consensus. It is not clear however "whether the development of a European identity meant increasing individuals' sense of belonging to the Union or whether it was aimed at making

them identify with other citizens of the Union; that is, identifying with fellow citizens to the exclusion of non-citizen residents" (O'Leary 1996: 39).

4. To identify the personal scope of the European Union. It confers upon its citizens a series of rights, freedoms and obligations that are to increase the sense of belonging to the common house. Therefore, the key question here concerns who really is a citizen of Europe.

European citizenship in the Maastricht Treaty

In order to realise the above mentioned objectives the Maastricht Treaty provides the following provisions:

Article F (2) TEU
The Union shall respect fundamental rights, as guaranteed by the European Convention for the Protection of Human Rights and Fundamental Freedoms signed in Rome on 4 November 1950 and as they result from the constitutional traditions common to the Member States, as general principles of Community law.

Article 6 EC
Within the scope of application of this Treaty, and without prejudice to any special provisions contained therein, any discrimination on grounds of nationality shall be prohibited.

Article 8 EC
Citizenship of the Union is hereby established. Every person holding the nationality of a Member State shall be a citizen of the Union.
Citizens of the Union shall enjoy the rights conferred by this Treaty and shall be subject to the duties imposed thereby.

Article 8 (a) EC
Every citizen of the Union shall have the right to move and reside freely within the territory of the Member States, subject to the limitations and conditions laid down in this Treaty [...]
The Council may adopt provisions facilitating the exercise of these rights [...] acting unanimously on a proposal from the Commission and after obtaining the assent of the European Parliament.

Article 8 (b) EC
Every citizen of the Union residing in a Member State of which he is not a national shall have the right to vote and to stand as a candidate at municipal elections in the Member States in which he resides, under the same conditions as nationals of that State.
[...] Every citizen of the Union residing in a Member State of which he is not national shall have the right to vote and to stand as a candidate in elections to the European Parliament in the Member State in which he resides, under the same conditions as national of that State. Both rights shall be exercised subject to detailed arrangements adopted by the Council, acting unanimously on a proposal from the Commission and after consulting the European Parliament; these arrangements may provide for derogations where warranted by problems specific to a Member State.

Article 8 (c) EC
Every citizen of the Union shall, in the territory of a third country in which the Member State of which he is a national is not represented, be entitled to protection by the diplomatic or consular authorities of any Member State, on the same conditions as the nationals of that State.

Article 8 (d) EC
Every citizen of the Union shall have the right to petition the European Parliament in accordance with Article 138 (d).
Every citizen of the Union may apply to the Ombudsman established in accordance with Article 138 (e). It is important to emphasise that these two rights are conferred not only on citizens of the Union but also on any natural or legal person residing or having his registered office in a Member State.

In the light of the rights enshrined in the Treaty and present developments within the European Union countries two questions seem to be of vital importance:

1. Does the idea of European citizenship actually realise the objectives assigned to it?

2. Is it a proper concept for the European Union preparing itself and facing the enlargement into the Central and Eastern Europe countries?

Limitations of the European citizenship

European citizenship is based on the rule of member state nationality and the procedure within which nationality is conferred and defined by each member state. According to O'Leary "the member states thus have ultimate control of access to, enjoyment of, and even forfeiture of, the rights of citizenship of the Union. As a result, no direct link, political or otherwise, has been created between Union citizens and the Union, although this link could be regarded as a fundamental ingredient of citizenship at national level. The use of nationality as a base for Union citizenship also demonstrates that member state sovereignty, rather than promotion of individual rights, remains of ultimate concern to the architects of the Union Treaty" (O'Leary 1996: III). The policy of individual member states in this field is usually not so much liberal.

Traditionally, nationality is based on the rule of soil (*jus soli*) or the rule of blood (*jus sanguinis*). Germany as one of the most restrictive countries adopts the *jus sanguinis* as the fundamental principle, while France is known for using the more liberal rule of *jus soli*. The UK preserved *jus soli* for a long time but since adopting the 1961 Commonwealth Immigration Act has become more restrictive and moved towards *jus sanguinis* adopted within British Nationality Act, signed in 1981. In 1994 Germany promised limited citizenship rights to third generation immigrants, provided that their parents had lived in that country at least ten years and one of them had been born there (Newman 1996: 156). France, following the course adopted by other EU countries, became more restrictive in this matter and in its bill of 1993 concerning immigrants established the rule of *jus sanguinis*.

Therefore, the Union citizenship is fully determined by national citizenship. The Member States, not the European Union, decide who might receive the privileges of Union citizenship. According to Evans the reason of this situation is the will to preserve the direct link between Member States and their nationals and exclude any possibility of expansion of union rights behind the context of this relationship (Evans 1995: 86–110). This practice is contradictory to the rule expressed in a decision of the Court of Justice, which ascribing to the Member State the competence to determine who their nationals are, at the same time emphasised the need to realise this competence in accordance with the objectives of European law (free movement of persons, Community's standards in the field of fundamental rights). Several organisations like the European Parliament had wanted European citizenship to be determined on the basis of principles enshrined in a form of constitutional document incorporating the European Convention of Human Rights. The Maastricht Treaty, however, did not follow this path as several states (like Great Britain) which have not accepted this Convention within their legal framework did not want to incorporate them via the European Union (Newman 1996: 157). In other words, the Member States were not completely prepared to "denationalise" the issue of "union citizenship".

In consequence, the use of "national identity" as a fundamental rule of determination of citizenship led to creation of the whole group of second class citizens and non-citizens of the European Union who became excluded from certain basic rights.

1. There is growing evidence that most Member States expect migrants from developing countries to return home after satisfying their needs on the labour markets. The case of Germany is significant here. It is extremely difficult for Turkish migrants to obtain the status of citizenship even after living there for two or more generations. There are estimations that in the European Union about 10 million people are legal residents without having status of citizenship.

2. Since the second part of 1970s there has been increasing evidence of racism in Europe strengthened additionally by the economic recession (Newman1996: 161). In several European countries the position and role of neo-fascist and far-right parties have risen. Recent developments with the Haider Liberty Party in Austria are a good example of this phenomenon. It should be noticed that also the media play a certain role in petrification and dissemination of negative stereotypes concerning immigrants and linking their presence with increases of crime, terrorism, drug smuggling (Ford Report 1991).

3. Since the 1970s immigration and family reunification policies in Europe as well as policies on admission and employment have become more stringent. There is a similar situation with asylum policy. It should be emphasised that asylum seekers are treated as illegal immigrants. Moreover, the average acceptance rate for asylum status is very low 9% (Benyon 1994: 502).

4. Apart from Belgium, France, the Netherlands and Britain, in other European countries there is a lack of legislation that might be the legal base for combating racism and discrimination. France, for example, denies the existence of ethnic and national minorities which in a sense legitimises some forms of racism. There is a similar situation in Germany which, housing about 6 million immigrants, denies to be a country of immigrants and rejects any evidence of discrimination and xenophobia (Commission of the European Communities 1993: 75).

In general, the European Union created a situation which has a negative impact upon the victims of racism and constructed a non-accountable legal framework introducing policies contributing to discrimination (Newman 1996: 163). That is why the European Parliament in its resolution of February 1989 called for freedom of movement on the same conditions for all legally resident workers living in a member state irrespective of their nationality. This resolution, however, was rejected (Official Journal 1989: 47).

The Maastricht Treaty hardly changed the existing situation. Although Article K2 of the "third pillar" says that all matters belonging to its area (asylum policy, immigration policy, cooperation in the field of internal affairs) should be realised according to the European Convention of Human Rights and Fundamental Freedoms, it must be noticed however that this Convention is not an integral part of the Treaty and is not binding for the jurisdiction of the European Tribunal.

Thus, the union citizenship based primarily on national citizenship, where the rule *jus sanguinis* dominates, is of exclusionary character towards foreigners. It makes them in fact the non-citizens of the European Union.

I. The right of residence and moving established according to Art. 8(a) is in fact limited by two factors: possession of sufficient resources and possession of sufficient medical insurance. The conditions are not described *explicite* in the Treaty but in the secondary legislation giving effect to the Treaty. This legislation comes from the period preceding the Maastricht and is contained within three directives (90/366; 90/365; 90/364). The role of the conditions (limitations) envisaged in those directives is to ensure the situation in which member state nationals and their families will not become a burden of the social security policy of the host Member state. Though the Court of Justice has refused the subsistence minimum to be a determining factor for free movement and residence, the Member States themselves are in fact free to determine who benefits from these basic freedoms envisaged in Article 8(a). This article is not therefore a guarantee of the right of free movement and residence because the very realisation of this right depends on the 1990 Directives that are quite restrictive. As the result, this article makes for the emergence of two groups of citizens. The first which is a beneficiary of freedom of moving and residence and the second which is excluded from this right (O'Leary 1996: 51). This is especially important in the light of the fact that the right of residence and free movement is a crucial factor of the idea of Union citizenship. Realisation of many other rights associated with Union citizenship depends in fact on the possibility to move freely and reside in another Member State.

II. Also the provisions of the Article 8(b) concerning electoral rights of Union citizens residing in an another Member state do not work for creation of a more direct link between Union and citizens. In fact, all important decisions concerning European citizens are not taken at the level of local governments and rarely in the European Parliament. All crucial matters are decided within the European Union Council or in national parliaments. Moreover, possibility to influence on the matters directly affecting citizens in their daily life envisaged in participation in local elections actually depends on competence exercised by this level of power. This, in turn, depends on decentralisation of power that varies from country to country.

III. Taking into account the fact that European citizenship was to develop or strengthen a sense of identity with the Union or other citizens of the Member States it must be noticed that a specific type of identity is being fostered. Namely this one which excludes of long term legally resident third country immigrants or citizens not meeting certain economic conditions. According to Herzog's Document "the Maastricht Treaty does not create a genuine citizenship of the Union. It simply grants citizens of the Member States rights *vis-à-vis* countries of which they are not nationals. The Union has virtually no obligations towards them" (European Parliament's Herzog Working Document 1993: 2). The adopting of Member state nationality as a base for Union citizenship means that the key factor for defining its content was the preservation of national sovereignty rather than the fostering of individual rights and democratic values.

The Amsterdam amendments on Union citizenship

The Treaty of Amsterdam practically did not change the existing situation regarding the idea of Union citizenship. It only added one statement to the Art. 8 that "citizenship of the Union shall complement and not replace national citizenship" (The Treaty of Amsterdam 1997; 86). It also moved the policy concerning common visa, immigration and asylum from the intergovernmental third pillar to the first pillar of the European Union. In this way it extended the democratic procedures of the European institutions to legislation in this area. It also improved the prospect of the principle of free movement of people within the European Community. An important change concerns the fact that anti-discrimination provisions were written into the Treaty and recognition of human rights was made an explicit criterion for accession to the Union. However, the derogations for the UK, Ireland and Denmark on freedom of movement weaken the unity of the European Community in this field and limit some rights of citizens (Duff 1997: XXIII–XXXVI).

Thus, the idea of Union citizenship (envisaged in the Maastricht as well as in Amsterdam Treaties) does not create any direct relationship between a European citizen and the Union – the relationship which seems to be a very condition of any kind of citizenship. Secondly, nationality used as a criterion of the European citizenship excludes in fact a significant part of a society from benefits of fundamental rights. These features of the Union citizenship are specially important from the perspective of the Union facing enlargement towards eastern and central Europe. The development of Union citizenship clearly suggests that it has proceeded according to the logic of elimination or exclusion of *the Other*.

History of exclusion

It seems, therefore, that Union citizenship reflects and reveals an internal mechanism of the European integration. This integration might be perceived as a specific continuation or extrapolation of the very tradition of Western culture which main principle was – as is illustrated in the work of Michel Foucault – the exclusion of the Other. The sources of this tradition go back to ancient Greece. "The Greeks had a relation to something that they called *hybris*" (Foucault: 1965: XI). It was not, however, a relation of condemnation. The Greek Logos did not treat *hybris* as an enemy.

In the Middle Ages a relation to the other, the obscure, the unclear and the incomprehensible adopted a form of relation to lepers. The mushrooming of the lazar houses in Europe had not only a medical meaning involving an isolation of the deadly ill. Important here was also a ritual to keep the sickness at a sacred distance in an inverse exaltation. The leper – though excluded from this world – by its very existence was a witness of God, His anger and His grace. Foucault says that "abandonment is his salvation; his exclusion offers him another form of communion" (Foucault 1965: 7). When at the end of the Middle Ages leprosy disappears as a plague the practice of exclusion is used for vagabonds, criminals and "deranged minds". Especially the latter case was deeply explored in relation to something called *madness, dementia, insanity*. Perhaps Western reason owes its depth to these obscure forces. "The Reason-Madness nexus – writes Foucault – constitutes for Western culture one of the dimensions of its originality; it already accompanied that culture long before Hieronymus Bosch, and will follow it long after Nietzsche and Artaud" (Foucault 1965: XI).

Whereas the Renaissance was an explosion of unlimited madness the classical age managed to tame it using a strange act of force. Descartes, in turn, in his act of uncompromising and total doubt rejects all dreams, illusions, mistakes, insanity, phantasms that could disturb the absolute clarity and certainty of knowledge. Due to this act Reason, Cartesian *cogito* confirms itself in its contact with truth – contact not spoiled by any illusions and phantoms. As a consequence, it is possible to define a truth as a clear and explicit notion moving away on the margin everything that seems to be unclear, incomprehensible and mad. According to Foucault the adventures of the Cartesian doubt seems to suggest that in the seventeenth century the threat was overcome and insanity removed from the domain where a subject preserves his right to truth. It was a strengthening of human *ratio* which gave an impetus towards the all process of Western rationalisation.

In the social dimension of the classical epoch the relationship towards madness and insanity appeared in a massive phenomenon of confinement. It involved the whole body of measures that enabled and imposed work upon all those who could not live without it. Confinement, as a way of closure of the other bears the sign of an imperative of labour. It was a measure to eliminate the problem of "mendicancy and idleness as the source of all disorders" (Foucault 1965: 47). Confinement was the answer to an economic crisis the whole Europe experienced in the seventeen century – namely, reduction of wages, unemployment and scarcity of coin. The houses of correction, *hospitals general* were used as a shelter for the unemployed, the idle and vagabonds. The confinement served as a source of a cheap labour in the periods of full employment and high salaries and during periods of unemployment as a means of protection against disorders and uprisings. The economic and moral postulate of confinement was a result of a certain experience of labour. "Between labour and idleness in the classical world – says Foucault – ran a line of demarcation that replaced the exclusion of leprosy. The asylum was substituted for the lazar house. [...] The old rites of excommunication were revived, but in the world of production and commerce" (Foucault 1965: 57). The practice of confinement in the classical age was a milestone in the history of unreason. It enabled madness to be perceived within the horizon of poverty, incapacity to work or inability to integrate with the group. In the following period until the end of the eighteenth century classicism does not cease to confine. It creates the shelters for the debauched, spendthrift fathers, prodigal sons, blasphemers, libertines. Through segregation the modern world wanted to eliminate all those who within the social order seemed to be non-social. It gave a birth to a new sensibility that drew a line, elevated a barrier and chose new banished. This sensibility manifests itself in the gesture to set apart – the gesture that was once used to eliminate lepers.

The *Great Confinement* played not only a negative role of exclusion but was also an important factor for mobilisation and organisation of a society. Due to exclusion of the other, the non-rational the world itself became more rational, ordered and uniform. The very presence of the non-social, the useless allowed the organisation of the social entity more efficiently. As for Descartes the non-rational sphere of insanity, dream, illusions was a foundation of clear-cut and obvious truth as in the social domain existence of the *other, stranger* was a splendid reservoir of sense and principle that organised life.

At a certain stage of history "European Reason" creates the East as its different other. The East – writes Foucault – is a part of the universal Western ratio: East understood as a starting point, as a stunning place where all nostalgia originates and promises the return. East subjected to the colonising Western mind but at the same time somehow inaccessible because it will always be a limit and night of beginnings. East is all the West is not and has to search for its primordial truth.

In that sense the integration of Europe after the Second World War from the very beginning has followed the model of the *Great Confinement*. It was directed against Not-Europeans who as *the Others* found themselves on the other side of the iron curtain. The process of unification was therefore another example of the European reason and by the same token the very embodiment of the logic of *exclusion*. It was the logic which brought into being always a new *other* – leper, madman, vagabond, unemployed, woman, child, Jew and eventually not-European – who might have testified to the Western rationality, health, purity, rightness, superiority, etc. The Yalta conference was only a completion and the beginning of European history governed by logic establishing its enemy or the Other – against whom the West could have effectively integrated. The period of the Cold War – especially in fifties and sixties – was in fact the years of the greatest achievements of the European unification. Fear of external threat, of the soviet bloc – of the Other – worked perfectly as a main engine of the unification machinery.

The logic of exclusion, as was described earlier, found its continuation in the idea of Union citizenship that reflects the true character of the integration process. Therefore this concept might focus all obstacles and barriers for enlargement which – according to common sense – is associated with inclusion rather than exclusion of the other. As a result, it seems that enlargement of the

Union to Central and Eastern countries apart from economic, legal and technical problems has to overcome the whole European tradition of "citizenship" which is based on the exclusion of the other. Thus, the success of this process would need a sort of new vision of Union citizenship – citizenship defined not *against the Other* but *towards the Other* in a sense of *dialogue and responsibility for the Other*.

Conclusion

The idea of Union citizenship seems not to realise the objectives assigned to it. Namely, built upon the national identity it does not reduce democratic deficit and does not create a European identity based upon a direct link between citizens and the Union. Therefore, it does not increase a sense of belonging to the common house among Members states nationals. Free movement of persons, based in fact on the economic criteria, excludes some nationals from benefits of this right, making, as a result, second-class citizens.

Secondly, Union citizenship reflects in a sense a capability of the Union to further enlargement. As a continuation and embodiment of the logic of exclusion – being a fundamental principle of the European development – it does not seem to be a good device which might create convenient conditions and environment for eastern enlargement.

Further reading

Foucault, M. (1965), *Madness and civilization. A history of insanity in the Age of Reason*. London: Random House Inc.
O'Leary, S. (1995), *European Union Citizenship. The options for reform*. London: IPPR.
Lehning, P. B. & A. **Weale** (eds.) (1997), *Citizenship, democracy and justice in the new Europe*. London: Routledge.
Meehan, E. (1993), *Citizenship and the European Community*. London: Sage.

References

Beynon, J. (1994), *Policing the European Union: The Changing Basis of Co-operation on Law Enforcement. International Affairs*. Vol. 70, No. 3.
Bulletin EC Supplement, 7/85.
Bulletin EC, 12/1974.

Commission of the European Communities: Legal Instruments to Combat Racism and Xenophobia (1993), Luxembourg: Office for Official Publications of the European Communities.

Duff, A., (ed.) (1997), *The Treaty of Amsterdam. Text and Commentary*. London: Federal Trust.

European Parliament Working Document, A3-0437/93, 21 December.

European Parliament's Herzog Working Document on Citizenship of the Union and **Foucault**, M. (1965), *Madness and Civilization. A history of insanity in the Age of Reason*. London: Random House Inc.

Fundamental Rights for the Committee on Institutional Affairs, 1993 PE 211.308.

European Parliament Report drawn up on behalf of the Committee of Inquiry into Racism and Xenophobia on the findings of the Committee of Inquiry, (Rapporteur: Glyn Ford) Luxembourg: Office for Official Publications of the European Communities, 1991 (so called Ford Report).

Evans, A. C. (1995), "Union Citizenship and the Equality Principle". In: **Antola**, E. & A. Rosas (eds), *A Citizens' Europe. In search of a New Legal Order*. London: Sage.

Newman, M. (1996), *Democracy, Sovereignty and the European Union*. London: Hurst & Company

O'Leary, S. (1996), *European Union Citizenship. The options for reform*. London: IPPR.

Stanisław Konopacki

Citizenship in a Global Context

Introduction

The great amount of literature devoted to globalisation usually deals with an analysis of global processes including world-wide operation of financial markets, multinationals, trade patterns, flow of information, international organisations and international law challenging the modern institution and sovereignty of the nation state. Not enough attention, however, is drawn to the human consequences of the problem in question. It seems that the issue of the new role and position of an individual in a global context should be raised more explicitly. In other words it is a matter of the impact of global developments upon the meaning and significance of citizenship traditionally determined – also in the European Union dimension – in terms of national identity.

The global condition

One of the essential features of the global condition is a compression of time and space due to the development of new means of transport and communication. After Virilio one might argue that it is not "the end of history" but rather "the end of geography" which has been witnessed over the past hundred years. In other words, it means that distances do not matter any more, that they have become a social product being in fact a function of capability to overcome them. The typical equipment of a contemporary individual – mobile phone, fax, laptop, walkman, credit card – allows him/her to participate in social life "from the distance". Very soon the invasion of the progress – injected to our body various gadgets like: respirators, intelligent enzymes, biological computers – will help us to transcend the limits of biological time. Yet, invention of new means of transport and communication had serious social and cultural consequences. The possibility of fast travel and communication not involving the face-to-face contact between interlocutors eroded and undermined the stability and safety of the local totalities and gave rise to the process labelled by Tönnies as the transformation from *Gemeinschaft* to *Gesselschaft*.

The second important characteristic of the new developments refers to the divisions implicit in the economy and organisation pattern of contemporary industrial and service sectors. According to Dunlap "the company belongs to people who invest in it – not to its employees, suppliers, nor the locality in which it is situated". This statement does not express a simple relation of "belonging" or ownership but the possibility of taking part in the decision making process. In one of his latest works *Globalization* Bauman notes that the employees coming from the local communities do not have the right to decide upon the matters which might have an impact on their lives (volume of production, rate of unemployment, development of the company, etc.). Only those who are the owners or shareholders, to whom the company belongs, are to determine its fate (Bauman 1998:). Calculating the effectiveness of their investment they are free to move the company to a new place offering better conditions and surplus value. They are in no way space-tied, determined by geographical conditions. Having in mind their own business they are free to leave the local community without work and sources of life but with the burden of wound-licking and damage repair. Bauman argues that "the mobility acquired by 'people who invest' – those with capital, with money which the investment requires – means the new, indeed unprecedented in its radical unconditionality, disconnection of power from obligations: duties towards employees, but also towards the younger and weaker, towards yet unborn generations and towards the self-reproduction of the living conditions of all; in short, freedom from the duty to contribute to daily life and the perpetuation of the community" (Bauman 1998: 9) .

These two phenomena: new conditions of transport and communication as well as mobility of locally unbound capital produce the whole group of excluded and the space of human isolation and solitude. Traditional spaces are replaced by privately owned spaces of public consumption where the access is determined by ability to pay. The social universe is polarised between elites travelling more and faster than ever before and pariahs who are tied to the local space they inhabit. These privileged are emancipated from the constraints of local conditions and they search for the security being a state of "non-neighbourhood", invulnerable isolation and immunity from local interference. Those excluded, on the other hand, are cut off from the benefits of technological achievements and deprived the possibility of psychological, cultural and political development. The only space where the two groups meet are the shopping malls which are so constructed as to keep people moving, looking around, keep them diverted and entertained no end – but in no case for too long – by any of the endless attractions; not to encourage them to stop, look at each other, talk to each other, think of, ponder and debate something other than the objects on display – not to pass their name in a fashion devoid of commercial value... (Bauman 1998: 25).

There is another aspect of the formation of the space of isolation and exclusion. The separation of the well-off from the poor sector of society leads towards the increasing suspicion against others, resentment of strangers, intolerance and obsession of "law and order". The latter might be only realised within community that is racially, ethnically segregated and uniform. Therefore, nowadays the city designed for the sake of security is becoming more and more concerned with danger than with safety. According to Nan Elin "in our postmodern times the fear factor has certainly grown, as indicated by the growth in locked car and house doors and security systems, the popularity of 'gated' and 'secure' communities for all age and income groups, and the increasing surveillance of public spaces" (Bauman 1998: 47). With walls built not only around the city but also across it, contemporary societies have prepared themselves to cohabitation with unwanted citizens. Instead of togetherness, separation and fear have become their main feature.

According Bauman the process is accompanied by the development of the electronic database, which is in fact an updated cyberspatial version of the Benthamian Panoptikon. The storage of information on all details concerning the citizens is a means of selection, estrangement and exclusion. It serves those moving on the global scale to be freed from conditions that bind the others to their local community. In Bauman's words "certain people it admits to the extra-territorial cyberspace, making them feel at home wherever they go and welcome wherever they arrive; certain others it deprives of passports and transit visas and stops from roaming the places reserved for the residents of cyberspace" (Bauman 1998: 51).

Therefore, we witness the process of globalisation that is being complemented by the parallel phenomenon of territorialisation. In other words, the both are two sides of the same coin glossed as a *glocalisation*. On the other hand, the freedom of movement and new technologies of information initiate the opposite tendencies: privileges and deprivations, wealth and poverty, power and powerless, freedom and constraint. Cited by Bauman, John Kavanagh argues that

globalisation has given more opportunities for the extremely wealthy to make money more quickly. These individuals have utilised the latest technology to move large sums of money around the globe extremely quickly and speculate ever more efficiently. Unfortunately, the technology makes no impact on the lives of the poor world. In fact, globalisation is a paradox: while it is very beneficial to a very few, it leaves out or marginalises two-thirds of the world's population" (Bauman 1998: 71).

The wealthy part of the world denies the other, poor part the same right to move – the right that is understood as a precondition of freedom and prosperity.

Therefore, absolutely legitimate is a question concerning possibility of citizenship in a global context – context of the total polarisation of two sectors of contemporary societies where their mutual communication appears to be very difficult if not completely impossible. In moral terms it is a question about possibility of morality understood as the responsibility for the *Other*, recognition of his dignity in the condition of globalisation where the *Other* is in fact excluded, estranged and humiliated.

The global citizenship – roughly understood as a recognition of social, economic and political rights and obligations of all human beings – would need an overcoming a whole tradition of exclusion on which a concept of citizenship is founded. Paradoxically, some signs of such a possibility might be traced within the context of postmodern thought.

The postmodern condition

The idea of postmodernism has already grown with many dissertations and papers, which emphasise its multidimensional and ambiguous character. Wolfgang Welsch argues that *postmodernity* and *postmodernism* are not an invention of philosophers, artists or art theorists. On the contrary; "rather our reality has become postmodern. In the age of planes, telecommunication all diversity has become so spaceless that everything seems to overlap and simultaneity of the unsimultaneous has become a new reality. Genuine has become a state of overall simultaneity, mutual diffusion of ideas and expectations" (Welsch 1988: 4). He states that "radical postmodern pluralism tears off the fetters of unity being a hope of totalism which might be realised only totally" (Welsch 1988: 7). In that sense, in the name of pluralism, postmodernism fights all tendencies towards uniformity; it stands for pluralism ways of life, patterns of acting, thought and social ideas. It heads towards a real pluralism supporting it in line with the rule of differentiation. "Instead of neutralising all variety by ordless muddle it intensifies it through limitation. Instead of soothing all difference it gives a strength to contradictions" (Welsch 1988: 3). Such a pluralism, however, realises through the reference to unity. The unity which is not a uniformity annihilating all variety in overwhelming indifference but the unity supporting variety and pluralism. "Unity – according to Welsh – is one of preconditions for production, perception and realisation of pluralism" (Welsch 1988: 18). It is a structure of the wholeness being shaped in transformations, links and combinations.

The radical pluralism of reality corresponds with the pluralism of different types of rationality. This very fact, argues Welsch, necessitates a new concept of reason which – preserving the borders between different rationalities – enables their mutual penetration and confrontation. The author of *Unsere postmoderne Moderne* suggests a concept of new postmodern reason which he identifies as "transversal reason". What are its characteristics? The "transversal reason" is limited and open at the same time. It runs from one configuration of rationality to the other, articulates differences, makes links, debates and makes changes. These procedures are of horizontal and processual character. It does not make any total syntheses; but if it makes them it is accompanied by the consciousness of their particularities. Thus, it does not cancel pluralism – contrary, it elevates pluralism to the position of fundamental form of reason" (Zeidler-Janiszewska 1991: 131). The aim of transversal reason is neither differentiation (*dissensus*) nor identification (*consensus*) only a form of international explanations which never perpetuate any state as a ready one. It is not a synthetic reason, which would play the role of remedy for heterogeneity. It is rather a way of "explanation of heterogeneity of links, differences and identities". As Anna Zeidler-Janiszewska finds out

Welsch designs in fact a concept of postmodern reason, which describes the best possible manner of individual participation in cultural variety of contemporary praxis. [...] Thus, the transversal reason would describe the type of interpretative capabilities of a subject which preserves pluralism as a general superior value in the contemporary culture (Zeidler-Janiszewska 1991: 132).

The reason so conceived is a contradiction to any authority once playing a role of legislator and provider of senses, values and standards of behaviour, which individual was bound or subjected to follow. Authority used to destroy a natural tissue of direct contact between people; it created distance annihilating not only all closeness but also an essential moral relationship. Instead of direct sensitivity to a fate of his/her neighbour, man – enslaved by an authority (of *Truth, Law, Ethics,* etc.) – has become insensitive to his pain and toil. All obedience to authority creates a distance that enables non-human behaviour.

The *Other* Heading

In the context of Europe a good example of this new reason conceived as a recognition of the radical pluralism and *the Other* is the philosophy of Jacgues Derrida. As is commonly known, Derrida is a representative of deconstructionism which is a mutation of postmodernism. One of his recent book *L'autre cap* (The Other *Heading*) reveals a more political dimension of this current (Derrida 1992).

The ambiguous title of the book that might be understood as the *other cape, direction, course* is an announcement of particular intellectual journey of its author. It is an expression of searching for a new identity of Europe or rather of a new way of thinking on that identity. According to Derrida traditional European identity used to be conceived as an enclosure in itself, leaving *the alien, the other* behind *the limit*. To think on Europe in the other way is to think on the European identity in terms of *the other, difference, pluralism, and aporias*. Thus, the other course (*l'autre cap*) is not a proposal of a new goal, vision but rather a transformation of traditional thinking. Derrida argues that "it is necessary to make ourselves the guardians of an idea of Europe, of a difference of Europe, but of a Europe that consists precisely in not closing itself off in its own identity and in advancing itself in an exemplary way toward the other heading or the heading of the other" (Derrida 1992: 29). It is difficult to avoid paradoxes that in political and ethical realm assume a form of *responsibility*. If this responsibility is to be freed from Eurocentrism – that is from thinking on European integration as a West-European integration – it is necessary to think on Europe in *the other* way. Namely, that not only Europe is responsible for *the other* but also that its identity is to be constituted by *the other*. Moreover, this identity is to develop – according to Derrida – as recognition of pluralism, variety, otherness and difference. At the same time however it is to acknowledge some *universal* values as rejection of violence, racism, etc.

The same duty dictates respecting differences, idioms, minorities, singularities, but also the universality of formal law, the desire for translation, agreement and univocity, the law of the majority, opposition to racism, nationalism and xenophobia. The same duty demands tolerating and respecting all that is not placed under the authority of reason. It may have to do with faith, with different forms of faith. This same duty surely calls for responsibility, for the responsibility to think, speak and act in compliance with this double contradictory imperative – a contradiction that must not be only an apparent or illusory antinomy [...] but must be effective and with experience, through experiment, interminable" (Derrida 1992: 78).

In this way Derrida rejects the easy solutions of either total unification or total dispersion. He is an advocate of the Enlightenment values of liberal democracy but is also aware that these very values are never enough to ensure respect for *the otherness* (Naas 1992: XLVI). There is therefore a need for such a definition of European identity, which combines both *universal values* and *difference*. Europe "must not be dispersed into a myriad of provinces, into a multiplicity of self-enclosed idioms or petty little nationalisms, each one jealous and untranslatable. [...] But, on the other hand, it cannot and must not accept the capital of centralising authority" (Derrida 1992: 39).

At the start of the 21st century, for Europe being at the crossroads, postmodernism might provide a useful discourse for meeting the challenges of contemporary world. One thing is obvious. Facing solution of qualitatively new problems and perspective of the eastern enlargement, Europe needs a profound revision (deconstruction) of its foundations, which are the pillars of its construction. One must emphasise however that postmodernism does not offer easy solutions and total plans and projects. It only points at the direction (*le cap*) where Europeans should search for solution and answers to their problems and needs. The signs showing the way are: *new identity* – determined by the other – and *responsibility* – towards the other. They are bound by recognition of *difference* and *universal values*.

Postmodern subsidiarity

The very tangible example of this new reason and recognition of the other which might provide a ground for the global citizenship is a principle of subsidiarity. In the context of contemporary phase of European integration, it might be seen as an embodiment of a political commitment of the transversal reason. The first and most important feature of subsidiarity is ambivalence that also characterises the postmodern condition. In the preamble to the Maastricht Treaty we read: "Resolved to continue the process of creating an ever closer union among the peoples of Europe, in which decisions are taken as closely as possible to the citizen in accordance with the principle of subsidiarity" (Treaty on European Union 1992: 4). On the other hand, in Article 3B we find the following passage:

In areas which do not fall within its exclusive competence, the Community shall take action, in accordance with the principle of subsidiarity, only if and in so far as objectives of the proposed action cannot be sufficiently achieved by Member States and can therefore, by reason of the scale or effects of the proposed action, be better achieved by the Community (Treaty on European Union 1992: 13–14).

It is to be noticed that although in the preamble the need of decision making as close as to the citizen is emphasised in the further part of the document the partition of competence only between the Community and Member States is mentioned, leaving out a citizen.

Therefore, two cited above sections are fairly compatible and make subsidiarity a blurred and ambiguous concept. After all, ambiguity permeates a whole body of the Maastricht Treaty. It is a very complex document created as a result of numerous compromises between the member states, which did not have a clear vision of future Europe. Moreover, a concept of subsidiarity contains two meanings introducing an extra factor of ambiguity and lack of transparency. A negative aspect of the principle discussed expresses a postulate of non-interference. It means that a superior power should not disturb a lower power or citizens in their activity. Whereas, its positive element envisages help and support of efforts of those subjects which in their activity are not self-sufficient. According to Millon-Delsol, the idea of subsidiarity is a negation of division of competence established once for ever between various powers. It is an expression of searching, always unstable, balance between a need of interference on the one hand and non-interference on the other. It is a way of setting up the life in the world permeating with pluralism, variety, ambiguity; in the world where the limits between different actors of political scene are blurred- actors traditionally identified as community, international organisations, nation states, regions, local communities. Subsidiarity therefore appears to be an effort of overcoming theory and practice of modern reason having tendency to eliminate all that cannot be precisely identified, planned and arranged. It is, in a sense, a way of emancipation of Europe from all attempts of introduction of ideal order based on unquestioned authority of scientific and objective reason.

As is found out by Millon-Delsol: "against to ideology and global theories developed during last two centuries, subsidiarity focuses a thought directed against all systems, gives lie to all "isms". Rejecting all prescriptions and remedies "[...] showing relativity of doctrines – it insists on more trust to be given to individual judgements and political decisions" (Millon-Delsol 1995: 54–55). Thus, it is against the modern concept of science, objective knowledge – locating the source, and centre of its legitimisation in the sphere of universal truth. Power, decision making is not located forever in a one centre. According to the principle of subsidiarity, decisions may be taken on different levels; the point is that the process proceeds as close to a citizen as possible. Subsidiarity – freed from the cult of ideology, objective truth and the only valid theory – is an incentive for rethinking social relations in the context of growing autonomy of man. It is an effort to find a balance between individual freedom and various centres of power in situation of ever changing conditions of political and social life.

The very first source of the principle of subsidiarity was a tradition of Christian culture. It is in the encyclical *Quadragesimo Anno* where it has found its final shape. Reading of this document suggests that the only and fundamental value – which should be an essence of any social order – is human freedom and dignity. It is, however, the dignity of an individual who in the postmodern age does not possess a permanent and stable nature. Subsidiarity would be therefore a sort of recognition and esteem for individual whose the most important feature is lack of solid identity, *essence*. Thus, it is a recognition of the dignity of individual being in the process of incessant becoming. Moreover, it is an attitude of responsibility for an individual and active support in its effort to build an ever-changing identity. In this way, it inscribes itself into the philosophy appreciating only one value – dignity of human being.

Thus, subsidiary seems to be a form of the committed transversal reason. This reason, apart from describing pluralism of reality and participation of individuals in its various practices also acts for them. In that sense subsidiarity would be a beginning of "new morality"; morality which essence lies in recognition of pluralism and tolerance for *the other*. It appears to be a regulative rule of conduct and establishing the relations between different actors of political life in the world deprived of objective truth, solid foundations and ground. For the present and future phase of European integration, in the face of chaos, pluralism and contingency, it might be a way of salvation of man and his dignity. Since – argues Jacques Delors – "subsidiarity starts with moral protection enabling recognition of dignity and responsibility of individual, which are the purpose of all society" (Definition and the scope of the subsidiarity 1994: 9).

Feminism and citizenship

The practical example of the intellectual struggle for recognition of dignity and difference as well as responsibility for otherness presents the feminist debate on citizenship which has emerged since the end of eighties. There are commonly known arguments concerning a lower position of women in the contemporary societies, their under-representation in the higher levels of decision-making, oppression and need for liberty and equal treatment in political, social and family life. Feminism has questioned women's gender roles, their economic dependency on men, position in the labour market, sexual harassment, etc. The crucial purpose of all feminist ideas and movements is the realisation of women's liberty and substantial improvement of their condition. According to Juliette Mitchell and author of the bestseller *Woman's Estate*, it might be only achieved if all four structures, in which women participate, are totally transformed – Production, Reproduction, Sexuality and Subordination. At that time a popular slogan was coined "the personal is political" expressing rejection of the gap between private and public sphere. It conveyed a thought that the private problems should be open to political debate and state intervention. Also, they are to enrich politics (Voet 1998: 24).

The very popular word which described women's condition in the society was "patriarchy" expressing domination of females by males. However, the more developed and profound feminist debate centred around the equality-difference problem which addressed a question of whether females should claim equal respect as men or rather they should aim at recognition of their difference.

In this context, three main strands of feminist thought might be identified which addressed the equality-difference issue.

Humanist feminism

Young conceives humanist feminism as "revolt against femininity" (Voet 1998: 26). Women should have the same opportunities like men and the reason why women are not as active and powerful as men is that they did not make enough effort to get into the social life and significant positions. Male position in the social hierarchy and their behaviour are the pattern to follow by women. Thus, this type of feminism drawing on recognition of individualism and humanism demands equal rights and duties for all mature people. Interest of females is best expressed in words "Let us be included as citizens and forget that we are women". Humanist feminism focuses mainly upon relations between citizens and state rather than on relationships between citizens. It concerns rights only and not activities, opinions and virtues. Also, it mentions as the only duty of a citizen obeying the laws of the state and to pay taxes. That is why claiming for political rights, civil and social rights it is perceived as legalistic. The problem, however, does not concern the formal, legal position of women in modern western societies which is rather satisfactory. At stake is the actual and material position of females which is far away from the ideal. But this is not noticed by humanist feminism.

Woman-centred feminism

According to this view, women's suffering results from the rejection and depreciation of unique female values and performance by authoritarian masculine culture. Female bodies and activities are perceived as a reservoir of significant values for society and politics (Voet 1998: 27). In contrast to humanist feminism that is rather moderate and tries to adjust women's interests to the existing ideal, this variation of feminism is much more radical in its potential to change the world. It involves a proposal to include a female-based identity politics in contemporary liberal democracy as well as promotion of superior female morality to be used as a base for politics and citizenship. Woman morality, rooted in femininity and motherhood is conceived as an altruistic kind of ethical judgement.

Woman-centred feminists demand equality of "voice and access" which would include equal civil, political and social rights for all adults. Moreover, they are not in favour of gender-neutral citizenship but suggest to rethink citizenship from the perspective of the female. Thus, Pateman underlies the paradox of being included as citizens and excluded as women and argues that the terms 'men' and 'women' need to be included in the debate on citizenship. Moreover, "the meaning of sexual difference has to cease to be the difference between freedom and subordination" (cited after Voet 1998: 29)

Deconstructionist feminism

This type of feminist thought tries to transcend the equality-difference dualism, conceived as a legacy of the Enlightenment which should be overcome. Through rejection of the binary logic of Enlightenment: public/private; rational/ irrational; man/woman; culture/nature it aims at returning to the situation that does not create false opposition and obscure alternative options. By that deconstructionist feminists seem to suggest that it is not a nature of 'women' which should be taken as a basis for feminism. They are advocates of more pluralism in politics and society which has nothing to do with equal and universal citizenship proclaiming equal right for all people. Individuals with their separate interest and needs cannot be satisfied by the same model because some of them would be even more marginalised. Also, in their opinion, a differentiated citizenship is not a solution as it might stigmatize and isolate certain groups. The deconstructionist feminist answer to this paradox appears to have also a paradoxical character: "we can easily avoid a notion of equality that excludes difference and a concept of difference which excludes equality" (Voet 1998: 29).

Thus, the equality-difference debate absorbed feminist attitude on citizenship. Humanist feminism stresses equality between men and women whereas woman-centred feminism tries to maintain gender difference. Deconstructionist feminism, on the other hand, aims at transcending equality-difference opposition advocating general pluralism rather than only pluralism of gender.

Apart from all differences among various strands of the feminism-citizenship debate one thing seems to be common to them. It is a profound effort to defend and save rights and dignity of woman and as a result of any "different" or "other" who has been for a long time a victim throughout the history. Here, very instructive are Carter's words: "equal rights for women, who make up half the population, are a prerequisite for achieving justice. But protecting women's rights is organically linked to promoting the rights of the poor and disadvantaged and to ending discrimination based on the arbitrary grounds of race. This is not only because the poor are most often women, and black women suffer from dual discrimination, but primarily because women's rights will only be secured in a context of respect for the rights of all and of policies designed to ensure a just society" (Carter 1988: 196). Thus, the feminist debate on citizenship opens up the question concerning equal rights and proper position of all human beings in a world society.

The cosmopolitan citizenship

This concept of citizenship has its modern roots in cosmopolitan thought of the Western enlightenment. Advocates of this tradition argued that human beings share a common ethical identity and obey a common moral law. They demanded trans-state or global economic and political institutions and power reflecting a common moral character of human race. Moreover, they claimed a common universal system of judgement necessary to evaluate real political entities (Hutchings 1999: 12).

It is the Kantian philosophy where we find the first strands on the idea of world citizenship within the modern political thought. He argues that we have ethical duties to the rest of the human race that transcends our obligations to fellow citizens. The cosmopolitan law demands from people to share their hospitality with strangers as fellow "citizens of a universal state of humanity" (Kant 1970: 206). It is an appeal to join with fellow nationals to transcend the morally limited and vernacular space of the sovereign state. The Kantian idea represents a statist view on world citizenship that implies only compassion for others. Despite its limits and stressing that moral sphere cannot be reduced to co-nationals it provides a pathway to the politics of dialogue and consent.

The idea of cosmopolitan citizenship expresses an appeal to honour the rights and recognise the obligations towards the whole human race, not only to fellow nationals with whom with share the boundaries of the common state. In other words, it appears to be an embodiment of recognition of the others contained in postmodern thought and the rule of subsidiarity mentioned above. It is a device of transcending the belief that citizenship is inextricably linked with the nation state. Another aspect refers to the fact that in the present stage of globalisation modern state has lost partly its ability to protect the rights citizens. Facing this issue, the theory of cosmopolitan democracy repeats some views typical for postmodern thought and argues that the nation state is not the sole moral community (Held 1995: 18). Moreover, it emphasises the role of transnational and sub-state arrangements reflecting the political and ethical content of the rule of subsidiarity.

In the literature, there have been discussed three motives for creating a new idea of world citizenship rights and duties (Linklater 1999: 47). Firstly, in the contemporary universe of the world-wide interconnections, citizens in pursuing their interests and rights cannot rely only on national institutions. Secondly, a dense network of international organisations created for management the ever more interdependent world lacks a democratic legitimacy as their decisions are taken without popular assent. Thirdly, sovereign states should not treat themselves as the only and ultimate moral community when examples of transnational harm increase. They cannot build their autonomy by creating heteronomy for others. Also, in order to be correct with the proclaimed moral values they should work for building an international public space that allows in legitimate cases to encroach on state sovereignty rather than expressing compassion towards foreigners. Moreover, eliminating distinctions between citizens and aliens and creating the space for representation and voice of outsiders are vital needs of the contemporary democratic societies (Linklater 1999: 48).

It is however a more recent political thought which stresses a more active attitude towards citizenship which would work for the creation of wider communities of discourse. There is a conviction within this version of cosmopolitan citizenship that universalisation might be combined with practises which eliminate economic and social exclusion. Advocates of this view argue that widening the limits of political community does not imply the creation of a new centre of power demanding supreme loyalty. It is rather a question of promoting a variety and multitude of political spheres representing a level of sub-state loyalty as well as transnational and nation-state allegiances. In line with the rule of subsidiarity, citizens are able to claim their rights and express their needs on different layers of public space. On the other hand, the role of world citizenship is to establish a broad community of discourse; to create a political framework where power and force has been abolished in favour of dialogue and consent. Moreover, the idea of cosmopolitan citizenship apart from proclaiming a sympathy to others also emphasises the need for personal responsibility for the environment. It conveys commitment for treatment the vulnerable with compassion and effort to engage aliens in communities of discourse on equal terms. This ideal is based on the conviction that autonomy of self needs not be realised by creation of heteronomy of others (Linklater 1999: 51).

The real embodiment of cosmopolitan citizenship would be a solidarist international society where individuals are its main members and which is ready to encroach the state sovereignty whenever human rights are violated. Its main function is to create conditions for "limitless communication" and working for a variety of global communities of discourse which build up the heterogeneity of international society. Solidarist society implies defence of human rights, global justice and environmental management according to international law, changing by the same international society in line with moral standards. It can abolish some gap between duties of co-nationals and commitments to the rest of humanity that has been present in modern states. According to Habermas "the cosmopolitan condition is no longer merely a mirage. State citizenship and world citizenship form a continuum whose contours, at least, are becoming visible" (Habermas 1996: 515).

Conclusion

The cosmopolitan citizenship seems to be the answer to the contemporary condition of global capitalism. The alternative expressed by some conservatives – that there is a need to de-globalise capitalism, to return to the limits of nation states, increase protectionism, strengthen the power of trade unions and, by the same, to reduce the flow of capital and labour – does not seem to be possible. Capitalism cannot be de-globalised. Instead, democracy and civil society should be globalised. It should be mentioned that it is a democracy and civil society which were a fundamental base for capitalism – *not vice versa*. According to Barber, over the span from seventeenth to nineteenth centuries democratisation preceded a full development of industrialisation. Civil and democratic institutions form a framework for capitalism; they adjust it to the needs of people, shape its human face trying to keep it in line with the standards of equality and justice. Globalisation of economy (accompanied with the same process in technology and information sector) without similar globalisation of democracy means that capitalism got out from its framework and became wild, anarchic, which is destructive for the both democracy and capitalism (Barber 2000: 13). Therefore, the only solution is to globalise civil society and democracy. They should catch up with capitalism beyond the boundaries of nation states and re-establish in international scale the set of similar institutions that were inherent for the traditional nation states. It is a challenge that has to be faced in order to create a more human global world. The concept of cosmopolitan citizenship appears to be the very first step in this long way.

References

Barber, B. (2000), "Globalny jean". *Gazeta Wyborcza*, 1–2 July.
Bauman, Z. (1998), *Globalization*. Cambridge: Polity Press.
Carter, H. A. (1988), *The Politics of Women's Rights*. London: Longman.
Definicja i zakres zasady subsydiarnosci (1994), Strasbourg: Wydawnictwa Rady Europy.

Derrida, J. (1992), *The Other Heading. Reflections on today's Europe.* (translated by P. A. Brault, M. B. Naas). Indianapolis: Indiana University Press.

Habermas, J. (1996), *Between Facts and Norms: Contributions to Discourse Theory of Law and Democracy.* Cambridge: Polity Press.

Held, D. (1995)*, Democracy and the Global Order: From Modern State to Cosmopolitan Governance.* Cambridge: Polity Press.

Hutchings, K. (1999), "Political Theory and Cosmopolitan Citizenship". In: **Hutchings**, K. & R. **Dannreuther**, *Cosmopolitan Citizenship.* London: Macmillan.

Kant, I. (1970), "Perpetual Peace and Idea for Universal Hostory from a Cosmopolitical Point of View". In: **Forsyth**, M., H. M. A. **Keens-Soper** & P. **Savigear** (eds), *The Theory of International Relations: Selected Texts from Gentili to Treitschke*, London: Allen & Unwin.

Linklater A. (1999), "Cosmopolitan citizenship". In: **Hutchings** K. &R. **Dannreuther** (eds), *Cosmopolitan Citizenship.* London: Macmillan.

Millon-Delsol, C. (1995), *Zasada pomocniczości.* Kraków: Znak.

Naas, M. B. (1992), "Introduction: For example". In: **Derrida**, J., *The Other Heading. Reflections on today's Europe.* Indianapolis: Indiana University Press.

Treaty of the European Union (1992), Office for Official Publications of the European Communities, Luxembourg.

Voet, R. (1998), *Feminism and Citizenship.* London: Sage.

Welsch, W. (1988), *Unsere postmoderne Moderne.* (Acta Humaniora, Weinheim).

Zeidler-Janiszewska, A. (1991), "Kulturowy kontekst koncepcji rozumu transwersalnego". In: **Zeidler-Janiszewska**, A. (red.), *Postmodernizm w perspektywie filozoficzno-kulturoznawczej.* Warszawa: Instytut Kultury.

Tony Spybey

European Nation-States and Globalisation

The Origins of a State System and of Globalisation

After the collapse of the Roman Empire and the period known as the Dark Ages, European civilisation developed not in the form of a single imperial hierarchy but instead as a number of independent states. This distinguishes it from the other civilisations of China or India or Islam. European civilisation came to be known as Western civilisation since Europeans crossed the Atlantic to inhabit the Americas and went on to dominate much of the rest of the world too. Part of that domination has taken the form of a pervasive culture, the world's first truly global culture. The development of the European model of the state and the pervasiveness of Western culture are both dimensions to the process now popularly known as globalisation. Stated very simply, the European state system has provided the model for the global state system and Western culture has become the global culture.

We can develop our view of the globalisation process into four dimensions if we adopt the model from Anthony Giddens' work on structuration theory and the concept of inter-societal systems:-

Global Communications (the Global Communication System)

The media by which Western culture became so pervasive but also a significant part of the globalisation process in their own right.
In conceptual terms it is the means by which the global culture is signified.

The Nation-State System (the Global Polity)

From the sixteenth century onwards Europe developed as a set of independent states competing for politico-military power. Out of this process emerged the model for the modern nation-state and the system of nation-states became adopted as the form of organization for the global polity.

In conceptual terms it is the means by which global power is legitimated as authority.

The Global Economy (the Capitalist World-Economy)

At the same time, by a process of colonial exploitation and the extension of its trade, Europe drew a significant proportion of global economic transactions into its own market system operating on the principles of capitalist economics. The capitalist market system became adopted as the form of organisation for the global economy.

In conceptual terms it is the means by which the global allocation of resources is legitimated.

The World Order (the Global Military Order)

Colonialism was a process by which the world outside of Europe was largely divided up between the European states on the basis of their naval power. Other areas, such as China, were coerced into dealings with Europeans on their terms. The European notion of the balance of power became adopted as the world order.

In conceptual terms it is the means by which sanctions (to enforce the world order) are legitimated (after Giddens 1985: 277).

The way in which all of this came about is a significant part of the history of the world over the past six centuries and here we may emphasise some significant features in order to understand the development of the European state and the imposition of cultural domination as globalisation.

The Emergence of European States and the Establishment of Oceanic Navigation

Most historians are agreed that the sixteenth century was the time when, significantly in terms of world history, European states began to make their presence felt upon the rest of the world. Until that time Christian Europe, or Christendom as it would more normally have been referred to at the time, had been effectively contained by the rival Islamic religion which occupied the whole of the land area to the east, the Middle East, and to the south, North Africa. The

Crusades represented attempts by Christian knights to regain the Holy Land from Islam but their successes were only temporary. The population of Europe was small at the time and European armies were unable to make much of an impression upon the more powerful Islamic civilization. Success for Europeans came not on land but by sea and yet, as emphasized already, the subsequent territorial expansion did not involve the creation of a hierarchical European empire. Instead adventurers representing the crowns of different European states competed to seize overseas colonies and trading enclaves for their royal patrons. The pioneering voyages from Portugal and Spain were in the first place continuations of the Crusades. There were large red crosses on the ships' sails, larger versions of those which had been displayed earlier on the Crusading knights' tunics, and sailors who died on the voyages were deemed to have died as Crusaders. To circumvent the flanks of Islam was regarded as a worthy Christian purpose in its own right but the more Earthly goal was to gain direct access to trade with India and China. As it was the spices, the silks and the other goods which Europeans increasingly desired had to be obtained via Islam with a substantial mark up on prices. Furthermore, the powerful city-state of Venice controlled the eastern Mediterranean with its armed galleys and Condottieri mercenaries and maintained a monopoly of trade with Islam, imposing its own price mark-up on top of the existing one. There were therefore huge gains to be made for anyone who could break these arrangements. This is what spurred on Christopher Columbus and Vasco da Gama in their establishment of ocean routes but they required royal patronage in order to be able to achieve anything. European expansion when it came was a combination of individual initiative and the backing of the developing European states. We shall look now at the first two examples of European states entering the global arena.

Portugal

The first of these expansionary European states was Portugal, a small country but one established early in the development of modern Europe. Throughout the fifteenth century Portuguese ships pressed southwards down the west coast of Africa in search of a trade route into the Indian Ocean at a time when it was not known for sure that there was a passage around the southern cape. This was an enterprise begun by one of its princes, Dom Enrique, who is known in English as 'Henry the Navigator'. The progression from the Middle Ages to modernity are important for understanding the origins of both the European state system and globalisation. Henry was an intensely medieval figure, a crusader knighted on the battlefield at Ceuta in North Africa. Yet, whereas the crusades were affairs of the Mediterranean, the oceanic exploration which he sponsored was to take Europeans out into the wider world and on to the global culture which we see today.

Henry was fifth in line to the Portuguese throne and therefore unlikely to accede. So he devoted the considerable resources at his disposal, mainly in the form of a religious foundation, to the establishment of what would be seen today as a centre for the study of navigation. This was at Sagrés on the edge of Portugal's Atlantic coast, literally looking out to the wider world. Between 1418 and 1498 maritime expeditions representing the Portuguese state set out from Lisbon in search of the southern cape of Africa and a route into the Indian Ocean. They mastered the wind ellipses of the Atlantic in order to complete the round trip more easily and so developed oceanic navigation in practice. It was a long-term enterprise and it did not find its goal until long after the death of Henry when in 1498 four 'caravels' under the command of Vasco da Gama finally reached India.

On the final leg of the voyage the expedition enlisted the help of a pilot, Ahmad ibn-Majid, a Gujerati Muslim from India. They picked him up at Malindi, one of a string of African cities along the east coast. The Swahili had been converted to Islam and their cities become wealthy through the trading of goods from the African interior with the Arab Islamic civilization further north. This was part of the long established Indian Ocean trade that Europeans wanted to break into and it is one of the curiosities of such developments that a Muslim should have helped a European state finally overcome the land blockade effectively imposed by the Islamic empire's occupation of North Africa and the Middle East.

The Portuguese expedition subsequently landed at Calicut to find a vigorous trading port in which they were not welcome. Subsequently the use of cannon by larger fleets would deal with that situation but the immediate result in any case was a cargo of pepper landed in Lisbon. This undercut in price the existing supplies which were carried overland to Europe through Islamic territory to Alexandria and thence to Venice. The pepper brought back by the Portuguese was traded in competition through an existing commodity market at a fifth of the price of the Venetian pepper. The centre of this activity was the Flemish city of Antwerp, the focus of European banking and finance at the time. These pioneering ocean voyages by European states such as Portugal have to be set against the background of a developing European capitalist economy.

Spain

During the Portuguese pursuit of an eastern route to India, the Genoese adventurer Cristoforo Colombo, in English Christopher Columbus, arrived on to the scene. Italy was not to develop as a nation-state until the nineteenth century and Genoa was one of Venice's chief rivals as an independent city-state. Each owed its existence to trade but Genoa was less powerful, continually embattled and therefore less successful. An experienced seaman already Columbus was nevertheless shipwrecked off the Portuguese coast in 1476, but his unscheduled arrival was helped by the fact that his brother Bartolomeo lived in Lisbon. He stayed in Portugal for some time and subsequently sailed to England and probably Iceland but more importantly to Madeira. This was already a Portuguese possession strategically placed off the west coast of Africa with a developing trade in sugar and slaves to work on its plantations. He lived with his family for a while on one of the neighbouring islands and it was during this period that he developed his plan for a western route to China across the Atlantic. Unfortunately this was in competition with the existing Portuguese plan for an eastern route to India and it was rejected.

Undaunted he subsequently he took his scheme to neighbouring Castile. There he suffered a further rejection from the Duke of Medina Sidonia whose successor later commanded the Spanish Armada against the English. Eventually he gained access to the royal court and convinced the pious Queen Isabella of the advantages for Christendom of circumventing the territories of Islam. This was at the time of the expulsion from Granada of remaining Islamic forces of occupation. There were more years of frustration and delay but he finally sailed in 1492 under the joint flags of Isabella of Castile and Ferdinand of Aragon. Their marriage was instrumental in the creation of the new and powerful state of Spain, although at the time of Columbus's voyage the two parts still had separate constitutions. State building and the creation of overseas links, such as these examples, were a feature of the development of Europe and its creation of a global culture.

Columbus reached neither China nor India and his voyages failed to provide the immediate commercial gains that Vasco da Gama had achieved with the importation of pepper and other spices. But it opened up to the Spanish, and subsequently to other Europeans, the potential of the Americas, a continent named after an acquaintance of Columbus's, Amerigo Vespucci. He worked with Columbus on his second and third voyages before sailing on his own account as a surveyor of the American coastline for the Spanish government. It is he also who is credited with the term 'New World'.

Vespucci was from Florence, another Italian city-state of the Renaissance. These city-states were the economic centres of the existing Mediterranean trade; whereas Portugal and Spain were nation-states extending European trade out into the world. Yet for several centuries the new nation-states were dependent for finance and banking upon mercantile city-states, not those of the Mediterranean but those of north western Europe, Antwerp and Amsterdam.

The Treaty of Tordesillas

Portugal and Spain are the earliest examples of European states entering the global arena for politico-economic reasons. They struck out against Islamic military power. The Portuguese broke into the Indian Ocean trade that had existed for centuries and the Spanish began to take African slaves to their American colonies to replace the labour of the indigenous civilisations which they destroyed. In 1494, only two years after Columbus's first voyage, Portugal and Spain sealed the Treaty of Tordesillas. This sought to divide the world's potential trade and conquest between the two countries. It was an agreement that had been mooted for some time, supported by the papacy which was keen to see catholic countries extending their power and influence in the world. The idea was to create a north-south line in the Atlantic that would divide Portugal's sphere of influence to the east from Spain's to the west. King John II of Portugal successfully negotiated a line further to the west than at first envisaged and this bisected Latin America longitudinally to give Portugal the colony of Brazil. To this day Brazilians speak Portuguese whereas the rest of Latin America speaks Spanish, such are the long term consequences of even these first global steps by Europeans. The pope who blessed the Treaty was Alexander VI, the infamous Borgia pope, and this probably says much about the venal side of such agreements.

The Treaty of Tordesillas was of course a huge piece of European arrogance but it does vividly illustrate the global outlook of Europeans which at the time was unmatched by any other civilisation. Islamic teaching regarded ocean navigation as impossible and although the Chinese admiral Cheng Huo had reached East Africa almost a century before the Portuguese and with a much larger fleet there was no desire in the Chinese imperial court to develop the route. Cheng Huo was a eunuch in the service of the emperor and not an independent adventurer like da Gama or Columbus. Nevertheless, it was unrealistic for the Portuguese and Spanish to think they could maintain their Treaty because the Dutch, the French and the English, all seafaring powers themselves, were soon to be in search of their own colonial empires. After 1492 the progress of the European states outside of Europe and the Mediterranean was hardly impeded by Islam. The earlier Crusaders had encountered a superior Islamic culture in the Middle East, one that they were pleased to emulate in many ways, but in later centuries European culture eclipsed that of Islam in economic wealth, technical developments and political influence.

The Ottoman Empire was the final incarnation of the Islamic Caliphate and it survived, albeit in decline, until the early twentieth century. Then it made the mistake of taking the German side in the First World War and this gave Britain,

France and the USA the excuse to carve up the Middle East for themselves mainly in the interest of securing the rights to oilfields. The states of the Lebanon, Syria, Iraq, Palestine, Jordan and Saudi Arabia were established and influential Arab families installed as their rulers. The 1922 Cairo Conference, where these decisions were ratified, was a major milestone in the formation of the modern Middle East and the subject of much resentment amongst Islamic people. Recent manifestations of Islamism or, as Europeans like to call it Islamic Fundamentalism, are the legacy of this. However, the realisation of the European global view has irrevocably turned the world into a state system based upon the European model. This is the fundamental link between the European nation-states and globalisation.

The Modern World-System

One way of conceptualising the development of global connections by people representing the European states is through the work of the French historian, Fernand Braudel, and the American sociologist, Immanuel Wallerstein. Both have interpreted the events described in the previous sections as the beginnings of what Wallerstein refers to as 'the modern world-system'. Both interpret the trade which followed from the pioneering ocean voyages as the spread of European capitalism. In the case of Vasco da Gama's voyage to India the shipping of pepper began immediately with the return of the three surviving ships. Moreover, there was investment in such voyages by speculators and the commodities acquired could be traded on existing European markets, notably the one centred on the mercantile city of Antwerp during the sixteenth century.

The location of Antwerp in north-west Europe is significant because Wallerstein sees the 'modern world-system' as developing a 'core' in north-west Europe and a 'periphery' in the areas exploited by Europeans. Spain's American colonies of course formed part of the periphery; but also central Europe, lacking a trading sector, entered what he describes as a 'second serfdom'. Its landowners were content to live from their feudal tithes supplemented with revenue from the German and Dutch merchants who shipped the grain; but it was the latter who gained most from the arrangement leaving central Europe to stagnate. Of even greater significance, Portugal and Spain lacked the commercial infrastructure to exploit their overseas colonies to greatest advantage and so in Wallerstein's terms they became a 'semi-periphery' of the world-system, set between the north western European core and the colonial periphery. Much of the wealth shipped back from Spanish America, mainly in the form of silver, was used up in maintaining the courts of monarchs such as the Habsburg Charles V who was not only King of Spain but also Holy Roman Emperor with landed possessions in central Europe and the Mediterranean. The financial dealings involved were to a great extent brokered by the merchants and bankers of Antwerp. That is the reason for Wallerstein's emphasis on the developing 'capitalist world-economy' as the wealth creator of this 'modern world-system'.

Wallerstein's modern world-system represents a particular approach to the creation of globalisation and a globalised world. His work has often been criticised as economistic, since the world-system is based upon the capitalist world-economy. For Wallerstein capitalism transcended even the borders of those European states which created it and rendered their rulers dependent upon the dealings of merchants and bankers, if only for the taxation potential of enhanced trade. This meant that mercantile activity enjoyed a great deal of freedom so long as it contributed to the royal exchequer. As a state grew more powerful the cost of maintaining a permanent standing army and navy for defence, plus the cost of administering a bureaucracy that was effective in collecting taxes and administering expenditure, each required in itself ever growing amounts of revenue. The combination of powerful states and vigorous mercantile sectors points significantly to the separation of polity and economy in the spread of European civilisation. This is another defining characteristic of European development and one that has been carried into the contemporary globalised world. We speak of the public sector, meaning the arena of government and politics, and the private sector, meaning the arena of business and economic activity. By contrast the imperial systems which were Europe's adversaries during its period of growth and expansion had one hierarchy embracing polity and economy which tended to constrain the kind of vigorous independent mercantile activity which gave rise to capitalism.

Wallerstein argues that there have been several cases of 'world-economies' developing in the history of the world. By this he means systems of economic exchange which have embraced large geographical areas, such as the long standing Indian Ocean trade into which Vasco da Gama forced entry. In all cases other than Europe however a 'world-economy' was taken over by a 'world-empire' and this politico-military control constrained economic expansion. The sole exception, according to him, is the 'modern world-system' or 'capitalist world-economy' created by Europeans which has not been overshadowed by the political organisation of Europe in the form of nation-states. This arrangement has been so successful that the whole world has adopted the combination of politically independent nation-states and an inter-dependent world economy.

International Relations

If the approach of Wallerstein is overly economistic, a complementary framework with emphasis on politics and the nation-state may be derived from the study of International Relations. This is usually taken to be a sub-discipline of the study of Politics and it is based upon the development of the European state system and what emerged from that on the global scale. The relations between the European states are seen as increasingly significant after the Treaty of Westphalia which ended the Thirty Years War in 1648. This war also defined the division between Protestant northern Europe and Catholic southern Europe.

The European state system is sometimes referred to as the Westphalian system since the treaty was a milestone in the development of the modern map of Europe and therefore the definition of European states and their borders. But that is not all, there is also the codification of the protocols of diplomacy. The separation of these formal inter-state links from trading links is another aspect of the separation of polity from economy, in modern terminology the difference between the public sector and the private sector. International Relations therefore represents a politically oriented approach to European development to complement the economistic approach of Immanuel Wallerstein.

Globalisation

Around 1990 the so-called 'cultural turn' in the social sciences began to include the appearance of the term, globalisation, as an alternative to the world-system of Immanuel Wallerstein or the study of International Relations. As stated earlier the spread of European culture, especially with the input of twentieth century American culture, has meant that Western culture has become the world's first truly global culture. The difference between the concept of globalisation and world-system or international relations is culture itself – and communication. The means of spreading the culture is an important part of the culture.

The media of communication:
• from sailing ships through all the developments that have led to air travel;
• from the electric telegraph through all the developments that have led to fibre-optic cabling and the Internet or World Wide Web;

• from radio through all the developments that have led to television and satellite broadcasting;

• from recording cylinders to tapes and CDs and all the developments in sound reproduction that are available today.

These are all significant parts of the global culture.

The appearance of the term globalisation came at a time when electronic technology in communication had already been developed to a very high degree. The pervasiveness of television and the growing use of computers with e-mail and Internet links created a situation significantly different from any that had existed before. This is the view of several observers (see for instance Giddens 1990; Robertson 1992). The consequences of this constitute a qualitative change in the process of modernity that has been referred to as 'reflexive modernisation' (see Beck, Giddens and Lash 1994).

The 'electronic revolution' has produced a plethora of communications and a dramatic expansion of access to knowledge of all kinds. The impact of this has caused people to be more reflexive about their situation and their relationships with others. Communication is information and information tends to cause questions to be asked. In turn this contributes to the undermining of traditional forms of authority. In the West globalisation has been associated with the demise of the state and state authority. In the former Communist countries the impossibility of restricting or censoring the electronic media was associated with the demise of the Soviet Union and the pulling down of the Berlin Wall.

The Consequences of Globalisation

According to Roland Robertson (1992: 62), globalisation produces outcomes that are 'up for grabs'. The West may have begun the process of globalisation with its intercessions into other parts of the world and the implanting of Western institutions. Western culture has proved attractive to most of the people who have come into contact with it. But having begun the process, having created a global culture, the West will not necessarily continue to dominate globalisation. If it means anything globalisation means that the whole world participates. This cannot occur, on such a scale, without some changes taking place in the process as the result of the sheer scale of participation.

Another of Robertson's principles is that globalisation consists of a process of interpenetration between the global and the local. He states this in the rather difficult language of Talcott Parsons's structural functionalism:

...we are, in the late twentieth century, witnesses to – and participants in – a massive, twofold process involving the interpenetration of the universalization of particularism and the particularization of universalism... (Robertson 1992: 100).

The most important point here is that this is a principle of the continuing globalisation process. It is the way in which the global culture is reproduced. The local is as much a part of the process as the global. In fact, in order for globalisation to exist at all it must by definition be reproduced in all the localities that exist. Expressed this way, the conclusion is unavoidable that the reproduction of globalisation in local milieu must have significant effects on the continuing process.

The case of Japan is significant here. This is a society that kept itself closed from the West until the second half of the nineteenth century. Then during the twentieth century the Japanese began to devour Western institutions whilst at the same time retaining a strong culture of their own. Progress was brought to a halt with defeat after the disastrous militaristic imperialism of the Second World War but with rehabilitation at the hands of the US occupying forces after the war the process was intensified. The result was a Japanese version of industrialism with all its attendant institutions drawing from Japanese culture. By now industrialisation was becoming global and so there emerged a strong Japanese contribution to the continuing globalisation process.

An obvious example is the motor industry that really began with Henry Ford's development of assembly line production during the first decades of the twentieth century. So-called 'Fordist' manufacturing was the hallmark of successful industry for any country during the twentieth century. The Japanese reproduced the organisation of the motor industry but inserted into it some of their own cultural traits. *Kanban*, or 'just-in-time' stock control, characterises the broader organisation of Japanese industry and its component supplies. *Kaizen*, or 'quality circles', characterises Japanese workers' approach to their work and the importation of 'groupism' into the workplace. Each of these has been associated with the principles of Confucianism which form a strong and consistent part of the socialisation process in Japanese family life and education. 'Groupism' in Japanese society is held to have its origins in the Samurai period when peasants organised themselves into *ie* groups for their own protection. The Samurai are of course considered to have evolved into thrusting Japanese managers and all of these characteristics may be seen as local inputs into the global institutions of motor manufacturing and its management. The outcome of this has been that Western motor manufacturers have all seen the advantage of bringing facets of Japanese manufacturing into their organisations. This is often referred to as 'post-Fordism'.

Globalisation and the Nation-State

As already stated, globalisation tends to undermine the authority of the nation-state. Global communication brings to the attention of the citizens of the nation-state alternative focuses of authority. On a grand scale there is the United Nations Organisation or regional groupings like the European Union. On a lesser scale there have appeared, for example, organisations like Greenpeace. This campaigning organisation works globally and in its sphere of interest, environmentalism, it is often listened to with more authority than the governments of nation-states.

Some writers believe that the nation-state is too large to engage the trust of the individual but too small to play much of a part in the global arena. In response to the latter, the European states have combined as the European Union in order that they may have more influence. In this respect the Japanese writer, Kenichi Ohmae, has referred to a process of 'triadisation'. The triad that he is referring to consists of three focuses of politico-economic power that have appeared in the world towards the end of the twentieth. They are North America, Europe and East Asia and may be expressed more extensively as follows:

1. The USA has combined with Canada and Mexico to form the North American Free Trade Association, NAFTA for short.

2. Europe has taken the form of the European Union and most European countries are now members. Further entrants from eastern Europe are expected in the foreseeable future.

3. There is no such formal association in East Asia but where Japan took the lead, Hong Kong, Singapore, South Korea and Taiwan followed. Since then Indonesia, Malaysia, the Philippines, Thailand and other countries in the area have achieved considerable industrialisation. These clearly form an East Asian economic bloc.

This global triad represents the elite of the globalised world and therefore points to new forms of inequality between nations. And yet there is counter evidence. The systems of fibre-optic cabling which provide the networks for computers and the Internet is expensive and therefore disproportionately represented in North America, Europe and East Asia. Yet satellite broadcasting, although expensive to set up, operates regardless of distance. Therefore it is used quite widely in the less developed countries. India, one of the poorest countries in the world in terms of per capita income, is also one the largest users of satellite broadcasting.

Summary

1. European civilisation developed not as an imperial system with a single hierarchy like other civilisations but as a set of independent nation-states.

2. The European model of the nation-state and the nation-state system became adopted by the rest of the world.

3 From the sixteenth century onwards the Europeans began to implant their institutions throughout the world by the process of colonialism.

4. During the same period the economies of the world became influenced by European capitalism to form a capitalist world-economy.

5. By the second half of the twentieth century through the process of globalisation Western culture had become the world's first truly global culture.

Further Reading

Beynon, J. & D. **Dunkerley** (2000), *Globalization: The Reader*. London: Athlone Press; New York: Routledge.

Giddens, A. (1985), *The Nation-State and Violence*. Cambridge: Polity Press.

Holton, R.J. (1998), *Globalization and the Nation-States*. Basingstoke: Macmillan.

Robertson, R. (1992), *Globalization: Social Theory and Global Culture*. London: Sage.

Spybey, T. (1996), *Globalization and World Society*. Cambridge: Polity Press.

Wallerstein, I. (1979), *The Capitalist World-Economy*. Cambridge: Cambridge University Press.

The Authors

David Dunkerley PhD is Professor of Sociology at the University of Glamorgan, Wales. His recent books include *Globalization: The Reader*, Routledge, NY, 2000 (with J. Beynon) and *Wales Today*, University of Wales Press, Cardiff, 1999 (with A. Thompson). He is the author/editor of 11 other books and of numerous journal articles.

Lesley Hodgson is a Doctoral Candidate in Sociology at the University of Glamorgan, Wales. She has recently published in *TransAtlantic Studies*.

Stanisław Konopacki PhD is an Adjunct in the British and Commonwealth Studies Department at the University of Łódź, Poland. His recent books include *European Integration and Post-Modernism*, Adam Mickiewicz University Press, Poznań, 1998 and *From Accession to Membership*, European Institute, 1998. He also published widely in periodicals on European integration, contemporary philosophy and modern art.

Tony Spybey PhD is Visiting Professor of Sociology at the University of Glamorgan, Wales and Research Professor of Sociology at Staffordshire University. He has recently published *Globalization and World Society*, Polity Press, Cambridge, 1996 and *Britain in Europe*, Routledge, London, 1997. He has also published extensively in both book form and refereed articles on similar matters. He is currently the Editor of the journal *Sociology*.

Andrew Thompson PhD is Head of Sociology at the University of Glamorgan, Wales. His books include *Wales Today* and *Nation, Identity and Social Theory*, both published by University of Wales Press, Cardiff, 1999. He has also published in key journals on national identity, civil society and citizenship.